Family Revolution

Family Revolution

MARITAL STRIFE IN CONTEMPORARY
CHINESE LITERATURE AND VISUAL
CULTURE

Hui Faye Xiao

UNIVERSITY OF WASHINGTON PRESS   *Seattle and London*

the
modern language
initiative

THIS BOOK IS MADE POSSIBLE BY A COLLABORATIVE GRANT
FROM THE ANDREW W. MELLON FOUNDATION.

This book was also supported by a Book Publication Award
from the Friends of the Hall Center for the Humanities
at the University of Kansas.

University of Washington Press
PO Box 50096, Seattle, WA 98145, USA
www.washington.edu/uwpress

Library of Congress Cataloging-in-Publication Data

Xiao, Hui Faye.
Family Revolution : Marital Strife in Contemporary
Chinese Literature and Visual Culture / Hui Faye Xiao.
pages cm. — (Modern Language Initiative)
Includes bibliographical references and index.
ISBN 978-0-295-99349-2 (hardback : acid-free paper)
ISBN 978-0-295-99350-8 (paperback : acid-free paper)
1. Chinese literature—History and criticism. 2. Families
in literature. 3. Marital conflict—China. 4. Marriage in
literature. 5. Family life—China. I. Title.
PL2275.F34X53 2014
895.109'3355—dc23   2013043530

For my family on both sides of the Pacific Ocean

CONTENTS

It has been ten years since I first conceived of this project. In 2004, I went back to China on a research trip and came across the mega-hit TV serial *Chinese Style Divorce*. Everyone I knew in China was watching it and talking about it. Like many melodramas about marital strife, the serial revolves around a middle-aged woman's desperate effort in improving her wifely quality to protect her middle-class marriage. This viewing experience stirred mixed feelings in my heart— shock, indignation, and intellectual curiosity—and motivated me to explore the ways in which the pervasive rhetoric of individual self-development contributes to the reconfiguration of gender subject and domestic space in contemporary Chinese society.

In the following decade, I have been guided, assisted, and cheered by numerous people along the way, who have made the completion and publication of this book possible. First of all, I cannot thank enough Gary G. Xu, my graduate advisor who was always patient and supportive, encouraging me to carry through this long-term research project. Gary and his wife Chia-wen often invited international students to their place. Their hospitality created many unforgettable moments of familial warmth for us who were far away from our homelands.

I am also greatly indebted to Keith McMahon, my mentor at the University of Kansas (KU). He sets me a perfect role model as a productive writer, great scholar, and charismatic teacher. Despite his tight schedule, Keith has provided me with timely guidance and help in many difficult situations. Vickie Doll, the Chinese librarian at KU, is the most efficient person on campus who always gets me new research materials at unbelievable speed.

My research has been sponsored by various programs and institutions at different points. Thanks to the Illinois Program for Research in the Humanities, the National Endowment for the Humanities, the College of Liberal Arts and Sciences at KU, the Center of East Asian Studies at KU, and the Office of International Programs at KU for providing me with essential financial and administrative support in the forms of fellowships, office space, international travel grants, and summer research funds. I owe particular thanks to the Hall Center at KU, which awarded me a research leave in 2011 that allowed me to complete two new chapters of this book. I am also grateful to the Andrew W. Mellon Foundation and the Friends of the Hall Center for financial aid to defray part of the publication costs.

No list of acknowledgments can be complete, but I just want to take this opportunity to thank the following mentors, colleagues, and friends who offered me advice, assistance, thoughtful feedback, and moral support at various stages of my academic career: Rania Huntington, Nancy A. Abelmann, Robin Visser, Yan Hairong, Shao Dan, Maggie Childs, Yan Li, Crispin Williams, Elaine Gerbert, Megan Green, Randi Hacker, John Kennedy, Victor Bailey, Chris Forth, Ben Chappell, Nathan Wood, Dave Tell, Tony Rosenthal, Akiko Takeyama, Rebecca Nickerson, Chenwei Zhao, Tonglu Li, James Welker, Lawrence Chang, Shuyu Kong, Lin Danya, Liang Luo, Jingyuan Zhang, Chris Lupke, Ban Wang, Russell Berman, Ke Li, Matthew A. Hale, Feng Xuefeng, Chen Xuehu, Lü Li, and many others.

It has been a wonderful experience working closely with Lorri Hagman at the University of Washington Press; Tim Roberts, the managing editor of the Modern Language Initiative series; and my copy editor, Laura Iwasaki. Their efficiency and professionalism made things move fast and smoothly. I am also indebted to Marites Mendoza, an intern editor at the University of Washington Press, and two anonymous external readers for their insightful comments and suggestions that helped to strengthen the book. Of course, I am solely responsible for any errors in this book.

Portions of chapter 4 were published under the title "'Love Is a Capacity': The Narrative of Gendered Self-Development in *Chinese-Style Divorce*" in the *Journal of Contemporary China* (2010). A short version of chapter 1 was published under the title "Science and Poetry: Narrativizing Marital Crisis in Reform-Era Rural China" in the journal *Modern Chinese Literature and Culture* (2011). I have made extensive revisions to both chapters after acquiring new materials in my international research trips in 2010 and 2013. Thanks to the editors of both journals for allowing me to include these essays in this book.

In chapter 4, I commented that any married man or woman's professional advance should be regarded as a "two-person career." Actually, my book project involves more than two people. It is all about teamwork. The completion of this book demands a great deal of labor (domestic and professional), financial and emotional support, care, trust, and affection from many beloved ones in my life, particularly my husband, Hu Gang; parents, Ren Meihua (also my first teacher) and Xiao Juxi; and members of my extended family in China. Their life experiences, memories, stories, and sometimes discontents, complaints, and debates equip me with firsthand data attesting to the unprecedented transformation of the meaning and form of marriage and family. To them, I dedicate this book with my deepest love and gratitude.

Family Revolution

Introduction

Family Revolution, Divorce Representations

In China in 2003, a further liberalization of the regulations for marriage registration eliminated the need for individuals to seek permission to marry or divorce from their work units (*danwei*). Partly as a result of the state's loosening control on people's private lives, the divorce rate in China has skyrocketed. In 2004 more than 1.61 million Chinese couples filed for divorce, a 21.2 percent increase from the previous year's rate, earning 2004 the title "the year of divorce" (*lihun nian*).[1] Following this trend, the divorce rate has soared for seven straight years, as globalization and urbanization sweep through China and cause massive migration and dislocation.[2] Recent statistics show that 2.68 million Chinese couples filed for divorce in 2010, an 8.5 percent increase from 2009.[3] Beijing, Shanghai, Shenzhen, and Guangzhou are listed as the top four cities with the highest divorce rate.[4] In these economically developed areas, the rate is seven or eight times that of 1980.[5]

Having witnessed revolutionary changes in their family life, "many Beijing residents say one of the profound changes in their society is the surge in divorce."[6] Commenting on the evolution of marriage law in the past decades, Xia Yinlan, chair of the Research Center of Marriage and Family of the China Law Society, proclaimed, "China is the freest country in terms of divorce" (*Zhongguo shi lihun zui ziyou de guojia*).[7] At the 2010 conventions of the National People's Congress (NPC) and Chinese People's Political Consultative Conference (CPPCC), Hei Xinwen, a congresswoman, pushed through a

Table 1. Marriage Rate and Divorce Rate, 2002–2010

Year	2002	2003	2004	2005	2006	2007	2008	2009	2010
Marriage Rate %	6.10	6.30	6.65	6.30	7.19	7.50	8.27	9.10	9.30
Divorce Rate %	0.90	1.05	1.28	1.37	1.46	1.59	1.71	1.85	2.00

Source: Ministry of Civil Affairs, "Minzheng bu fabu 2010 nian shehui fuwu fazhan tongji baogao."

controversial bill aimed at complicating the divorce procedure in the hope of lowering the divorce rate.[8]

In the wake of this family crisis, divorce has become a focus of national attention and a battlefield of disparate political ideologies, judicial codes, intellectual discourses, and cultural representations. This book offers the first full-length qualitative study of popular narratives of divorce and marital discord in fiction, film, and television dramas produced and released mainly between 1980 and 2010. In multiple ways, literary and cultural representations of divorce interact and cooperate with, and, at times, contest, legal, eugenic, scientific, and, sociopolitical discourses to inform and articulate new ideas, values, and beliefs about family, marriage, and divorce. Beyond the modern liberal conception of divorce as a private practice that terminates a heterosexual conjugal relationship, divorce also represents a central trope of national crisis, social change, gender transformation, and individual revitalization at transitional moments in modern Chinese history. At the nexus of the public and the private, the old and the new, the traditional and the revolutionary, divorce in the cultural imagination provides a critical index of the dialectics of rupture with the past and reformation for the future.

The idea of home becomes more meaningful under hostile social circumstances.[9] Seemingly a cure for the ongoing marital strife and family crisis in contemporary Chinese society, popular narratives of divorce channel the desire of Chinese audiences for a new domestic culture couched in terms of private home ownership, a cosmopolitan lifestyle, and a naturalized gendered division of labor. This reconfiguration of the domestic interior does not simply indicate lifestyle changes or wealth accumulation. Rather, it acts more as a pivotal mechanism that demarcates gender/class distinctions and reproduces the post-socialist subject who yearns for middle-class private freedoms of consumption, domestic management, autonomous life choices, and self-governance.[10]

Narratives of marital strife thus not only highlight the impact of China's increasing capitalization and globalization on personal life but also engage in popularizing and sentimentalizing the development-oriented reform mentality. Celebrating a radical break with the personal and historic past, these narratives seek to reconstruct a privatized domestic interior as the ultimate shelter of "authentic humanity," or the personalized antidote to the political trauma of the socialist revolution and the relentless exploitation of the post-socialist market economy. Despite the fact that a higher percentage of divorce lawsuits were initiated by women since the 1950s, mainstream divorce representations tend to reproduce the "victim narrative," enhancing the cultural stereotype that, once divorced, women will become undesirable and worthless, just like unwanted used commodities.[11] In order to avoid such a miserable fate, it is suggested that women in unhappy marriages should struggle for the self-development of gendered, that is, wifely and maternal, qualities, instead of seeking a divorce. Evading the problem of structurally uneven development along regional, ethnic, class, and gender lines, these divorce narratives pinpoint women's self-cultivation of gendered qualities as the precondition for the improvement of life quality and as the ultimate cure for family disintegration and social unrest.

This study focuses on the intricate relations linking history, society, and cultural representations, examining divorce as an individual practice, a social institution, a representational strategy, and a pedagogic project of future-oriented developmentalism. It both provides an overview of the transformation of marriage and family under the sociocultural conditions of post-revolutionary China and investigates the ways in which popular narratives of marital friction and divorce endorse, promote, and contest the operation of official ideologies, judicial practices, and intellectual discourses in regulating the reconfiguration of family ethics, gender/class difference, and subject positions.

DIVORCE IN MODERN CHINA: HISTORY AND REPRESENTATIONS

It is generally agreed that divorce was rare in premodern China due to overwhelming social pressure.[12] In the majority of a limited number of divorce cases, the husband initiated divorce proceedings. Under the Qing dynasty (1644–1911) civil laws, the male side of the family could expel (*xiu*) the wife for any of the "seven conditions" (*qichu*) that can be traced back to the teachings in the *Book of Rites* (Liji), but a wife could request divorce only on very limited grounds.[13] After the overthrow of the Qing dynasty, the traditional legal code and cultural conventions concerning marriage and divorce were denounced by reformist intellectuals. The definition and structure of the family underwent radical changes—the family was transformed into, ideally, the cradle of "free" individuals who would grow up to be modern citizens with autonomous life choices.

As a part of the May Fourth family revolution, divorce signified a break from Confucian family structures and an emancipation of the individualist spirit. The May Fourth generation sought to establish the enlightenment structure of feeling "in staking uncompromising and nonnegotiable claims for individual freedom and autonomy."[14] In addition to free love and free marriage, reform-minded social activists and intellectuals also advocated free divorce as the essential means for asserting individual autonomy in terminating unhappy marriages and solving women's problems.[15]

In 1912, Tang Shaoyi, Cai Yuanpei, Song Jiaoren, and others founded the Society of Social Reformation (Shehui Gailiang Hui), aiming to modernize Chinese society in the spirit of humanism and scientism. They endorsed a series of new social customs including heterosexual monogamy, individual financial autonomy, free marriage and free divorce.[16] In 1920, Li Dazhao published "Understanding the Change of Modern Chinese Thoughts from an Economic Perspective" (You jingji shang jieshi Zhongguo jindai sixiang biandong de yuanyin), arguing that the legalization of free marriage and free divorce is a necessary precondition for abolishing the patriarchal system and achieving gender equality.[17] Hoping to reform the Chinese people's "feudal consciousness," the progressive intelligentsia also transplanted the Western idea of romantic love to Chinese soil in an effort to establish a modern companionate marriage that would nurture modern national subjects. In the drive to replace arranged marriage with companionate marriage, divorce was practiced and represented as the essential means of reforming the domestic sphere and modernizing the structure of feeling.

Lao She's novel *Divorce* (Lihun; 1933) illustrates such an intellectual yearning for modernizing the domestic via divorce. This novel zooms in on the marital crisis of Mr. Li, an urban-based proto-intellectual who yearns for romantic love, and his illiterate wife from the countryside, who remains nameless throughout the novel. Due to their radically different educational backgrounds and cultural habits, Mr. Li and his wife speak different languages and lack common interests. However, interventions by Mr. Li's colleagues keep this precarious marriage from falling apart. Performing the role of Mr. Li's surrogate patriarch, these colleagues discourage him from pursuing emotional autonomy and the freedom to divorce. Mrs. Li's aging body, however, bound by traditional customs and strained by household duties, cannot provide the visual pleasure sought by Mr. Li's gaze:

> [Mr. Li] dared not look at her [Mrs. Li] again. High-heeled shoes, voluptuous curves, flesh-colored silk stockings, painted lips, long narrow eyebrows . . . all these were at least two hundred years away from [Mrs. Li].[18]

Failing to catch on to modern bourgeois fashion, Mrs. Li is ridiculed for her awkward position in the Enlightenment intellectual's rosy picture of romantic love and sexual modernity. Investigating the discursive construction of sexual modernity, Michel Foucault examines the ways in which modern individuals "were led to focus their attention on themselves, to decipher, recognize, and acknowledge themselves as subjects of desire."[19] In modern China, the imported discourse of sexual modernity, inspired by Freudian psychoanalytic theories and "projected in literature, media, advertisements, and cultural theory," centers on heterosexual desire and behavior as the most important defining attribute of modern subjectivity.[20]

The middle-aged rural woman, with her desexualized body and bound feet, is represented as a *"walking human deficiency."*[21] The deterioration of her physical body and reproductive capacity goes against the Enlightenment teleology of social progress and national modernization. Epitomizing residual Chinese feudalism, the crippled and unenlightened woman is set up as the target of criticism in this divorce narrative narrated from the male perspective. In this view, the success of family reform is reliant on the (self)-reformation of "traditionally deformed" Chinese women, who are viewed as "the 'useless' and logically disposable body parts in a 'fast-forward' moving time-regime."[22]

The marital mismatch in Lao She's novel is a fictional (and dramatized) account of the real-life problems facing the "romantic generation of modern Chinese writers" such as Lu Xun, Guo Moruo,

Yu Dafu, Wu Zuxiang, Xu Zhimo, and Hu Shih who were caught between the old and the new, between aspirations to romantic individualism and practices of filial piety.[23] Imprisoned inside incompatible marriages, the men they were and wrote about epitomize the frustration of the male desire for a modern lifestyle.

Meanwhile, alternative accounts of the marital crisis from the other side, or from "the crippled sex," rarely reached the public eye.[24] One exception is Lu Xun's short story "Divorce" (Lihun; 1925), a narrative that takes a rural woman's point of view in an effort to expose the residual patriarchal domination in a divorce case. As the story shows, with little change in the fundamental socioeconomic structure, the touted modernization of divorce proceedings does not provide much protection for women's rights and interests. Changing the official term from *xiuqi* to *lihun* does not democratize the legal practice that is still entrenched in the unequal gender and class relationships of the patrilineal community.

In addition to Lao She and Lu Xun, a number of women writers dealt with the subject of divorce in their creative writings, but from drastically different perspectives. For instance, one of the most widely read stories by Zhang Ailing (also known as Eileen Chang), "Love in a Fallen City" (Qincheng zhi lian; 1943), sums up the cultural stigma, financial insecurity, and existential angst that Bai Liusu, a twenty-nine-year-old divorced Shanghai woman, endures during the war and political turmoil of 1930s China.[25] Instead of setting an example of the May Fourth–style independent "new woman," Bai seeks the "old-fashioned" recourse, that is, a second marriage that will secure a stable future with more socioeconomic resources.

Similarly, in another story by Chang, "Red Rose, White Rose" (Hong meigui yu bai meigui; 1944), Wang Jiaorui, a Singaporean Chinese living in Shanghai, also considers remarriage the only exit from an unhappy union and a failed extramarital romance. Their seemingly anachronistic choice reveals Chang's insight into the double standard at work in the bourgeois conjugal family—something which was often overlooked by advocates of romantic love and free marriage/divorce. As Haiyan Lee has noted, "while men can live a double life and make brief excursions into the world of adventurous affairs, for women, love is still a lifelong quest, the success or failure of which spells a lifetime of security (and perhaps happiness) or misery."[26]

Chang's later work "Stale Mates: A Short Story Set in the Time When Love Came to China" (Wusi yishi—Luo Wentao san mei tuanyuan; 1956) reveals an even more sarcastic attitude toward the May Fourth generation's idealization of romantic individualism and blindness to the double standard.[27] Rather than launching a family revolution, divorce—a supposedly modern practice of individualistic rebellion—ironically leads to a revival of "feudal" polygamy, one of the main targets of the Enlightenment intellectual discourse.

It is true that Eileen Chang and many contemporary Shanghai women writers concerned themselves with the question of gendered domesticity, "the formation and stabilization of the urban family";[28] however, Chang's trademark cynicism also guides readers to question this emerging discourse of gendered domesticity. Embedded in the power structure marked by unequal gender relationships of bourgeois conjugality and sexual modernity, how free, really, is free love and free marriage/divorce?

In her novel *Married for Ten Years* (Jiehun shinian; 1943), Su Qing, Chang's close friend, characterized another type of Shanghai woman who sought financial independence after divorcing her husband and shaking off the constraints of the traditional extended family. Compared to Chang's old-fashioned female characters, the autobiographical figure of a divorced Shanghai woman is more attuned to the imported image of Nora, the woman rebel in Henrik Ibsen's *A Doll's House*. Due to the translation and promotion of Ibsen's work by Chinese male intellectuals, Nora had become "an important archetype of the Chinese woman in search of independence" at the turn of the twentieth century.[29]

Despite their drastically different attitudes and approaches to the social issue of divorce, these literary works attest to the expanding legal freedom to divorce in Republican China. With the most liberal divorce laws in the world at the time, both the 1930 Nationalist and the 1931 Jiangxi Soviet civil codes granted men and women equal rights to marriage and divorce. In 1939, the Soviet government in the Shaanxi-Gansu-Ningxia Border Region also promulgated a new marriage law that stipulated "free will" (*ziyou yizhi*) and "affection" (*ganqing*) as the essential basis of marriage. Gu Yuan's black-and-white woodcut print *Appealing for Divorce* (Lihun su; 1943) depicts rural women in this region taking advantage of the new marriage law to initiate divorce proceedings in the 1940s.[30]

However, there was a huge gap between social reality and legal intent that was shaped by elitist May Fourth ideals and Communist revolutionary rhetoric.[31] It was not until the 1950s that the enforcement of the New Marriage Law became a nationwide campaign and, together with the Land Reform, dramatically changed Chinese family life and redefined the relationship between the state and the individual—especially for rural women.[32] The Chinese Communist Party (CCP) regime established the four cardinal principles of the New Marriage Law enacted in 1950: free marriage, gender equality, heterosexual monogamy, and protection of women's, children's, and senior citizens' legal rights.[33] This law, theoretically at least, "granted women their right to sue for divorce" and the "right to property and inheritance."[34] Emphasizing its importance, Mao Zedong declared: "The marriage law . . . is next in importance only to the Great Fundamental Law [the Constitution]."[35] Along with the family revolution, the Land Reform provided women equal rights to land.[36] For the first time in China's long history, women could stand on a more equal footing with their husbands, as Article 7 of the law stipulated.

Aiming for a totalistic revolution that was not limited to the political realm, state power inserted itself into the private sphere to revolutionize people's everyday practices. As a result, "[n]o institution has experienced the vicissitudes of the political, economic, and social changes that have marked the PRC's first half century more sharply than the family."[37] Because the divorce rate rose sharply after its promulgation, the New Marriage Law got its nickname of "divorce law." In the early years of the People's Republic of China, divorce "tower[ed] over all other categories of civil cases."[38] From 1950 to 1953, nearly two million divorces were granted.[39] Redefined by the state ideology as *funü*, or female subjects empowered by the political movements organized by the party-state, Chinese women often initiated divorce and used it as an essential vehicle for breaking away from arranged marriages and to pursue personal happiness.[40] Unlike what modernization and liberal feminist theories predicted, rural and working-class women—rather than urban-based educated women—benefited more from the political campaign of "revolutionizing the family,"[41] though many gender-specific problems still remained.[42]

The story "Registration" (Dengji; 1950), by the "peasant writer" Zhao Shuli, draws a picture of how the New Marriage Law changed traditional customs concerning courtship and marriage, especially in rural China.[43] His earlier work "The Marriage of Young Blackie" (Xiaoerhei jiehun; 1943) was also adapted for comic books, films, and local operas in an effort to reform the "feudal consciousness" of peasants and to politicize their ethical world.[44] "The Marriage of Young Blackie," Zhao's most widely read story, seeks to educate the masses about the new ideas of free love and free marriage under the CCP regime and to denounce traditional customs such as child brides, arranged marriages, and selling women.

The central story line of "The Marriage of Young Blackie" revolves around members of the younger generation fighting against their superstitious parents for free love and free marriage. This was a common plot in the May Fourth literature, but it often led to a tragic ending with the younger generation's failure or death. Set in the CCP revolutionary base in Shanxi, this age-old formula gets a new treatment.[45] Pursuing her rights to free marriage, Xiaoqin, Third Fairy's daughter, refuses to go along with the traditional practice of arranged marriage and thus establishes herself as a role model for the younger generation of Chinese women. Loyal to her handsome and hardworking peasant lover, Young Blackie, and prudent in her contacts with the opposite sex, Xiaoqin becomes a new role model of political consciousness and sexual behavior for the emerging subject of socialist Chinese women.

Acting as a negative foil for the younger generation of Chinese women represented by her daughter, Third Fairy, a middle-aged rural woman, is represented as the repository of superstitious beliefs and the "feudal" mind-set. In addition to her political "backwardness," Third Fairy is also portrayed as sexually improper. She likes to wear fancy clothes, heavy makeup, and gaudy trinkets in an age-inappropriate manner and flirt with young men in the village. Setting up the characterization of such a coquettish and sometimes hysterical middle-aged woman as the target of ridicule reveals, ironically, the misogynist rhetoric embedded in CCP political campaigns for women's liberation and family reform. While granting younger women more rights to "free love, free marriage," family reform also intended to establish a more prudish sexual culture that would banish polygamous, promiscuous, and age- and class-inappropriate sexual behaviors. Thus, the "everyday occurrence in the life of village sexuality" became "the object not only of a collective intolerance" but of an entire biopolitical discourse that constructs a connection between one's political identity and one's sexual performance.[46]

In this light, it is not too hard to understand why Fang Ji's controversial short story "Let's Make Life Even Better" (Rang shenghuo biande geng meihao ba; 1950) evoked severe criticism with its highly problematic portrayal of a loose rural woman as "a proper role model for new China's women."[47] Similar trends in gender representations can also be found in early PRC film productions such as *City without Night* (*Buye cheng*; dir. Tang Xiaodan, 1957), *Tight Encirclement* (*Tianluo diwang*; dir. Gu Eryi, 1955), *Sentinel under the Neon Lights* (*Nihongdeng xia de shaobing*; dir. Wang Ping and Ge Xin, 1963), and *Two Stage Sisters* (*Wutai jiemei*; dir. Xie Jin, 1965). These films tend to feminize the class enemy who attempts to corrupt the "socialist new men" and sabotage the socialist cause, highlighting their eroticized bodies for voyeuristic gaze while holding them outside of the proper moral and ideological boundary. Inscribing sexual differences in the Maoist rubric of class struggle, not unlike the frequent characterization of the femme fatale in classic Hollywood cinema, the misogynist rhetoric embedded in these popular narratives is enhanced through associating the female body with dangerous and improper (classwise) erotic pleasures.

The reformation of political and moralistic vision goes hand in hand with a new imagination of the female body and libidinal economy.[48] Rather than desexualizing Chinese women as the conventional wisdom asserts, the new legal culture, moral code, and cultural production still construct a highly eroticized woman's body for popular consumption, at the same time associating eroticized femininity with ideological Otherness, such as residual feudalism, a bourgeois lifestyle, and dangerous urbanism.

Compared to narratives of free love and free marriage, cultural representations of "free divorce" were limited in number. A few peasant-oriented stories about divorce were published immediately after the release of the 1950 New Marriage Law. These works, including "The Story of Qunni's Divorce" (Qunni lihun ji), "Li Fengjin," "Feng Junying Gets a Divorce" (Feng Junying lihun), "Erqiao Gets a Divorce" (Erqiao lihun), "Little Husband" (Xiao nüxu), were all published as cheap pamphlets between 1950 and 1954. Aiming to promote the New Marriage Law among local peasantry, all these stories were set in rural areas and narrated in colloquial style. The protagonist was often a rural woman who was encouraged to "speak bitterness" (*suku*) (a term to be fully discussed in the following two chapters) about her "feudal" marriage and to initiate a divorce for self-emancipation (*fanshen*). In order to make the revolutionary rhetorics of *suku* and *fanshen* more accessible to peasants, most of whom were illiterate, these propaganda pamphlets borrowed narrative techniques from indigenous artistic forms such as local operas, vernacular storytelling, and "linked pictorials" (*lianhuan hua*).

However, the political campaign of family revolution turned out to be short-lived. After 1953, the top-down movement of marriage reform was not encouraged as much because the party-state was concerned that the soaring divorce rate might affect social stability and consequently the legitimacy of its regime. During the Cultural Revolution (1966–76), Red Guards saw divorce as "a manifestation of promiscuity and unethical behavior unbefitting a true Communist."[49] Such puritanical sexual morals brought the divorce rate to a historic low. Accordingly, between 1953 and 1976, literary, dramatic, and artistic representations of divorce were also rare.

Of course, there were still a few deviant works published during this period. One is the short story "Divorce" (Lihun), published in *People's Literature* in 1957, on the eve of the disastrous Great Leap Forward (1958–61). It paints a glorious picture of agricultural collectivization, prioritizing a message of political propaganda over realistic depictions of marital conflict. However, beneath its surface of ideological didacticism, the characterization of Lin Xingchun, the peasant wife, is indicative of new changes in gender politics and rural family life.

Lin Fang, the male protagonist of the story, is attracted to a city girl while he is working in Shanghai. Determined to divorce his peasant wife, Xingchun, he pays a visit to his hometown. To his amazement, he finds that Xingchun has become a competent laborer on the farm, despite her delicate constitution, and an independent decision-maker at home. While Lin Fang is away from home, she looks after his mother and their toddler son. Outside the home, she also participates actively in political meetings and community activities, learns to read and write, and often offers counseling and mediation on domestic affairs to other village women. At the end of the story, Lin Fang is so impressed by the drastic change in his home village and his wife that he decides to stay with her. The happy ending, typical of Maoist narratives of marital strife such as Xiao Yemu's "Between the Two of Us" (Women fufu zhijian; 1950), Deng Youmei's "On the Cliff" (Zai xuanya shang; 1956), and Shen Fu's film *Spring is Splendid Color* (Wanzi qianhong zong shi chun, 1959), reduces the disruptive potential of the family crisis and reinforces the proper domestic and ideological boundaries.

A more well-known exception is the 1959 film *Song of Youth* (Qingchun zhi ge; dir. Cui Wei and Chen Huaikai). The film is based on Yang Mo's novel (1958) of the same title, which has been acclaimed as a classic bildungsroman celebrating a petit bourgeois student's evolution into a steadfast revolutionary. Lin Daojing, the female protagonist, divorces her first husband because he prioritizes esoteric scholarship and domestic bliss over class struggle and nationalist resistance against the Japanese invasion of China. This woman-initiated act of divorce signifies a rupture of the male-dominant bourgeois domestic order in favor of her ultimate embrace of the Communist revolution and mass movement.[50]

One meaningful discrepancy between the novel and its filmic adaptation is particularly worth noting. In the original literary text, Lin becomes involved in various romantic relationships with four men and cohabits with two of them. The film downplays Lin's sexually libertine attitude, which is typical of progressive female characters in the May Fourth generation's literary works, such as Ding Ling's "Diary of Miss Sophie" (Shafei nüshi de riji; 1928). Yu Yongze, Lin's first husband, calls her "my wife." Additionally, a close-up shot of a framed wedding picture on the wall emphasizes the fact that Lin is legally married to Yu. The emphasis on the legally sanctioned domestic sphere in which the woman revolutionary is properly situated indicates a conservative turn in CCP gender ideology.

Compared to *Song of Youth*, some lesser-known works include Sun Qian's story "A Strange Tale of Divorce" (Qiyi de lihun gushi, 1956) and Feng Cun's short story "A Divorce Case" (Yige lihun anjian). Sharing a similar structure with Bu Wen's story "Divorce," "A Strange Tale of Divorce" also depicts a triangular relationship between an urbanized husband, his peasant wife left behind in a rural village, and his new lover—a city girl. However, the ending of the latter story turns out to be drastically different from the former, due to the male protagonist's ideologically wrong choice: he loses his job, his wife, his children, and above all, his girlfriend because he insists on getting a divorce. The relentless punishment of the urbanized husband cancels out the possibility of making serious reflections on the vast gap between city and country and on the unequal gendered division of labor. Instead, it turns the divorce narrative into a conventional cautionary tale in which the socialist government steps in to play the role of a substitute Confucian patriarch to maintain the time-honored family ethics against divorce. Through the means of political discipline and administrative punishment, the fusion of residual family ethics and the emerging political order was made possible.

Published in the Henan-based minor literary magazine *Torrents* (Benliu) in 1957, "A Divorce Case" tells a different story of divorce. In this piece, the husband and the wife cannot solve their domestic conflicts despite their common socialist ideals and political status (model workers and members of the Communist Youth League). As a result, they file for divorce. Although the CCP bureaucrats criticize them for this "bourgeois" practice, in the end the couple's divorce petition is granted, thanks to their perseverance. This story has often been read as an intellectual's gesture of rejecting the party-state's "political control over personal life."[51] However, such a dichotomist view of the political versus the personal reduces the meaning of the political to the interventionism of the rigid party-state bureaucracy. Such a limited view fails to address the unequal power relations and gendered division of labor in domestic politics. As depicted in Feng Cun's story, while the husband devotes himself wholeheartedly to the sublime cause of socialist construction, the wife has to occupy herself with devalued housework and a woman's reproductive duties.

If we agree that capitalist modernization separates work and home through spatial compartmentalization (e.g., suburbanization), then it can safely be concluded that socialist modernization tends to redraw the boundary between outside and inside by redefining the meaning of "work" (*gongzuo*). The state-touted gender equality only means women stepping outside the domestic sphere, taking up men's work, not men retreating inside, doing women's work that is hardly counted as work. Usually only paid, nonagricultural, non-household-based labor is considered to be formal work, while housework is trivialized as "household chores" (*jiawu huo'r*) performed mainly by women inside the boundaries of the home. Such a pattern of spatialized gender inequality, justified by the reinvented meaning of work, exposes the persistent patriarchal power structure in socialist gender politics and family life, which left room for the return of male centrism in post-revolutionary China.[52]

REVOLUTIONIZING THE INTERIOR
IN POST-REVOLUTIONARY CHINA

In 1978, the Third Plenum of the Eleventh Party's Congress marked the end "of a prolonged period of revolutionary transformation of

Chinese society and the beginning of a new era of consolidation, adaptation, and modernization."[53] When post-revolutionary China changed its agenda from pursuing "revolutionary modernity" to seeking global capitalist modernity, the reconstitution of class power and social relationships informed the redefinition of gender, family, marriage, and divorce. Conditioned by a free market economy and legal reforms, post-revolutionary divorce politics is manifestly different from that of the Republican or Mao era.

In 1980, the New Marriage Law was superseded by the Second Marriage Law. Divorce rates dramatically increased following the promulgation of this more liberal marriage law. "The Great Fission of Yin and Yang" (Yin yang da liebian), Su Xiaokang's well-known work of reportage literature, documents a wide range of real-life, often sensational, divorce cases filed during this period.

Article 25 of the Second Marriage Law stipulated that divorce could be granted on the grounds of "the breakdown of mutual affection" (ganqing polie). This move to legalize domestic sentiments recognized the essential significance of affection and feelings in marital life. The reorientation of legal discourse and practices was in alignment with the celebration of individual freedom and romantic sentiments among 1980s intellectuals.

After the Cultural Revolution, the resurging discourse of liberal individualism remapped the intersections of society, family, and state. As a counterdiscourse to the hegemonic official ideology, it had enormous liberating power, particularly when combined with a wave of feminist writings in Chinese literature in the 1980s, such as Zhang Jie's groundbreaking literary works "Love Must Not Be Forgotten" (Ai, shi buneng wangji de; 1979) and "The Ark" (Fangzhou; 1982). Complementary to liberal individualism, Freudian theories were deployed to render the individualized psyche the primary site producing heterosexual desires, affects, and the essential foundation for identity formation. However, an overemphasis on liberal individualism and personal privacy also tended to obscure a critical vision of the socioeconomic consequences of marriage and divorce.

In the following decades, the pace of China's marketization and globalization accelerated. During this period, "restrictions on divorce were further relaxed as a result of the 'fourteen articles' issued by the Supreme People's Court on 21 November 1989."[54] Article 8 stipulates that the court may grant divorce "when a petitioner files for a second time, even if he or she had been the offending party in an extramarital affair."[55] The Second Marriage Law was amended in 2001, replacing direct involvement by the state in domestic affairs with financial compensation for the "the weaker or disadvantaged party" (*ruozhe*) in divorce cases. The family is redefined as an economic unit rather than a political entity or production unit, as it was in the Mao era.

Indicating the state's retreat from the citizen's bedroom, the Second Marriage Law and its 2001 amendment are often hailed for their emphasis on private freedom in marriage and divorce. Correspondingly, divorce is often represented as a project of materializing domestic reformation and individual autonomy in the private realm. Complementary to the legalization of the private, a new popular culture capitalizing on domestic interiority has begun to take shape. Intensified transnational commodity and cultural flows since the 1980s have fostered the circulation of a global middle-class culture in various mass products including films, TV dramas, domestic fiction, commercial advertisements, women's magazines, and household management and home remodeling handbooks from Euro-America, South Korea, Japan, Taiwan, Hong Kong, and other parts of the developed world.

Localizing such a global middle-class culture, indigenous divorce representations do not simply recognize social anxiety about the current family crisis but play a key role in fueling the individual desire for a new future-oriented project—building a better tomorrow not by socialist revolution but by investing in the reformation of the domestic interior. Meanwhile, as a trope of rupture and radical change, divorce is also mobilized as a social practice and representational strategy of negating a personal and social past that was associated with the collectivist ethos and state interference with the private realm. Through such a dialectic movement of reformation and rupture, interruption and reconstruction, the historical scheme of remapping the temporal order is predicated on a restructuring of the spatial (dis)connections between state/individual, work/home, public/private, and outside/inside, down to the most intimate levels of people's everyday practices in marriage and divorce.

Such a trend of spatial segregation and social compartmentalization is part and parcel of the historical process of modernization. Talking about the formation of capitalist modernity in Second Empire Paris, Walter Benjamin places particular emphasis on the division between work and home together with a new sense of the public and the private:

> For the private individual, the place of dwelling is for the first time
> opposed to the place of work. The former constitutes itself as the inte-
> rior. Its complement is the office. The private individual, who in the
> office has to deal with reality, needs the domestic interior to sustain
> him in his illusions.[56]

Nancy Armstrong and Gillian Brown have analyzed the historical
formation of this domestic interior from a gender perspective and
address the pivotal role of bourgeois women therein.[57] Teasing out the
tangled relationships between domestic interior, bourgeois individualism, and class identity, Nancy F. Cott argues that "the discourse of
domesticity was a prime means by which members of the ascendant
middle class understood themselves as men and women and presented
themselves to the world."[58]

Interiority (or the lack thereof) is also a contested issue in discussions of modern and contemporary Chinese literature. Chen Xiaoming, a Chinese literary critic at Beijing University, announced the
advent of "an age of no interiority."[59] For Chen, the New Urbanites
Fiction (Xin Shimin Xiaoshuo) of He Dun and Chi Li mirrors a postmodern Chinese social reality characterized by glamorous appear-
ances of global capitalist modernity without any fundamental interiority or transcending spiritual values.

In a rebuttal to Chen's claim, Xiaobing Tang provides a brief genealogy of the notion of interiority in contemporary Chinese intellectual
discourses. In the early 1980s, Liu Zaifu wrote a seminal discussion
of human subjectivity that could be read as a correlative to the notion
of interiority. Comparing the operating strategies of subjectivity and
interiority in resisting "the dehumanizing force" of a historical teleology, Tang contends:

> If the discourse of subjectivity, inspired by belief in a humanist uni-
> versality, once served as a veiled plea for positive creative as well as
> political freedom, then interiority could be viewed as a defense of
> negative freedom, the right to resist by escaping and turning inward.
> Both concepts, in agreement with the Enlightenment tradition of anti-
> despotism, affirm human liberty through the possibility of a reflec-
> tive, critical consciousness.[60]

Then, through a close reading of He Dun's stories, Tang pinpoints
"an emerging form of interiority, which is closely related to a new
sense of private interior space and eventually to the necessary mechanism of interiorization."[61] Tang focuses particularly on the prevailing social practice of interior design and decoration as well as its

literary representations. Drawing on Jean Baudrillard's theory about the "sign language of commodities," he suggests that "interior design, by instilling a sign-consciousness in our most private and personal sphere, serves to acculturate us to the system of sign-objects—namely, to interiorize the political economy of the sign."[62]

Tang's discussion of the evolution of the concept of interiority from the 1980s humanist discourse to the 1990s consumerist culture is intriguing. However, in addition to the commodity aesthetics of interior design, social practices and cultural representations of divorce not only internalize "the political economy of the sign" but also form a dialogic relationship with shifting intellectual discourses and official ideologies to articulate a psychic and emotional structure of interiority. This emerging discourse of private interiority operates not simply as a strategy of resistance on the part of intellectuals but, more frequently, as a pivotal mechanism of negation, differentiation, segmentation, and domination along the division lines of class, age, gender, and ethnicity.

During the post-revolutionary years, socialist experimentation was replaced by the intellectual pursuit of "universal human nature imagined as the essential ingredient of cosmopolitan worldliness."[63] With the bankruptcy of radical revolutionary ideology and the expansion of global capitalism, the spiritual pursuit of the ultimate authenticity of universal humanity has often been imagined and realized within the domestic interior. As China sees unprecedented social mobility and border-crossing population flows, a strong yearning for retrieving the lost home prevails in the cultural imagination. On the one hand, radical marketization and privatization dis-embed people from the network of political and social collectivities. These social pressures catalyze the breeding of *homo economicus*—the new species of cosmopolitan modern being who is attuned to the demands of a global market economy and is regulated by the conduct code of neoliberal (self-)governance. On the other hand, as post-revolutionary Chinese citizens become increasingly cynical and suspicious of Maoist socialism and revolutionary collectivism, home—usually understood as the modern nuclear family based on heterosexual monogamy—becomes *the* utopia, the last shelter for dis-embedded individuals to secure some emotional comfort and spiritual transcendence above all the historic vicissitudes of the dramatically changing times.

While Dai Houying's influential novel *Ah, Humanity!* (Ren ah ren; 1980) and Tian Zhuangzhuang's banned film *Blue Kite*

(Lan fengzheng; 1993) vividly illustrate the destruction of private domestic space by political violence during the heyday of the socialist revolution, Yu Hua's novel *To Live* (Huozhe; 1993) and the 1994 filmic adaptation directed by Zhang Yimou, which was also banned, strike a sharp contrast between intimate familial bonding and the bloodsucking—both literally and metaphorically—party-state. In order to counter political totalitarianism, these post-revolutionary literary and cinematic narratives established the antagonism of the cold-blooded state toward the heartwarming family.

Radical revolutionary ideology—sometimes lumped together with Confucianism as a loosely defined mainstream Chinese culture or "feudal consciousness"—is regarded as the very obstacle to the restoration of both individual autonomy and domestic order, which is similar to the way May Fourth iconoclasts viewed Confucianism. In a wave of globalizing consumer culture, the privatization of home ownership and lifestyle is touted as an essential means of "increasing citizens' autonomy and power."[64] Therefore, the construction of a private domestic interior is predicated on a celebratory rhetoric of rupture with the revolutionary modernity. Often a reaction to the "repressive" revolutionary modernity and its structure of feeling, post-revolutionary representations of divorce play a key role in negotiating with the past and remapping a new domestic space that safeguards the reproduction of a future-oriented generation through privatized financial and affective investments.

All these converging forces of legal, psychohistorical, and cultural discourses have led to the internalization of the domestic sphere on three levels:

First, the sweeping privatization of home ownership gives spatial forms to China's socioeconomic differences and the middle-class dream of a "private paradise," a historic process dubbed "spatialization of class."[65] The subjectivizing effect of the neoliberal ethics of self-governance and private accumulation is particularly noteworthy, because "[p]rivatization was a deliberate shift in China's governing strategy to set citizens free to be entrepreneurs of the self." However, the exercise of private freedom and individual rights is allowed only "within the political limits set by the socialist state."[66] Little legal or institutional support is offered to encourage individual participation in social movements to assert civil rights or manage public affairs. Under such sociopolitical constraints, the domestic site turns out to be the safest site for the performance of the individualized subject and the exercise of newly acquired power to fulfill dreams of self-realization, private accumulation, and consumption. Meanwhile, the dismantling of the state welfare system, along with decreased social trust, forces Chinese individuals to "fall back on the family and personal network of *guanxi* [social connections]."[67] In the process of the individualization and differentiation of Chinese society, "the family remains the most important reference point for the individual's self-identity."[68]

Second, beyond the neoliberal rationale of private ownership and market individualism, the revolution in the domestic interior is also invested in constant articulations of a new structure of feeling and libidinal economy. Popular divorce narratives tend to translate the historical rupture and social fragmentation into a personal problem related to inner feelings and private desires that need to be solved within the domestic domain. Alleviating the prevailing sense of disorientation and anxiety about massive social and domestic dislocation, a rich lexicon of individual sentiments, emotionality, self-expressions, and private intimacy has been invented and circulated in these narratives. The sentimentalization of domesticity, or the domestication of sentimentality, seeks to enshrine the last resort of an affective haven by cutting its links with the tumultuous exterior, be it socialist revolution or cutthroat capitalism. The success of this strategy, however, remains a question to be addressed, and the interconnectedness of the artificially divided realms of outside/inside, public/private, male/female and so on, merits investigation.

Third, domestic fiction and divorce melodramas, with their dominant interior setting, overflowing sentiments and feelings, and exclusive focus on family relations, among other representational conventions and generic features, are often marginalized as "feminine" genres. Targeted mainly at middle-class female audiences dwelling in the domestic interior, these popular narratives not only inscribe a new gender and class position but also feminize the confined domestic space as a privileged venue in which this position is desired, imagined, and performed. These narratives reveal a trend of spatialization of gender: if the projection of ideal manhood is often invested in earning private home ownership by venturing into the outside world (read: market economy), then the defining mark of femininity is portrayed as the skillful management of consumption, reproductive sexuality, and the affective economy associated with the home. Hence, the radical reconstitution of gender, family, and class relationships has been re-narrativized as an interruption and reconstruction of a feminized interiority that is now embedded in the new social, affective, and spatial order in the making.

MIDDLE-AGED DIVORCEES IN A POST-FEMINIST AGE

Claiming to provide a panoramic view of contemporary Chinese society, Hu Fayun's reportage literature *The Fourth-Generation Women* (Di sidai nüxing; 2000) collects "real-life" cases of conjugal and domestic conflicts facing contemporary Chinese women who grew up in the reform era. Hu includes a letter from a woman named Silan who tells readers that her husband has quit his job in a government agency to start a private business. The man's professional evolution— "plunging into the sea of business" (*xiahai*), a typical career trajectory for male urbanites in the 1990s—brings their nuclear family (husband, wife, and child) more material wealth, but less "quality time" together. At the end of the letter, Silan cries out: "How I wish that we could return to the past when we were poor, but when he would spend every night with our child and me!"[69] Connecting Silan's letter to the social issue of family disintegration in a transitional period, Hu, a prominent male writer, comments:

> Only because of this type of "boudoir lament" [*guiyuan*], and only because of women's longing for family life and familial love, has this world not become a crazy machine driven by man's greed for fame and success. As a result, men in this world not only pursue social recognition and material wealth but also care about their women and families.[70]

Hu's unreserved praise for women's timeless "natural" attachment to family life does not tackle the man/outside versus woman/inside dichotomy but instead perpetuates this gendered division of space. On the one hand, he associates men's social success with achieving fame and wealth in a highly competitive market economy. On the other hand, he returns women to the domestic site where their only obligation is to guard modern men's emotional well-being by acting as an antidote to the alienating forces of market capitalism. This fantasized timeless image of a feminine homemaker situated in a binary structure of family versus market reproduces the "universal" significance of domestic interiority.

The spatial segregation and temporal universalization reduces the complex relations of women and history into a singular mode.

While history has been decontextualized and de-territorialized into a cultural sign standing for the universal and eternal male-centered power structure, women are abstracted as the embodiment of the pure feminine interior uncontaminated by the "dirty" politics and money of the masculine outside. An oppositional dichotomy of man/culture versus woman/nature is naturalized through such a vision of history.

Seeking to resist the hegemony of a male-centered master narrative of socialist revolution, this type of introspective feminine narrative has become so prevalent in a post-revolutionary age that it has given birth to a new master narrative that renders women as prediscursive and apolitical creatures situated at the heart of the domestic interior. Subverting the gender politics of China's "revolutionary modernity," post-revolutionary Chinese intellectuals criticize representations of socialist subjects in Maoist Chinese literature as lacking psychological depth, creative individuality, and universal humanity with a sexual core. Seeking to reconstruct a universal sexualized and psychologized modern subject of desire, divorce narratives in post-revolutionary China often center on a revolution of the inner structure of feeling that has been launched within the confines of the private domestic sphere. This redrawing of the boundary between work and home supports the received wisdom that one's innermost true self can be displayed only in the private realm of the domestic, while one's social identity is only a disguise that has nothing to do with the interior authenticity of the modern subject. As Teresa de Lauretis warns, "'the personal is political' all too often translates into 'the personal instead of the political'."[71]

What is often overlooked is that the construction of such an ideology of interiority can never be effective without the regulation of the party-state ideology. With the accelerating marketization and dismantling of the socialist welfare system, the nuclear family is transformed from a political entity into a self-sufficient economic unit, or from an extension of the socialist work-unit system and an ideologically charged (re)production site into a privatized space. The domestic interior now serves as a feminized incubator of a better-quality new generation ensured by the future-oriented accumulation of vast financial and emotional investments.

On a national scale, state policies seek to expand the individual freedom of consumption and promote the stability and self-sufficiency of the middle-class family.[72] Such a private "harmonious" interior is embodied by the fantasized figure of a young, sexy, yet dutiful housewife who guards the sweet home against the invasion of a competitive and exploitative capitalist outside. Feminine youth, "fashioned as the timeless object of male desire," now indexes a new desire for capitalist modernization and global consumer aesthetics in the place of the May Fourth romantic individualism or socialist revolutionary idealism.[73]

However, little attention has been paid to the population of middle-aged women and their gender- and age-specific problems. Ever since the May Fourth period, few Chinese feminist theories and practices have shown genuine concern for this particular social group or for the gender inequality of divorce practices. Since the May Fourth movement in 1919, "women's liberation" (funü jiefang) has often been reduced to "girls' liberation" (shaonü jiefang), with its focus on "free marriage."[74] The most visible and powerful May Fourth symbol is "the image of a daughter who left her patriarchal family in pursuit of free love."[75] Through the means of heterosexual courtship and "free marriage," the father's daughter was saved by the male, entered a conjugal family, and thus completed the cycle of "girls' liberation." However, women's subjugated status within the confines of domestic space remained largely intact.

Similarly, during the socialist campaign of women's liberation, middle-aged women were not the focus of state feminism. The Maoist "iron girl" (tie guniang), the role model of the socialist women's liberation campaign, was an unmarried young girl who participated actively in social production. Emphasizing the revolutionary zeal and productive power of the youthful body, the idealized femininity of the iron girl associates gender biopolitics, heroic collectivism, and labor aesthetics with the new socialist subject of youth. While the Maoist revolution focused on the liberation of women's social productivity, the gender problems of persistent patriarchy and the double burden shouldered by married women were frequently dismissed as trivial or vulgar personal problems.[76]

Even those divorce narratives published after the release of the New Marriage Law in 1950 failed to deal with with these issues. Rather, they attributed the unequal gendered division of labor to the residual forces of the "old society" and painted a glorious picture of gender equality in a "new China." What has often been overlooked is the fact that the conception of family as a naturalized physical space based on gendered division of labor was never seriously questioned. And the socially accepted feminine roles of being a wife and a mother within the domestic space remained a prominent marker indicating a radical rupture between one's girlhood and womanhood and consequently expelled middle-aged married women from the political agenda of women's liberation. The question "What happens after a daughter gets married?" was rarely raised or discussed.

In the post-revolutionary era, "the Maoist image of strong, heroic women was ridiculed as a symbol of backward obstacles to China's modernization" and supplied a ready excuse for the massive layoffs of women workers.[77] A whole cultural industry created in the name of the "beauty economy" (meinü jingji) has focused on how to look young and stay young, ideally forever. Countless rounds of beauty contests and pageants have objectified the female body as the eroticized target of the male gaze and promoted the bewitching glamour of the urban facade. The proliferation of glamorous youthful female images in a global popular culture places enormous pressure on middle-aged women and creates a profound sense of age anxiety.

In sharp contrast to the glamorous image of remasculinized male elites and resexualized young women, Chinese women growing up in the Mao era are often depicted as "over-liberated" and thus unfeminine in post-revolutionary divorce narratives. They hardly fit the feminine role model stipulated by postfeminist sensibilities that place great value on "the formulation of an expressive personal lifestyle and the ability to select the right commodities to attain it."[78] Going against the teleological time of progress toward a better tomorrow, the aging bodies of middle-aged women expose the irreversible traces of productive and reproductive labor. Resisting the cumulative changes that time and labor inflict on a woman's body, the commodification of young femininity emphasizes the wholeness and purity of the feminine body as the object of male desire and an effective trope of modernist glamour free from the pains and strains of strenuous labor. The constant reproduction of the fetishization of feminine youth in mass culture leads to a misogynist vilification of the middle-aged woman. While the sexualized and fertile youthful female body is upheld as the ahistorical gender norm, the middle-aged woman's body is rendered as abnormal, unfeminine, deficient, dirty, and pathological—it "can contribute neither to the continuity of the species nor to the pleasure of men."[79]

To address this concern, specific gender- and age-related problems facing middle-aged women in marital crises, as portrayed in literary and cultural representations of divorce, will be discussed in the following chapters. In particular, the "postfeminist presumption that feminism is dated, irrelevant, and inapplicable to current culture" will be problematized and countered.[80] Since the 1990s, American popular culture has developed a postfeminist master narrative of "retreatism," which tends to naturalize the gendered division of labor while evading structural social inequities and fetishizing "housewife chic."[81] In the Chinese context, the historical legacy of women's liberation is often discredited. Rather, it is suggested that in a "post-women's-liberation" era, the solution to marital strife and family crisis is to re-gender the "over-liberated" middle-aged Chinese woman within the domestic sphere.[82] Thus, the story of divorce is retold as a personal issue at the heart of a well-guarded domestic interior free from the moral or political interventions of kinship networks or socialist state mediation.

However, the construction of such an autonomous and feminized domestic interior is highly fragile and contested. What has often been overlooked is the fact that the "family revolution" goes hand in hand with China's metamorphosis into a "risk society" in which "the state reforms governmental institutions to redirect responsibilities and redistribute risks to the individuals."[83] As a result, the neoliberal rationale of optimizing individual gains through "free choices" penetrates the fabric of people's private lives and changes the rules of affective transactions. Hence, the question, again, is, how free (what freedom and whose?) is free marriage/divorce, as the mode of governance in post-revolutionary China shifts from socialist intervention in the private to the penetration of neoliberal market logic into the domestic interior?

CHAPTER ONE

Divorcing the Rural

Miss Science and Marital Crisis in the Reform Era

Members of the May Fourth generation often found themselves caught between the old "feudal consciousness" and the new "modern consciousness" when they struggled to modernize family life by practicing free love and free marriage/divorce. Decades later, during the post-revolutionary period, a renewed discourse of modernization replaced the Maoist rhetoric of class struggle and "continuous revolution" to reconfigure the entanglements between individual, state, and family. As a result of the shifting ideological and institutional environments, the male intellectual's moral quandary and identity crisis caused by the gaps between the traditional and the modern as well as between the rural and the urban once again became the essential subject of fiction about divorce and marital strife.

Breaking the political and moral constraints imposed by socialist ideology, the intellectual discourses centering on romantic love and Enlightenment humanism in the early 1980s redefined the form and meaning of love, marriage, and divorce. This chapter pays a critical visit to the very starting point of China's reform era through a close reading of two influential, award-winning stories about the marital crisis of Shi Ping, a peasant-turned-intellectual, and his extramarital affair with Qiu Fei, a woman scientist in Shanghai. In recontextualizing and reexamining the texts on social cultural conditions since the 1980s, this chapter is as much about the past decades as it is about current social problems, particularly the widening gap between the urban and the rural and the increasing tension between the educated elites and the masses in post-revolutionary China.

In the face of radical marketization and global consumerism, a wave of nostalgia for the 1980s is sweeping across China's cultural landscape. That period is often commemorated as a "euphoric decade," when Chinese intellectuals were idealistic iconoclasts who stood at the center of the cultural transformation that was believed to be a precondition for China's modernization.[1] Viewed through such a nostalgic lens, the 1980s intellectual-led "new enlightenment movement" (xin qimeng yundong) is comparable to the earlier May Fourth movement in terms of their allegedly common agenda of bringing Enlightenment thoughts, humanism, scientific knowledge, and modern consciousness to China. In the past few decades, many scholars have written critical works on the 1980s,[2] yet none of these studies considers the interaction between the dominant intellectual discourse of the decade and the drastically changing social life in the rural areas, particularly in the private sphere of the domestic interior.

Outside of the field of literary and cultural studies, Susan Greenhalgh provides an ethnographic account of Dengist China's turn to scientism in the 1980s, revealing the ways in which a group of cyberneticists "scientized" the one-child policy and how this radical policy affected Chinese society, particularly peasant family life.[3] However, this groundbreaking work focuses on the policymaking process, not on the day-to-day lives of the Chinese peasantry. Furthermore, Greenhalgh emphasizes the natural scientists' crucial role in the 1980s "scientizing moment" without taking into account the interaction, cooperation, and contestation between scientists and humanists in this transitional period. As a result, many pressing questions have been left unanswered: What structures of classification and domination were built up and sentimentalized in the process of institutionalizing scientific knowledge production and dissemination? What role did literary representations play in legitimizing 1980s intellectual discourse centered on the "emancipatory capacity of knowledge"? In what ways does an alliance of scientific modernity and literary representation affect the reimagination of private life in the domestic interior?

Two controversial short stories written jointly by Chen Kexiong and Ma Ming in the 1980s are illuminating in this regard. In both pieces, the power of scientific knowledge is constantly invoked to naturalize strategies of political domination and to intrude in people's marital life. The first story is "Return, Cries the Cuckoo" (Dujuan tigui). First published in the literary magazine *Youth* (Qingchun) in 1980, it won the national Youth Literary Prize and aroused a heated debate regarding the tension between "feudal" tradition and scientific modernity, a common theme of intellectual debate at this historical moment.

The story is narrated mainly from the point of view of Shi Ping, the male protagonist, a married peasant from a remote village. At the end of the Cultural Revolution, Shi is admitted into college for his literary talent. There, he falls in love with a girl studying nuclear physics, stirring up a deep dissatisfaction with his rural lifestyle. When graduation approaches, he is forced to make a choice between staying with the well-educated girl in the big city or going back to his peasant wife and young daughter in the countryside. After a long, bitter internal struggle, he finally decides to return to his peasant wife's side.

Discussing their motivation for composing such a morally ambivalent story, Chen and Ma revealed that they had witnessed many similar divorce cases when they attended Fudan University in Shanghai. Some of their fellow students came from the countryside, while many others had been "sent-down" youths (xiaxiang zhishi qingnian) during the Cultural Revolution. These students had gotten married and had children in their rural homes before leaving to attend university in a big city. Chen and Ma wrote this story to expose their marital problems and internal agonies.

One year later, in 1981, Chen and Ma wrote a widely acclaimed sequel, "Flying Afar" (Feixiang yuanfang), to their first story. As the title indicates, the second piece resonates with the Chinese intellectuals' desire to "march toward the world" (zouxiang shijie) and to reconnect with the global metropolitan modernity lurking on the distant horizon. Almost an allegory of this new global imaginary, "Flying Afar" completely rewrites the ending of "Return, Cries the Cuckoo": the male protagonist finally divorces his peasant wife and chooses to dwell permanently in the city in the hope of pursuing free love, individual development, and a modern lifestyle. Although the central plot about a man's difficult choice between his peasant wife and city girlfriend is reminiscent of some 1950s divorce narratives, the sequel revises the typical happy ending of those earlier works, such as Xiao Yemu's "Between the Two of Us" (1950) and Bu Wen's "Divorce" (1957), which favor the peasant wife and reunite the alienated couple.

This ideology of rural favoritism changed in the reform era. As sent-down youths returned to the city, the city itself also returned to the center stage of modernization. Here, the word "city" does not refer to any specific city but to a deterritorialized space of modernity in which the modern subjectivity and the values of modernity can be imagined and materialized. In addition, what is especially interesting in this new narrative of modernity is the explicit evocation of the power of modern science, mediated through poetic aesthetics, to resolve the protagonist's marital problems and internal conflicts.

It has been noted that the reconfiguration of the social stratification and power structure caused an "epistemological reorientation" in the 1980s.[4] This insightful analysis captures well the spirit of a historic moment marked by a dramatic paradigm shift. However, complementary to this "epistemological reorientation" that was thought to have taken place mainly on the rational level and in the public sphere, there was also a pervasive reconfiguration of the structure of feeling in the domestic and psychic interior, as a close reading of these two short stories reveals.

During the Cultural Revolution, intellectuals were labeled "stinky old ninth" (*chou lao jiu*) who were politically untrustworthy and romantically "unsuitable as lovers or husbands."[5] In the years after the Cultural Revolution, educated elites not only rose to dominate the emerging "technocratic class order"[6] but also reconstructed the familial order in which domestic power and affective value are reassigned based on access to scientific knowledge and urban civilization. Moreover, literary representations played a central pedagogical role in the process of romanticizing scientific modernity, replacing the "revolution plus love" formula with a new "science plus love" convention at the onset of the reform era. Even as it denounces the socialist state's intrusion into the domestic sphere, the early 1980s alliance of science and literature subjects the private realm to regulation through a new party-state ideology of scientific modernity.

ALLIANCE OF SCIENCE AND LITERATURE

A national craving for the scientific development and a fever for knowledge marked the early 1980s. As the Maoist ideology of class struggle and "continuous revolution" lost its appeal, the Chinese Communist Party (CCP) turned to science to regain its legitimacy as a ruling entity and to reorganize the political and economic order.[7] As a result of this policy reorientation, disenchantment with the Maoist revolutionary ideology and political idealism went hand in hand with the new enchantment with scientific modernity and the development mentality.

In the late 1970s, a large amount of Euro-American scientific writings were translated and published in China. "New industrial revolution," "information revolution," "fourth industrial revolution," and "third wave" (the title of a best-selling Chinese translation of Alvin Toffler's book) were all cultural buzzwords in the discourse surrounding the global technological revolution.[8] Laments over China's backwardness in this "third wave" of development could often be heard among Chinese intellectuals. The famous question once raised by Joseph Needham resurfaced and haunted Chinese intellectuals: "Why didn't China develop its own system of modern science?"

In 1978, a national science conference was held in Beijing, intended to serve "as a forum to promote . . . rapid and sustained development and technology."[9] In his opening remarks at the conference, Deng Xiaoping put forth the political tenet that "science and technology are the first productive force" (*kexue jishu shi diyi shengchan li*). In 1983, Zhao Ziyang, premier at the time, emphasized anew the notion that developing science and technology would be instrumental in narrowing the gap between China and developed countries.[10] As a result, social progress was equated with technological and material progress; rapid economic development would, so the discourse went, resolve all social problems.

Because technological expertise occupied the central position in economic transformation, scientists, and intellectuals more generally, were expected to be leading agents in the state's modernization program.[11] In 1977, the Chinese Academy of Social Sciences was founded to give institutional support to this program, referred to as the "Four Modernizations."[12] The new political slogan "without intellectuals there will be no modernization" (*meiyou zhishifenzi jiu meiyou xiandaihua*) gained popular currency.[13] An increasing number of technocrats were incorporated into the Party leadership or placed "in positions of authority."[14] New party members were drawn from an enlarging pool of college graduates instead of from peasants and workers, as had been the case in the early stages of the Party's history. Hence, the Party was transformed into "a party of technocratic officials."[15]

Abandoning radical Maoist educational policies aimed at leveling class distinctions, the government restored the national meritocratic "college entrance examination" (*gaokao*) system in 1977, and the educational system was reorganized to stress only academic success.[16] With all these institutional changes, the gap between a college

student's social status and that of a peasant grew. As a result, the lure
of the urban became more tempting. Sent-down youths were not the
only ones who chose to return to the cities where their families resided;
educated peasant youths also made great efforts to leave the rural areas
using the entrance examinations. This universal pattern of migration
from the rural to the urban through command of scientific knowledge and cultural power gave birth to an increasingly popular slogan, "Knowledge changes one's fate" (*Zhishi gaibian mingyun*), which
associated individual success with a university degree and marked the
path to social mobility and self-realization in post-revolutionary Chinese society.

This overhaul of the educational institution and social value system helped establish a unified linguistic market in which a new kind
of knowledge could realize its exchange value, like a commodity. Formation and "integration into the same 'linguistic community'" is a
necessary condition for establishing and consolidating such "relations
of linguistic domination."[17] Once marginalized and mistreated by
the Mao-era proletarian dictatorship, post-Mao Chinese intellectuals reversed the discursive hierarchy in which scientific knowledge—
closely associated with modernization, development, industrial
urbanity, and the vision of historic progress—became the legitimate
and universal language that prioritized mental over manual labor and
the industrial over the agrarian mode of production.

Numerous literary works and cultural debates further fueled the
enthusiasm for scientific modernity. The prominent poet Guo Moruo
made a landmark speech hailing the coming of "springtime for science" (*kexue de chuntian*) at the National Science Conference in
1978. Following this, the cultural and literary elite forged a strong
alliance with scientific workers, as illustrated by the mutual attraction
and admiration felt by the characters Shi Ping and Qiu Fei in "Return,
Cries the Cuckoo" and "Flying Afar." These characters' intimate
emotional ties best illustrate Li Zehou's philosophical speculation,
which was influential among 1980s Chinese intellectuals, that a holis-
tic modern subjectivity can be established only by a new knowledge
system of "science plus poetry" (*kexue jia shi*).[18]

Along the same lines, Lin Xingzhai, a literary critic, labeled "the
unity of poetry and mathematics" (*shi yu shuxue de tongyi*) as the
"ultimate realm of human civilization" (*wenming de jidi*).[19] In the
spirit of this new alliance of science and poetry, the mental labor
of creative writing was regarded as equivalent to scientific research,

because both propelled the modernization of the nation and thus shared an interchangeable cultural value and symbolic power. The best humanistic study is regarded as a result of "the synthesization of poetry and mathematics" (*shi yu shuxue de tongyi*).[20] Li Zehou traces this alliance of humanists and scientists back to Hu Shih's ideas of "scientism," which placed equal value on deciphering an ancient character and discovering a constellation.[21] An English literary critic, I. A. Richards, who taught at Tsinghua University between 1929 and 1930 and whose *Science and Poetry* has been translated into various Chinese versions since 1929, also influenced Chinese scholars of Hu Shih's generation. Richards advocated that literary studies, like other modern disciplines, should be done in a more systematic manner by incorporating methodologies from social sciences such as psychology and linguistics.

The intellectual discourse of the 1980s inherited this scientific spirit. Not only was scientific discourse incorporated into literary practices and social criticism; literary phenomena and historical events were also studied as sciences. In his preface to Gao Xingjian's influential book *A Preliminary Study of Modernist Fiction Techniques* (Xiandai xiaoshuo jiqiao chutan; 1981), Ye Junjian, a veteran Chinese writer, establishes a science-inspired correlation between the development of literary techniques and the evolution of technology that has brought human society from the age of craftsmanship, to the age of the steam engine, and finally to the age of electrons and atoms.[22] By the same token, Jin Guantao and Liu Qingfeng's seminal work *Prosperity and Crisis* (Xingsheng yu weiji) studies Chinese feudal society as an "ultra-stable structure" (*chao wending jiegou*) using natural scientific models such as control theory and systems theory. Their book has had a wide and long-lasting influence among college students, scientific workers, and humanist intellectuals since its publication. It was listed as one of "the most influential twenty books in the last twenty years of the twentieth century."[23]

Meanwhile, literary writers endowed their scientist characters with a humanistic interior world. The best-known works include Xu Chi's reportage literature, such as "The Light of Geology" (Dizhi zhi guang; 1977) and "Goldbach's Conjecture" (Gedebahe caixiang; 1978). These pieces popularized the notion of scientific rationality among general readers by highlighting the sublime figures of Li Siguang and Chen Jingrun, a geologist and a mathematician, as *the* national heroes of a new era who unswervingly dedicate themselves to the advancement of human knowledge and the development of scientific research despite economic difficulties and political adversity. Xu's works were lauded as "harbingers of the coming spring of the flourishing of scientific and cultural endeavors" and "glorious odes expressing the masses' yearning for the Four Modernizations."[24]

Another significant cultural event combining literature and science was the staging of Bertolt Brecht's *Life of Galileo* in 1979. This play portrays "a giant of science" who challenged authority in order to seek a universal scientific truth and free the modern humanistic spirit.[25] By the same token, the book *Adversities · Resolution · Success* (Nijing · lizhi · chengcai) put together dozens of biographical accounts featuring scientists such as Marie Curie and Alexander Graham Bell, artists such as Ludwig van Beethoven and Franz Schubert, filmmakers such as Chen Kaige, and many other Western and Chinese intellectuals. In these accounts, these prominent cultural figures are described as working hard against adversities and finally achieving success through "individual struggle and self-development" (*ziwo fendou*). Despite their drastically different backgrounds and disciplines, these figures' stories feature common themes containing buzzwords of the 1980s, namely, "knowledge" and "development."

Additionally, as a popular tool of "science vernacularization" (*kepu*), science-fiction books captured a vast readership and often became instant best sellers. For instance, the first edition of *The Adventures of Little Talent in the Future* (Xiao lingtong manyou weilai), the most popular children's science-fiction novel by Ye Yonglie, which fantasizes a utopian future of the technological sophistication and modernized urban life in twenty-first-century China, sold 1.6 million copies in 1978. From 1976 to 1981, China published 30,000 works of science fiction. In 1982, 120 magazines of popular science writing brought journal circulation to 1.7 million collectively.[26] It is suggested this particular literary genre, underdeveloped during the Mao era, was mobilized as "a lobby literature for the science community."[27]

More intriguingly, these youth-targeted science-fiction works often connect a utopian future with a literary imagination of a modernized domestic interior. For instance, "A Fantasy Story That's Not a Fantasy: Family Life of the Future" (Bushi huanxiang de huanxiang gushi: Weilai de jiating shenghuo), published in *Youth Science* (Shaonian kexue) in 1981, depicts such an imagined scene of future family life: a couple and their son sit comfortably on a sofa, using a telephone-computer whose name is Congcong (meaning "smart") to order the latest model of solar-powered toy motorcycle for the boy's birthday. Like their May Fourth predecessors, such as early Lu Xun and Zhou Zuoren, reform-minded Chinese men of letters once again resorted to the imported genre of science fiction to expose Chinese people to the latest scientific learning and the development mentality, which have been further humanized and sentimentalized with a rosy picture of the domestic bliss promised by modern technology and the pleasures of commodity consumption.[28]

The fever for modern scientific knowledge and the intellectual pursuit of humanism converge in what can be called a "development mentality." Exemplified by the political slogan "development is the ultimate truth" (*fazhan cai shi ying daoli*), this mentality makes economic development the top priority. During the 1980s, writers and intellectuals engaged in various ways in this central discourse of development and participated in the formation of the master narrative of "scientific modernity." Writers, poets, humanists, and cultural workers reassumed their historical mission of leading the masses along the path to modernization. Literature became an essential tool for reproducing the everyday structure of feelings and reconfiguring the relationship between the past and the future.

This zealous pursuit of scientism harks back to one of the major themes of the May Fourth movement. In the early twentieth century, reform-minded intellectuals turned to European Enlightenment rationality to envision a modernized new China. An import from the European Enlightenment, the modern concept of science was personified as "Mr. Science" and promoted as China's gendered savior. In *New Youth* (Xin qingnian), the flagship journal of the New Culture movement, the word "science" appears 1,913 times, more than four times as often as "democracy," the other May Fourth buzzword.[29]

Together, scientists and New Culture pioneers constructed a "scientific discursive community" (*kexue huayu gongtongti*) in the hope of calling upon the power of Western science to demolish traditional power structures and construct a coherent modern nation.[30] Wang Hui derives his term from Jean-François Lyotard's "scientific community," which refers to the intellectual group whose social influence radiates not only through scientific organizations and journals but also through the educational system and various cultural media and consequently blurs the boundaries between scientific and humanist discourses. The scientific discursive community takes shape through radical changes in educational institutions, knowledge production, and the social division of labor.

As science, the marker of industrial modernity, acquires its universal legitimacy outside disciplinary boundaries through the power of the scientific discursive community, human society also becomes a subject (or object) of scientific analysis and categorization. Like the May Fourth years, the decade of the 1980s was marked by the formation of such a community and its legitimization of the discourse of science. The intellectual group including both cultural and scientific workers who compiled the *Toward the Future* series was one of the most influential scientific discursive communities of the 1980s. Jin Guantao and Liu Qingfeng oversaw the publication of the series in order to popularize scientific methodology and modern consciousness. Jin, who graduated from the chemistry department at Beijing University, and Liu, who graduated from the Chinese department at the same university, appear to serve as a perfect example of the alliance of science and literature. In this sense, the romance between Shi and Qiu in the stories parallels the collaboration of Jin and Liu in real life.

THE SPLIT MODERN SUBJECT

Set in the context of the "scientizing moment" of the early 1980s, Chen and Ma's stories can be read as symbolic representations of the male intellectual's painstaking evolution from a member of the local agrarian community to a member of the urban-based "scientific discursive community." It may not seem that strange to include a poet (the male protagonist Shi Ping is a poet) in this community, given the fact that literature was also scientized in the sweeping wave of scientism in the early 1980s. The constant interaction and cooperation between science and poetry expanded the definition of both science and literature. Here, the word "science" refers to the systematized disciplinary knowledge and professional expertise (usually inscribed in and transmitted through written words) that institutionalize everyday choices and personal decisions.

Caught between the drastically different value systems of the two communities, the poet's struggle, uncertainty, and angst are projected onto his marital crisis, which leads to the complete destruction and rebuilding of his ethical and emotional worlds. At the very beginning of "Return, Cries the Cuckoo," the male protagonist Shi Ping is hurrying back to S city (Shanghai), where he attends F University

(Fudan University), after spending a summer at home. The meandering country road leads him to the vast world outside the village but also serves as an inconvenient link to his past. In a retrospective narration, Shi relates his life story: Born in a secluded mountain village, he consented to an arranged marriage at twenty-five and had a daughter with his peasant wife, Caifeng (who remains nameless in "Return, Cries the Cuckoo" and is identified only by her first name in the sequel, "Flying Afar").

In language that is lyrical and far removed from the everyday speech of "real" peasants, Shi's pre-university life is portrayed as quiet and peaceful, following the same pattern day in and day out. Every morning, he and his wife toil in the fields, and every evening, the country road takes them home. Such a lifestyle is compared to a clear creek that flows between the valleys, never changing its course. Caifeng's bright and gentle eyes are then compared to the flowing creek, thus feminizing the idyllic representation of an eternal Nature.

Even their arranged marriage—a "feudal" social practice reviled by intellectual and political elites since the May Fourth movement—is softened by its connection with the picturesque landscape. Erasing any imprint of the historic vicissitudes that China has endured, the idyllic aesthetic situates rural life firmly in the imaginary realm of the natural, beyond the reach of political campaigns such as the Land Reform, the Great Leap Forward, and the Cultural Revolution. Only on a personal rather than a political level—and then only very briefly—is the "up to the mountains and down to the villages" (shangshan xiaxiang) movement mentioned in a reminiscence from Shi's perspective: what distinguishes him from his cohorts are his literary writing skills, which he learned to develop with the help of some sent-down youths during the Cultural Revolution.

Shi's mastery of the medium of written language consequently changes his life path. He remembers the autumn evening when Caifeng told him about her pregnancy as they were walking home after a long day's labor. Excited at the good news, he sauntered down the country road, enjoying a grand symphony of colors, fragrances, and sounds of the harvest. That night, Shi wrote a poem titled "One Night, Coming Home on the Country Road" (Xiaolu yegui) in celebration of the golden harvest season. Untouched by the "curse of labor,"[31] nature is transformed by the indulgent gaze of the educated male spectator into an all-providing maternal figure who magically produces a natural bounty. Traces of sweat, dirt, drudgery, physical strain, and squalor in the daily lives of rural laborers are erased from this romanticized picture of an idealized natural order.

Following the publication of his poem, Shi composes more poems on the pastoral landscape, idyllic lifestyle, and traditional ethics of his village. At the end of the Cultural Revolution, he is recommended to the Chinese Department of F University as an emerging young poet.[32] At the university, he continues writing about his passion and nostalgia for rural life, delivering philosophical speculations on local traditions, and thus enjoys a certain renown in university and literary circles.

Ironically, the poetic construct of an aesthetic utopia does not help Shi Ping delve deeper into the everyday reality of his native village; instead, it breeds a profound sense of alienation from the family he left behind in the countryside. When Shi returns to the village during his first summer break, he is baffled by the banality of the unsavory village life that appears completely different from his memory of it. He finds the winding country road home narrow and bumpy in comparison to the wide and well-maintained asphalt highway in S city. As the object of aesthetic valorization in his first published poem, the country road connects Shi with a new world that promises a bright future. In its physical existence, however, this road of everyday life is like an unsightly scar that constantly reminds him of an abject past that has been sedimented into his self-identity.

Caifeng personifies the ambiguous position of the country road stuck between the future and the past. When Shi returns home during his first summer break, he wants to behave like a "civilized" urban resident by offering to shake hands with his wife whom he has not seen for a year. To his great disappointment, his wife does not react in a "civilized" manner. Rather, she blushes and dodges the proffered hand. While her maternal body once inspired his poetic celebration of Mother Nature's harvest season, Caifeng's lack of modern manners now brings him face-to-face with possible obstacles to his future metamorphosis into a citizen of modernity.

After spending a few days in the village, Shi gets bored and depressed. Compared to the high-rises in S city, the cottage in which his family lives seems particularly shabby and dilapidated. The divide between the urban and the rural has become not only a physical distance but a split between the two different systems of values, feelings, and sensibilities that people develop through their quotidian experiences. As the post-revolutionary program Reform and Opening Up

(*Gaige Kaifang*) has reestablished Shanghai as the model of metropolitan modernity in sync with global trends, "the rural hinterland seems to become almost a different 'time' as well as place."[33]

Grasped and amplified by the senses of the newly educated poet, rural poverty is reified as the abject Other of urban modernity that revolutionizes his sensibilities of everyday experiences. The despondent poet misses his school life in S city, of which his illiterate wife has no personal experience or even any remote knowledge.[34] Instead, she can only talk to him about their everyday chores and needs, which are no longer of interest to him. After just a year's separation, the unfathomable distance between the city and the countryside has driven a wedge between the peasant couple, causing each to lose access to the other's inner world.

Their miscommunication makes manifest a clash of two hierarchical languages. Linguistic exchanges are never transparent or free of ideology; rather, they always reflect power relations between the speakers.[35] In the story "Return, Cries the Cuckoo," Shi joins the class of cultural elites because of his mastery of a literary language used by post-revolutionary Chinese intellectuals, whereas his wife remains a member of the marginalized peasant class. Having internalized the universal power of knowledge, Shi prioritizes poetry over oral communication with his wife about their everyday life and memorizing English vocabulary over helping her work in the fields. The rural/urban divide manifests itself in a hierarchy of different systems of knowledge and language. Specialized and professionalized scientific knowledge inscribed in a written language is regarded as far superior and more meaningful than practical knowledge acquired from manual labor and day-to-day technical innovations, often passed on orally in the local dialect from one generation to another.

The incompatible linguistic systems used by husband and wife reproduce and perpetuate the enlarging social and economic differences between them: the feminine/rural language is particular and meticulous about physical details, practical skills, and the prosaic materiality of everyday life, whereas the masculine/urban language is lofty, conveying universal scientific truths that transcend local specificities and legitimize the modern subject. More often than not, the latter linguistic system is used as the standard language for representing—and oftentimes overriding—the former. The distance between the two linguistic systems reproduces the unfathomable distance between the countryside, which is closely tied to physical hardship and the local dialect, and the city, which is associated with civilization, mental labor, and the language of universal knowledge and modernity in the 1980s intellectual discourse.

Standing in contrast to the ascending male intellectual, the illiterate peasant wife is reduced to the subordinate state of unenlightened Other who must be expunged from the modern male-female relationship. A primitive body without an intelligent mind, the rural woman is exiled from the male intellectual's fantasy of an urban-based family life that cultivates modern citizens with an Enlightenment consciousness and "civilized manners." Unable to find a market in his rural hometown where he can realize the exchange value of his newly acquired symbolic capital and linguistic competence, Shi flees back to S city before summer break ends.

Shi's self-exile from his poeticized "pastoral life," the root of his literary creation, and his failure to reconnect with his peasant wife reveal an unbridgeable gap between lofty poetic longings and the mundaneness of everyday life. The peasant-turned-poet can deal with his tangible past rural experiences only as abstracted memories, nostalgia, and spiritual quest mediated through literary lyricism. In other words, only after being physically removed from the rural site and only through a "magical extraction of the curse of labor" in rural life is he able to resort to aestheticization and sublimation as ways of recuperating indigenous traditions.[36] The separation of the object of the gaze and the owner of the gaze is a necessary precondition for creating a pastoral landscape.

MISS SCIENCE: A WOMAN OF THE FUTURE

Shi Ping's tension-ridden marital relationship becomes even more vulnerable when a city girl enters his life. A foil to Shi's peasant wife, the character Qiu Fei in "Return, Cries the Cuckoo" is the gendered embodiment of scientific modernity. Qiu is a nuclear physics major at F University. Coming from a Shanghai-based intellectual family, this young woman stands at the frontier of urban civilization and natural science. Pretty, intelligent, and aggressive, she symbolizes exactly what Caifeng is not. In their very first meeting, Qiu impresses Shi with her sharp critique of his serial poem "Longing for the Country" (Xiang lian):

"Sure, some lines are very beautiful. But as for the overall motif, I cannot say I like it. Don't you think the 'oil lamp' and 'ox plough'

should be sent to a history museum? Are those signs of the outdated
rural life still worth your poetic passion in the late 1970s, a new age
marked by the wide application of computer technology?"[37]

Shocked by such a future-oriented view announced decades before
China enters the age of information, Shi tries desperately to defend
himself by alluding to the time-honored tradition of pastoral lyrical
poetry in classical Chinese literature. However, his poetic philosophy
of "returning to the roots of Chinese literature" does not convince
Qiu. She cuts him short and proclaims that poetry should keep up
with social reality, which is always changing and moving forward.
All of a sudden, she switches their discussion from verse writing to
her own major in order to illustrate her argument concerning historical progress and scientific advancement: "My major is nuclear physics. How I worship nuclear fusion!" She goes on and on, describing
in lengthy detail the whole process of nuclear fusion. The next day,
Qiu takes Shi to her lab. Pointing to her equipment, the odd shapes
of which suggest the mystical technological power of modern science,
she exclaims, "This is real poetry!" Then this Miss Science passionately declares that nuclear fusion will generate an explosive energy
that could cause a real revolution in the material world and usher
humankind into the modern era.

Though he knows nothing about nuclear physics, Shi surrenders
completely to the power of scientific knowledge embodied by the figure of the urban woman. From then on, they meet often, discussing
his poems, her research projects, and the future of the young generation. Even though they live on the same campus, Shi and Qiu exchange
letters frequently. In one long letter, he talks about his bold experi-
ment with new poetic styles. In response, Qiu tells him excitedly that
her lab is collaborating with Dr. Chen Ning Yang, a Nobel laureate
physicist, to work on a groundbreaking research project. Basking in
the bliss of discovering the immense revolutionary power of modern
science and technological innovation, Shi is inspired to compose a
series of narrative poems championing the reform and development
of social life and popular consciousness.

Normally, the cultural image of the modern scientist is gendered
male, from Mr. Science during the May Fourth movement to Chen
Jingrun and Li Siguang in the 1980s reportage of Xu Chi. In "Return,
Cries the Cuckoo," the urban/rural divide is powerful enough to
reverse the usual gender model of male mentor and female student.
Although Qiu Fei's role complicates such a male/female positioning,

often associated with the mind/body dualism, there is an additional layer of gendered power structure in the story: Qiu catches up with the latest international scientific developments through her cooperation with Dr. Yang, a male scientist whose Nobel Prize made him a household name in reform-era China. The reversal and subsequent reinforcement of conventional gender roles indicate that "male" and "female" are not merely biological concepts but relational positions in multilayered power networks.

Emphasizing the relational aspect of the notion of gender, Chandra Talpade Monhanty reminds us that

> [n]o one "becomes a woman" (in Simone de Beauvoir's sense) purely because she is female. Ideologies or womanhood have as much to do with class and race as they have to do with sex. . . . It is the intersections of the various systemic networks of class, race, (hetero)sexuality, and nation, then, that position us as "women."[38]

It is only through these interwoven power nexuses of class, gender, nation, the urban/rural divide, and educational institutions that a global network of hierarchical relations has been built up: the Chinese American Nobel laureate leads a young Chinese woman scientist to join the international scientific community; she in turn seeks to reform the peasant-turned-poet, who is torn between his past and his present, with her future-oriented scientific project; and at the bottom of this hierarchical chain of classification and distinction is the illiterate rural woman, the abject Other of the Modern, or the disturbing traces of a past that needs to be erased to make way for the birth of a modern subject.

That being said, it would be simplistic to conclude that Qiu Fei is simply a masculinized woman scientist, rationally predicting what China will be. Rather, her feminine appeal is constantly highlighted and superimposed on the urban space of Shanghai with all its modern facilities, educational institutions, leisure activities, and visual spectacles. Qiu first meets Shi at a college dance party. Ballroom dancing is an imported "Western" social activity. It regained its popularity in 1980s urban China after being associated with the "decadent" bourgeois lifestyle and was banned during the heyday of the socialist revolution. College dance parties at the time were often viewed as "a schooling in gender and sexual roles for young college students."[39]

Transgressing the conventional gender norm in dance halls of men leading and women following, Qiu takes the initiative and decides to teach Shi ballroom dancing. Constantly correcting his wrong steps, she gives the awestruck poet a first lesson in how to adjust his ungainly body movements to the pulsating rhythm of social dance, the very symbol of Shanghai's highly eroticized modern nightlife since the early years of the twentieth century. Later, Qiu takes Shi to the Bund, a riverside walkway in downtown Shanghai where young lovers go to display their physical intimacy in public. Here, on "the center stage of S city civilization," Shi, shocked at what he sees, receives an education in sexual modernity.

Charged with erotic energy, the night scene on the Bund is described as seductively charming: the gentle wind caresses the young lovers' faces and hair, and the lights from countless ships dance on the dark surface of the Huangpu River. In contrast to the pastoral image of the serene creek in Shi's hometown, the Huangpu River, artery for Shanghai's manufacturing industry and international trade, illuminates the modern ideals of unlimited mobility, constant action, and rapid changes. The dazzling spectacle of a vibrant modern space replaces the rustic landscape as the setting for a reform-era romantic drama.

A similar pattern of light and shadow can be found in the profile of the modern woman Qiu, whose youthful body is fused with the seductive night scene. Observed from Shi's point of view, Qiu's face is hidden in the dark, thus taking on almost mystical feminine charm. However, her eyes shine through the darkness, glistening with the light of hope for a brighter future. Qiu's future-oriented gaze changes the focus of the dynamic picture of urban nightlife, elevating a yearning for passion and intimacy to a strong commitment to social advancement and historical progress. Through such a well-balanced poetic account of darkness and light, spontaneous passion and progressive reason, scientific modernity is aestheticized by and synchronized with the everyday sensibilities of a feminized urban civilization.

Attracted by this woman of the future, Shi becomes more and more alienated from his wife, the woman of his past. Thus, upon graduation, he is confronted with a life choice: to return to his wife in the countryside or stay in the city with Qiu. With his future career development in mind, he determines to divorce his wife. He returns to the village to inform Caifeng of his decision. Caifeng reacts by staring at him in despair for a long time. However, unwilling to ruin his future, she silently acquiesces. The night before Shi leaves for the city, Caifeng kneels beside his bed to take a last look at him. Awakened by his wife's streaming tears soaking his face, Shi closes his eyes, struck by mixed feelings of sadness, helplessness, and guilt.

The next morning, as he prepares to leave for the city, Shi discovers an unexpected letter from his wife. (During the days when he was absent, his wife struggled in her spare time to learn to read and write.) Her farewell note indicates that she is willing to sacrifice her own happiness for his bright future in the city on one condition: he must take their young daughter to the city and send her to college so that she will not repeat her mother's suffering and misery. This is the first time in the story that the reader gains access to Caifeng's inner world. While his wife's tears did not change his mind, this gesture of self-sacrifice, mediated through the power of written language, miraculously short-circuits Shi's determination. Deeply moved, he breaks into tears and suddenly pleads with his wife for forgiveness. Thus, the story ends on a seemingly happy note: the male protagonist finally rejects the temptation of the technology-savvy Shanghai girl and instead heeds the call of traditional family ethics in the rural community by returning to his wife's side.

SCIENTIZE THE "HAPPY ENDING"

After its publication, "Return, Cries the Cuckoo" was widely read and discussed among general audiences and literary critics. Its vast readership ranged from college students to educated peasants. On one end of the spectrum of its literary reception was praise for the way the male protagonist's sense of responsibility aligned with traditional Chinese family ethics; on the other end was ridicule for a choice that was seen as decidedly old-fashioned, conservative, and hypocritical.

Wang Yinshu's opinion represents the first type of critique. Not a professional literary critic or an intellectual, Wang Yinshu is a young peasant working in the Nanyue Brigade of Ji County, Hebei. On the night of December 28, 1980, the brigade branch of the Communist Youth League organized a meeting to discuss the selection of stories for the national Youth Award. At this meeting, Wang Yinshu aired his opinion that "Return, Cries the Cuckoo" exposed and criticized harshly those modern reincarnations of Chen Shimei, a stock villain in traditional Chinese drama who abandoned his wife so that he could remarry for social advancement. Wang further emphasized that one should not pursue one's happiness and self-development at the cost of other people's emotional well-being.[40]

Essays in the official Party publication *Xinhua Daily* (Xinhua ribao) held opinions similar to Wang's. These pieces by literary critics condemned the male protagonist's extramarital affair as "bourgeois corruption." They compared the peasant-turned-poet to Chen Shimei, despite the irony that Chen, an official-scholar in premodern China, could be hardly counted as a member of the modern bourgeois class.[41]

Even those who praised the literary merits of the story regarded the ending as weak, conservative, and hypocritical. Conveying a message that contradicts the overall theme of the story, the hasty and anticlimactic "happy ending" is more like a question mark than a period. The idea that their daughter can escape a miserable life only by going to the city further emphasizes the urban/rural divide and destabilizes rural ethics. One critic, Wu Xin, argued that the backward economic conditions in the countryside made it impossible to build a "civilized spiritual life" anchored in a highly developed material civilization.[42] For this critic, therefore, the ultimate means of eradicating the peasant wife's misery would be to accelerate economic development. Civility and emotional autonomy were considered to be correlative with economic development. In this sense, although the authors touch on a significant issue in the reform era, the ending is out of step with the essential spirit of the times.

Another critic, Dong Jian, supported Wu's argument by positing that the marital crisis is a natural result of the conflict between the old and the new.[43] The woman nuclear physicist represents a new generation, while Shi's wife personifies the old, whose "feudalistic" mindset is determined by her total lack of education and day-to-day backbreaking labor. Thus, the narrative of the "personal" relationship in the story becomes a site at which various discourses ("socialist" morality, traditional ethics, romantic love, and modern consciousness) compete intensely for ideological legitimacy.

Under pressure from these harsh criticisms, Chen and Ma wrote a sequel to change the "feudal consciousness" of the much maligned ending. The altered ending calls the story's "realistic" style into question and draws the reader's attention to the shifting ideological lenses through which reality is perceived. Called "Flying Afar," the sequel suggests a justified move to divorce the rural past and strive for a spatiotemporal reorientation toward the boundless outside world and the modern future. This forward-looking vision and future-oriented narrative resonate with some of the most popular slogans of the 1980s such as "march toward the world" and "turning toward the future" (mianxiang weilai).

In the sequel, Shi lands a job as a literary magazine editor in P city (Beijing). He brings his wife to the city for a short visit, thus creating even more conflicts and miscommunications between them. In awe of the splendid cityscape at her first sight of it, Caifeng becomes completely disoriented by the profusion of unfamiliar everyday details. She does not know how to use a washing machine or any household electrical appliances. Ironically, modern technology increases her stress and frustration rather than relieving her burden of household chores. Her fear of the natural gas stove reminds readers of Shi's unease about the explosive power of modern machinery when he visits Qiu Fei's nuclear physics lab for the first time.

Moreover, Caifeng fails to dress and talk properly at a cultural salon organized by her husband's colleagues in the literary circle. She can neither appreciate nor pretend to appreciate the modernist paintings exhibited in the National Art Gallery. But by far her most shocking experience occurs when she witnesses young couples' public displays of affection, again reminiscent of Shi's own difficulty in adapting to sexual modernity under Qiu's guidance. Catapulted into metropolitan modernity, she fails to accumulate the kind of everyday knowledge and urban life experiences that would allow her to develop a new, modern subjectivity. Her very language has lost its validity in the context of urban modernity. Having no access to any legitimate linguistic authority, she becomes the silenced rural woman, lurking as an Other from an outmoded world and still tethered to the past, totally lacking the possibility of articulating an appropriately modern subjectivity.

Caifeng's failure to perform as a modern subject brings Shi Ping face to face with his abject past. Such a past threatens to shatter his fantasy of becoming a modern subject and to pull him back to the status of the undesirable Other. His strong sense of shame at Caifeng's failure indicates his awareness of the difference in status between rural and urban in the modern space of Shanghai. In order to complete a successful transformation, he finally chooses to drive away the wretched traces of his past and fully identify with the modern subject position. In the end, his wife leaves him to return to the countryside, and Shi is determined to get a divorce for the sake of a new life infused with a "modern consciousness." Because the split between the written word and everyday experience cannot be overcome within the aesthetic world of pastoral poetry, in the sequel the poet seeks to end his constant inner struggles by abandoning his "backward-looking" stance and succumbing to the power of modern knowledge and the development mentality.

"Flying Afar" highlights this link between modern science and private life choice by beginning with a wordy lecture, imparting systematic knowledge of important scientific discoveries to its readers: In 1912, German geologist Alfred Lothar Wegener discovered that the contours of the eastern coast of South America and the western coast of Africa match perfectly. Based on this groundbreaking discovery, he proposed the theory of continental drift. Three decades later, William Maurice Ewing at Columbia University discovered that earthquakes and volcanoes along "a great submarine canyon" and its branches had caused the drift of the continents.[44] This continuous drift, geologists predicted, might lead to a rearrangement and realignment of the continents.

Immediately following this uncanny lecture on geology, a series of curious letters and numerals further puzzle the reader: "YNX 7385, 1045, 8821 1420 0120 7344 0018." The story later reveals that these are telegraphic codes informing Shi that his wife will take the train to visit him in Beijing. Throughout the story, passages like this describe the penetration of scientific knowledge and modern technology into the very fabric of modern urban life. The hard facts and verifiable data reorganize the space of everyday life and give Shi's personal choice the luster of scientific objectivity, in the logic of which modernization is considered a value-neutral and rational system that comprises a series of quantifiable technical indices.

Echoing this scientifically informed beginning, the closing paragraphs of the story repeat this obsession with scientific rationality and the developmental mentality with a popularized account of earth science:

> Continents move eternally. Earthquakes and volcanoes erupt constantly. They may have brought immense damage to human life, but they also provide the possibility of new construction and new life. Who can make the earth stop moving?[45]

Drastically different from Shi's first poem eulogizing the birth of new life from the womb of Mother Nature, these descriptions of groundbreaking geological discoveries transform Nature into the object of scientific observation and analysis. Rather than aestheticizing the feminized details of everyday country life, the sequel shifts its spatial focus from the local to the global, and its temporal mode from looking back to contemplating the future. This forward-looking vision in Shi's personal choice actually mirrors the broader discursive trend of constructing the modern subject through an alliance of "science and poetry" in the 1980s intellectual discourse.

This trend suggests that scientific knowledge requires a narrative in order to achieve legitimacy, for "knowledge finds its validity not within itself . . . but in a practical subject—humanity."[46] Through the mediation of literature and culture, the relevance of abstract and sophisticated scientific advancement to everyday life can be easily understood. Thus, discursive scientific modernity and a development mentality are able to circumscribe all aspects of social life as a legitimate everyday narrative and an internalized constituent of the "modern consciousness." Within such a structure of domination, there is not much room left in which to explore their exact connotations and how their meanings are inscribed into the words of "ordinary language." Through such an alliance of science and literature, the urban-based educated elites become the architects of a new interior space in which abstract scientific terms and concepts find concrete form in literary and cultural representations of individual experience and the modern/urban lifestyle. The romanticization of reform and science was made possible through reorganizing and renarrating everyday practices in the domestic site.

CONCLUSION

During England's industrialization in the nineteenth century, an immediate result of increasing social mobility was "the difficult nature of the marriage choice."[47] At such a historic juncture, "personal" choice was often a choice of class identification, "a choice primarily of a way to live."[48] Compared to preindustrial society, the modern age promises average people more freedom in choosing marital partners and accruing material possessions, social status, and symbolic capital within a new system of social differentiation and stratification.

As post-revolutionary China has gone through a historic process of rapid industrialization and urbanization, it has seen some similar social practices and cultural phenomena comparable to those in industrializing England. The stories "Return, Cries the Cuckoo" and "Flying Afar" portray such a difficult choice between urban and rural life at the onset of China's post-Mao reform era. At this transitional moment as portrayed in the stories, social mobility is the privilege (and sometimes source of anxiety) of the male intellectual Shi Ping, while the peasant wife Caifeng, who has few resources, is adversely affected and left with not much choice. Su Xiaokang's "The Great Fission of Yin and Yang" also registers similar real-life cases of urbanized husbands divorcing their rural wives after the promulgation of the Second Marriage Law.

However, the issues of gender inequality and the urban/rural divide were often glossed over in the discourse of scientific modernity that dominated mainstream ideology in the early 1980s. Emphasizing the "scientizing moment" as a historical rupture from radical (often equated with irrational, feudalistic, and unscientific) Maoist governance, the intellectuals of the 1980s failed to subject modern scientism and its alleged universal values to critical scrutiny; neither did they reflect on the historical continuity of scientism and its discursive entanglement with developmentalism in modern China. China's zealous pursuit of modern science, born out of local aspirations for nation building and economic development, started at the turn of the twentieth century, further "intensified under Soviet tutelage in the 1950s," and in the 1980s the ideology of scientism reached its peak as China turned to a technocratic mode of governance.[49]

Regulating people's everyday lives with this new model of governance, the state started to abandon its previous practice of directly controlling practices of marriage and divorce by administrative means. Rather, dominant state ideology, intellectual discourse, and cultural products combined forces to align the domestic reform with the nation' new agenda of scientific modernization. Jia Pingwa's novella "Households in the Chicken Nest Lowland" (Jiwowa de renjia; 1983), adapted in 1985 into the award-winning film *Wild Mountains* (Yeshan; dir. Yan Xueshu), attests to such an ideological shift in its depiction of the unusual practice of "wife-swapping" in a small mountain village in northwest China: two peasant couples are divorced and then re-matched as a result of their drastically different responses to the unstoppable intrusion of science into their lives. While the couple who embraces the power of modern technology is shown in a positive light as the new hero and heroine of the time, the other household is cast as the embodiment of historic inertia in resisting the modernization of village life.

Similarly, a large number of literary and filmic narratives produced between the late 1970s and the mid-1980s engage with the intersection of affectivity, domesticity, and technological advancement in reform-era rural China. Films include *Son, Grandson and Seeds* (Erzi, sunzi he zhongzi; dir. Liang Tingzhao, 1978), *Not a One-Off Story* (Bing fei yige ren de gushi; dir. Zhang Fengxiang, 1978), *A Sweet Life* (Tianmi de shiye; dir. Xie Tian, 1979), and *Our Veteran* (Zanmen de tuiwubing; dir. Zhao Huanzhang, 1985). Among the literary works are Zhou Keqin's story "The Mountain Moon Doesn't Know My Thoughts" (Shanyue buzhi xinli shi; 1981) and novel *Xu Mao and His Daughters* (Xu Mao he ta de nüer men; 1980), which won the Mao Dun Literary Award and was adapted into a 1981 film of the same title dir. Wang Yan), as well as Zheng Yi's novella "Old Well" (Lao jing; 1985), which was also adapted in 1986 into a film of the same title directed by Wu Tianming. While the protagonists (often male) in these filmic and literary narratives tend to dedicate themselves to the cause of transforming the country and building a new life with the power of modern science, along the way they also win women's whole-hearted admiration and romantic love. The frequent repetition of this new thematic pattern of "science plus love" replaces the formula of "revolution plus love" that dominated the earlier literary and filmic canons in praise of Communist revolutionary ideology.[50]

In addition to literary representations, real-life stories published in youth-oriented popular magazines in the 1980s spell out a similar ideological pattern: "[l]ove stories of the period were consciously subsumed into this larger romance of modernization."[51] As is explicitly stated in a 1980 State Council official notice, family issues were particularly important because they "were related to building socialist material and spiritual civilization." Hence, the nationwide implementation of the Second Marriage Law in 1980 was considered essential to "a new era defined by the central task of realizing 'the four modernizations' in agriculture, industry, science and technology, and the military," a new era that reinvented the links between legalized conjugality, national modernization, and scientific productivity.[52]

The publication of "Return, Cried the Cuckoo" and "Flying Afar" coincided with the early 1980s "scientizing moment," when "the growing participation of scientific experts in the policy process . . . ushered in a more systematic, realistic, and data-driven process of policymaking."[53] Moreover, literary and cultural representations of science helped popularize scientific knowledge and created unified narratives that regulated the everyday sensibilities and imaginations of the private realm. As a result, romance associated with scientific modernity and metropolitan splendor became the legitimate articulation of feelings. At the same time, far removed from the proper domain of metropolitan modernity and urban domesticity, the feminized countryside became synonymous with a timeless and stagnant "small peasant mind-set" (*xiaonong yishi*), the abject Other lurking outside of the modern symbolic order.

Writers such as Chen Kexiong and Ma Ming contributed significantly to the formation of a new universal language of science and poetry by reconfiguring the popular narratives of romantic love, gender relationships, and domestic order in early reform-era China. The hierarchy among different genders and classes within the domestic sphere is justified by the depoliticized individual's efforts to overcome "feudal consciousness," which was often associated in 1980s intellectual discourse with the excessive political violence of the Cultural Revolution, in pursuit of development and modernization. Displaying the dialectics of rupture and reformation, these representations tap into a demand for the negation of the past as well as the cultural construction of a new domestic interior that is able to reproduce the modern national subject.

Catching the current of China's transitional times, reform-era divorce narratives engendered a developmentalist structure of feelings. Thus, the emerging discourse of interiority became an essential vehicle by which Chinese intellectuals could build up and sentimentalize the connections between the grand narrative of economic reform and tangible changes in people's social practices of gender, divorce, and marriage. This Enlightenment intellectual effort to liberate the interiorized individual by modernizing the domestic was continued and contested in the influential divorce narratives of the following decades.

CHAPTER TWO

Midlife Crisis and Misogynist Rhetoric

Male Intellectuals' Divorce Narratives

Wu Ruozeng's novel *Divorce* (Liyi; 1986) and Su Tong's novella "A Divorce Handbook" (Lihun zhinan; 1991) concern the midlife crises of urban-based male intellectuals. Urban modernity and historic progress do not solve their personal problems. Rather, new life circumstances under changing social conditions arouse new desires as well as new anxieties for these middle-aged intellectuals who seek to overcome their midlife crises through divorce.

Midlife, loosely defined as a transitional period between early adulthood and old age (thirty-five to sixty-five), is closely associated with anxiety over a decreasing libido and an increasing awareness of aging and death. In 1965, Elliott Jacques coined the term "midlife crisis," meaning "a period of crisis that is triggered by the realization of [one's] own mortality and a change in time frame from 'time since birth' to 'time left to live'."[1] Not simply a hormone-determined and age-specific psychological phase, the midlife anxiety depicted in the two divorce narratives is rooted as much in a breakdown of old meanings, values, and social order in post-revolutionary China as in personal awareness of "time left to live."

Images of jaded middle-aged men and women populate post-Mao Chinese literature, replacing the heroic figures of revolutionary youth that dominate May Fourth and Maoist literature. The most well-known character of this type is Lu Wenting in Chen Rong's influential story "At Middle Age" (Rendao zhongnian; 1980). Lu, the middle-aged female protagonist, is crushed by mounting stress. She is a remarkable ophthalmologist and strives, not as successfully, to carry out the role of "good wife and wise mother" (*xianqi liangmu*) at the same time. However, Lu's double burden was not read as a gender issue so much as a post–Cultural Revolution social problem of the "intellectuals' burden."[2] Similarly, the midlife crises of the male intellectuals in Wu's and Su's works go beyond age- and gender-specific personal issues and are represented as widespread social disorientation caused by a paradigmatic shift in post-revolutionary Chinese society and ruptures of its old emotional and ethical ties.

Wu Ruozeng's novel *Divorce* was first published in the prominent literary journal *October* (Shiyue) in 1986. It appeared in book form in 1987 and was reprinted several times due to its sweeping popularity. Its Chinese title, *Liyi*, literally means "to part and separate." *Liyi* is a legal term used in the classical Chinese of the Ming and Qing dynasties to refer to the act of a husband divorcing his wife.[3] Wu chose the term *liyi* for the title of his novel instead of *lihun*, the official legal term for divorce in contemporary China, because the former connotes a general sense of alienation, which resonates with the heated intellectual debate about alienation (*yihua*) in the 1980s. This debate was initiated by Wang Ruoshui's influential article "About the Concept of 'Alienation'" (Guanyu "yihua" de gainian). Drawing on early Marxism, Wang criticizes "the lack of concern for 'human nature' in Mao's doctrine," which results in estrangement "between the ruling ideology and the people who had been taught to believe it."[4]

Taking their cue from Wang's article, 1980s Chinese intellectuals attacked the dehumanizing nature of the Maoist regime that often manifested itself as the alienation and disruption of family relationships. Guo Xiaodong, a literary critic, argues that members of the younger generation growing up during the Cultural Revolution "bade farewell to the loving atmosphere of the traditional Chinese family and were catapulted into an environment in which expressing one's love was a crime." Then he labels this "homeless" generation as a bestial group who "were nursed with wolf's milk and schooled in the philosophy of class struggle."[5] Similarly, Liu Binyan, an overseas Chinese political dissident, states: "Of all the destruction, it is the damage to the people's spiritual world, what is called 'internal injury,' that is the most difficult to repair." As a result, Liu concludes, the word "love" disappeared from Chinese literature. The antidote to such an internal injury is to renovate Chinese literature with the idea of individualism and humanism, which constitutes the core of the subject of literary modernity.[6] Commenting on dominant literary trends in post-revolutionary China, Jianmei Liu has also observed: "Loaded with the social duty to reflect what was destroyed by the Cultural Revolution, 'scar literature' embraced love as a key to solving social problems."[7]

Against this cultural backdrop, Wu's novel *Divorce* can be read as a typical literary effort to cure the internal injury by aestheticizing the modern subject's quest for individual freedom and romantic love. Throughout the novel, the male protagonist's alienation and dislocation from both domestic order and social order are highlighted and psychologized, as suggested by the novel's subtitle: *The Interior Monologue of a Contemporary Chinese Man* (Yige dangdai Zhongguo nanren de neixin dubai). Li Bo, the male protagonist, is a sociologist studying contemporary Chinese urban culture. This professional background puts him in the advantageous position of constantly theorizing his personal experience of divorce and spelling out the prevailing sense of alienation and displacement among male Chinese intellectuals.

Blaming the opposite sex for the displacement felt by Chinese men, Wu suggests that over-liberated Chinese women make Chinese men look particularly weak and consequently cause the unbalanced situation of "ascending yin force versus descending yang force" (*yinsheng yangshuai*).[8] In this divorce narrative, Wu resorts to both the revolutionary rhetoric of "speaking bitterness" (*suku*) and the post-revolutionary discourse of "rule by law" (*fazhi*) to transform the *yin/yang* imbalance by reconceptualizing the intricate relationships between gender dynamics, individual desire, domestic order, and state control.

Compared to Wu's novel, Su Tong's "A Divorce Handbook" registers the more individualized and fragmented experiences of an urban male intellectual. The dominant market logic of capital accumulation and commodity consumption in the 1990s has overshadowed Shi Ping's enthusiastic embrace of scientific modernity and Li Bo's zealous pursuit of romantic individualism in the 1980s. As a result, this novella is haunted by a strong sense of disillusionment among middle-aged Chinese intellectuals, who find that an all-encompassing market economy and consumer culture deprive them of their privileges. The modern nuclear family is represented as a microcosm of such a repressive world and is synonymous with mechanical daily routines and overly feminine sentiments. For these men, divorce becomes a way of escaping from an increasingly materialistic world. Instead of making strenuous efforts to reform the domestic interior through the act of divorce as Wu depicts, Su translates the immense fear of post-socialist urban modernity into a complete rejection of any possible indication of interiority, be it psychic depth or domestic bliss.

Though reflecting divergent attitudes toward the 1980s New Enlightenment intellectual discourse, Wu's and Su's divorce narratives both highlight a misogynist rhetoric in their narratives of the male intellectual's midlife crises. This misogynist rhetoric posits that women are the embodiment of a madness that threatens the Enlightenment rationality of the male intellectual. Only through purging the pathologized and gendered Other who is associated with either residual revolutionary ideology or overwhelming post-revolutionary marketization can male urban intellectuals rework their traumatic memories, absorb the shock of modernity, and redefine male subjectivity.

Leo Lee has suggested that the May Fourth tradition of critical realism is marked by making the "distinction between self and society," between "I" and "they," a "part of a manifestation of individualism."[9] While Li Bo, the male protagonist of *Divorce*, consummates the division between "I" and "they" through his own suicide, which sublimates the midlife fear of impending death into a grand gesture of resistance to feminized social repression, in Su Tong's "A Divorce Handbook," the distinction between "self" and "Other" finally collapses, so "I" and "they" become one. This narrative tone of pessimism reminds one of the madman in Lu Xun's first vernacular story, "Diary of a Madman" (Kuangren Riji; 1918, who in the end realizes the futility of his struggles and gives in to the old social order. Marking the demise of the sublime intellectual subject constructed in 1980s New Enlightenment intellectual discourse, the representation of a problematic male subject in Su's "A Divorce Handbook" can be read as a parody of Wu's speaking-bitterness narrative.

DIARY OF A MIDDLE-AGED MAN

Wu Ruozeng was born in Heilongjiang in northeast China. He graduated from Nankai University in 1968, when the violence of the Cultural Revolution reached its peak. In 1980, he started publishing literary writings, which focused on exposing the atrocities of the Cultural Revolution and other political movements during the Mao era. In particular, Wu attacked two alleged sins of the Cultural Revolution, sexual suppression and total lack of individualism, and hailed the emerging modern subjectivity, or "gendered and psychologized subjectivity," during the post–Cultural Revolution years.[10]

All these leitmotifs can be found in the novel *Divorce*, which revolves around the stringent divorce procedure that an urban-based Chinese family would typically go through in the mid-1980s. It is one of the few full-length fictional works that dedicates itself to registering each step of a slow-moving divorce case and various social forces involved in the procedure. One critic calls the novel "an encyclopedia of contemporary Chinese marital life."[11] No wonder this book met with a warm reception and inspired countless letters to the author from his enthusiastic readers.

Renovating an important literary tradition of self-writing, *Divorce* is narrated in the form of the male protagonist's diary. Use of this device to construct a modern subject position is not uncommon in modern Chinese literature and is found in well-known works such as Lu Xun's "Diary of a Madman," Lu Yin's "Lishi's Diary" (Lishi de riji; 1923), Yu Dafu's *Nine Diaries* (Riji jiuzhong; 1927), Ding Ling's "Diary of Miss Sophie" (Shafei nüshi de riji; 1928), and Yang Gang's "Fragment from a Lost Diary" (1936). Using such a generic form to sustain "an integrated sense of self" enables the male intellectual narrator of *Divorce* to separate a distinctive modern subject—the first-person narrator's thoughts, feelings, and special experiences—from those of the ordinary masses.[12]

A brief preface precedes the intellectual narrator's interior monologue; in it, the character Nan Yang, a writer and a longtime bosom friend of Li Bo's, informs readers of the final outcome of Li's divorce case: "Li Bo killed himself when he was forty years old. Oscillating between love and marriage, he challenged two unbeatable forces and was consequently crushed by them."[13] He then reveals that Li Bo entrusted him with his diary before throwing himself into the deep waters of Amazon, a suburban nature reserve. In search of inspiration for new work, two years after Li's death, Nan Yang decides to have Li Bo's diary published.

Following the preface, Li Bo's 105 diary entries are faithfully reproduced, according to Nan Yang. They are divided into six parts, each corresponding to a different stage in Li's marital crisis and divorce procedure: part 1, "Separation" (Fenju), diary entries for May 3–August 23, 1982; part 2, "The First Prosecution" (Diyici qisu), diary entries for August 28–November 15, 1982; part 3, "Perplexity" (Kunhuo), diary entries for November 25, 1982–April 15, 1983; part 4,

"Hallucination" (Huanying), diary entries for April 26–May 31, 1983; part 5, "The Second Prosecution" (Di'erci qisu), diary entries for June 6–August 24, 1983; and part 6, "The Outcome" (Jieju), diary entries for August 25–27, 1983. The novel concludes with a letter sent by Li Bo to Nan Yang that reports Li's final thoughts before his suicide.

As these diary entries reveal, the completion of Li Bo's divorce lasts fifteen months. The first diary entry relates the events of May 3, 1982. On that evening, Li walks out on his wife without revealing any specific reason. The author's choice of this particular date is especially meaningful—an ostensible gesture of reenacting the eve of the May Fourth movement in 1919, a historical moment when modern youth broke out of their families in search of individual freedom. In his diary entry, Li describes himself as a polite, genteel, and long-suffering husband who proposes calmly: "I hope this matter can be solved in peace." Zou Huixian, his wife, reacts strongly to his words by yelling hysterically at him: "Out! Get lost! Fuck off!"[14]

After exiling himself from his home, Li spends a night alone in his office. Having left Xiaofang, their young daughter, to his wife's care, he never stops to consider the possible challenges facing a working mother who has to juggle a full-time job and the daily needs of a school-age child. Rather, he indulges himself by drawing a graphic mental picture of his wife's verbal and physical abuse of Xiaofang: "Most probably, Huixian would vent her anger on the child. She would yell frantically: 'Hurry up! Wash your hands and eat! Looking for your father? That son of bitch is already dead!'"[15]

Li continues to narrate this imagined domestic scenario: Finally Huixian would totally lose control of herself and give Xiaofang a good beating for no reason. Torturing himself with all these imagined brutal details of domestic violence, Li cannot stop crying. His excessive tears sentimentalize the very first journal entry, which ends with an emotionally charged exclamation, "Ah, my poor child!" For readers familiar with modern Chinese literature, this exclamation brings to mind the famous ending line of Lu Xun's "Diary of a Madman": "Save the children!"

Compared with Li Bo, self-cast as an emotionally sensitive father who cares about the welfare of the next generation, his wife is portrayed as a stereotypical "old-fashioned" middle-aged woman, a gendered emblem of the established power structure working against the male intellectual. Belying her given name, which means "virtuous" (with an exclusive emphasis on feminine virtues), she appears to be an irritable and violent beast who cannot control herself and cannot find valid access to the comprehensible linguistic order. Instead, she yells, curses, speaks in stumbling or fragmented speech, or simply keeps silent, seemingly lacking the ability to articulate her inner thoughts and feelings rationally and coherently.

What makes Zou Huixian look even more unreasonable and backward in her intellectual husband's eyes is her act of publicizing private matters, that is, going to her husband's work unit and the Women's Federation to speak out about her domestic grievances. As a result, Li's colleagues become aware of his troubled family life and try to persuade him not to initiate divorce proceedings. The party secretary of the Academy of Social Sciences where Li works also exhorts him to place his career development over his domestic affairs. The CCP cadre's criticism makes Li feel ashamed for lowering himself to the same level of those *"niang'r men,"* a colloquial, often derogatory, term referring to married women, particularly elderly ones whose concerns are often confined to domestic affairs.

SPEAKING BITTERNESS

In order to elevate his private (read: feminized) life from an isolated personal case to a general social problem facing all Chinese male intellectuals in the mid-1980s, Li chronicles personal observations and professional interviews of various urban-dwelling divorcees as part of his sociological research on marriage and family in contemporary Chinese society. For example, Wang Laijun, who works in the library of the Academy of Social Sciences, is a worker-turned-intellectual. While he was working in a factory, he married a female coworker. After graduating from college and finding a white-collar job as a librarian, he has an extramarital affair and divorces his wife, which earns him a bad reputation as "Wang Shimei."[16] Without probing into the details of Wang's divorce or mentioning Wang's wife's side of story, Li jumps to a sweeping generalization:

> In our everyday lives, people normally detest the crimes of murder, arson, robbery, and theft. However, people also sneer at the practice of divorce. They show scorn and discrimination and feel resentment! This is particularly true if the divorce is being initiated by an accomplished intellectual![17]

Relating back to his own marital crisis, Li reaches the conclusion in his May 4 diary entry that the real tragedy for Chinese intellectuals lies in their hopeless pursuit of spiritual fulfillment of which romantic love is an integral part.[18] Apparently, the populist sentiment against divorce is deemed a conservative and backward force, an obstacle to the birth of the modern subject and his quest for emotional fulfillment.

This strategy of class distinction is in line with the mid-1980s Chinese intellectual discourse on individual sexuality: "Narratives of 'repression,' denunciations of 'backwardness' and promises of 'pleasure' place the intellectual in a privileged position in which his knowledge is set against established power."[19] In liberal intellectual discourses, sexual liberation is closely linked with political liberation. It is believed that "once an 'individual' was 'free' to express and enact sexual desire, society would follow with increased democratization and choice, and totalitarian mentalities and approaches to governing would disappear."[20]

More intriguingly, the "backward" populist sentiment against liberal thinking is often gendered as female. Li's wife refuses to grant the divorce. Ms. Xiao, head of Li's work unit, also disapproves of his petition for divorce. Women cadres in the Women's Federation condemn his intention to divorce his wife as a manifestation of the polluting force of "bourgeois liberalization." In his July 29 diary entry, Li Bo records a head-to-head clash with such a populist attitude against divorce: When Li and Wang Laijun go to a dance party organized by their work unit, two "demure-looking" women roll their eyes and leave the ball immediately. Their apparent contempt triggers a highly emotional reaction from Li Bo, who describes the tension-ridden moment in his diary:

> At that moment, I can sense their very tangible feelings of hostility and disdain. How I wish I could throw myself at them and teach them a good lesson with my fists! Honestly, I never lack self-confidence! This kind of woman should go to hell! I would rather stay single for my whole life than marry such a woman! However, their attitude still hurts me badly![21]

Situated in such a dualistic structure of autonomous male individual versus coercive social norms (gendered female), the middle-aged man's marital crisis is sublimated to a universal moral dilemma that tortures male Chinese intellectuals. Instead of an interactive interpersonal relationship that always unfolds under specific historic and cultural circumstances, romantic love is reconceptualized as a universalized

abstract idea that sets the male intellectual apart from the masses and
ensures his privileged class and gender position. It is implied that only
these enlightened and individualized modern intellectuals who know
how to liberate their bodies and manage their marriages can manage
public affairs rationally and liberate the nation from totalitarian governance. Envisioning himself as a lonely fighter against an established
power structure, the male narrator posits domestic estrangement as the
source of Chinese intellectuals' existential angst and emotional crisis.

Analogous to early 1980s stories about divorce, Wu Ruozeng's
divorce narrative also attests to a strong belief in social evolution as
the ultimate cure for domestic disorder. In his May 4 diary entry, Li
relates his marital crisis to the general conditions of Chinese intellectuals and concludes:

> Chinese intellectuals are always psychologically repressed and emo-
> tionally unfulfilled!
>   Mankind should develop a material civilization first, then a spiri-
> tual one. A nation with underdeveloped material civilization will
> inevitably have an underdeveloped spiritual civilization![22]

Attributing his marital failure to the lack of historic progress, Li pinpoints an oppressive "old society," referring to the Mao era with its
economic underdevelopment and political intervention in this context, as the root of the tragic love lives of all Chinese intellectuals
(obviously gendered male). In his diary, he pours out all his anger,
angst, hatred, woes, overflowing tears, violent impulses, and bitter
feelings. The overall narrative is hyperbolic and emotionally charged.
Ironically, this central mechanism of integrating arbitrary complaints
of everyday hardships into a systematic class narrative is reminiscent
of the political ritual of speaking bitterness. Speaking bitterness is a
Mao-style political strategy that aims to raise collective consciousness
and amplify moral power by actively recollecting and reenacting past
bitterness.[23] In 1950s divorce narratives such as "The Story of Qunni's Divorce" (1951) and "Erqiao Gets a Divorce" (1953), the protagonists, normally rural women, often adopt this strategy to tell readers
about how they have endured physical pain and torture in "feudal"
marriages arranged in the "old society." Different from the Mao-era
peasants' political ritual of speaking bitterness about their physical
(exterior) wounds and sufferings in the "old society," Li's narrative
seeks to expose the psychological (interior) trauma inflicted on contemporary Chinese male intellectuals.

Whereas Mao-era illiterate peasants publicized their stories of bitterness primarily through oral and physical performances, the narrative of speaking bitterness in Wu's novel is inscribed in the written language. The numerous diary entries create a central stage on which the male intellectual protagonist can address his audiences directly, weep abundant tears, and exhibit a subject position with which audiences are invited to identify. Though lacking the sense of immediacy and face-to-face interaction of a performance, this new type of "writing bitterness" not only ensures a potentially larger audience but also marks the emergence of a privileged class member with a mastery of a different linguistic register and access to the modern technology of printing.

Despite their ideological and media differences, one important trait shared by both types of speaking bitterness is their heavy reliance on packaging ideological battles in affective terms. Throughout the middle-aged intellectual's diary, the excessive use of exclamatory words and dramatic exposé style is comparable to the theatrical mode of the Maoist "speaking bitterness meeting" (*suku dahui*) in which peasants gathered to tell their stories to large groups of spectators in order to arouse collective feelings and rupture old emotional and ethical bonds. Similarly, in Wu's speaking-bitterness narrative, the enunciation of a new subject position is contingent upon building a developmentalist structure of feelings in place of the old forms of familial relations and community ethics.

Enthusiastic letters written by numerous readers to the author not only attest to the popularity of the novel but also weave an interactive network between the fictional performer and his large audience. Though the male protagonist commits suicide in the end, his death does not mean the annihilation of the idealized male subject. Rather, this radical act is the realization of his belief that his self-destruction creates important "social values" (*shehui de jiazhi*).[24] Death means the elimination of the male body's biological functions, needs, and desires for sexual pleasure and material comforts. In this sense, death realizes the ultimate autonomy of the individual, severing all his physical, emotional, and social ties with a secular life that this divorce narrative associates with the debasing force of the female corporeality.

In other words, suicide completes the sublimation of such a privileged affective subject, whose emotional authenticity is reproduced not only through Nan Yang's ideal (male) reader's compassionate preface but also through the emotional engagement and identification that readers experience with the diary of speaking bitterness. Commenting on his effort to weave such an emotional communication into a larger tapestry of historic progress, Wu says: "I feel very delighted by the fact that not a single reader read the novel as simply a love story" because "literary works should capture the spirit of the times of the Reform and Opening Up."[25] Connecting private matters with "the spirit of the times," the intellectual's speaking-bitterness narrative is turned into the essential basis on which a privileged class and gender identity are expected to be constructed and performed.

LEGALIZING THE DOMESTIC

In order to reinvent such a class and gender subject position situated at the intersection of state, family, and individual, the author first turns to the revolutionary ritual of speaking bitterness to arouse public passions about the marital crisis of a male intellectual and then capitalizes on the post-revolutionary currency of rule by law to regulate and legalize domestic sentimentality. Since the late 1970s, the discourse of rule by law has been revitalized by intellectuals as a powerful weapon to fight the socialist collective mentality and to legalize a new individualized subject position. In "Democracy and Rule by Law" (Minzhu yu fazhi), published on July 13, 1978, in the Party mouthpiece *People's Daily*, rule by law was considered an all-powerful weapon for cleaning up the residual "feudalistic" influence of the Cultural Revolution.

This rekindled passion for legalism reverts to the May Fourth generation's heated debates about "rule by man" (*renzhi*) versus rule by law, emotionality versus rationality, and tradition versus modernity. In his 1915 *New Youth* article "Differences of Basic Thought between Eastern and Western People" (Dongxi minzu genben sixiang zhi chayi), Chen Duxiu argues that "'rule by man' had been the core of the Chinese legal tradition and was exceedingly vulnerable to emotions." In direct opposition to rule by man, rule by law, with its roots in the modern West, "was deemed objective, and thus above subjective interference."[26] Without a historicized analysis of the evolution of jurisdiction in various legal traditions, Chen, like many of his contemporary Chinese intellectuals, makes a simplistic equivalence between judicial institutions and cultural quintessences.

In the realm of civil laws, this tradition of rule by man is often closely associated with the famous (or infamous) judicial practice of "mediation" (*tiaojie*), a cornerstone of the Maoist mode of civil justice. This mode "called for judges to go down to the village to investigate and then marshal community and familial as well as official pressure to effect reconciliation, in a very time-consuming process."[27] Emphasizing the critical agency of the judges, the Maoist mediation, including "mediated divorce" (*taojie lihun*), seeks to find a "middle course" (*zhongjian daolu*) between radical reforms and populist emotions in order to strike a balance between community ethics, individual interests, and—most importantly—totalitarian state intervention.[28]

After the Cultural Revolution, judicial practices, particularly in the realm of civil law, changed from on-site investigation to investigating by adjudging at court. This shift was made not merely out of practical concerns (insufficient funds or staff) but also out of an ideological rupture with the Maoist mode. Having lost faith in the Maoist collective social movement based on a mobilization of massive passions, post-revolutionary Chinese intellectuals revived Chen's belief in the regulation of modern individuals by law and order. Analyzing the tension between rule by man and rule by law as reflected in Zhang Yimou's film *The Story of Qiuju* (Qiuju da guansi; 1992), A-chin Hsiau pointed out that the tradition of rule by man emphasizes the government's duty of morally educating the people. Hsiau further argues that, compared to the Maoist totalitarian political moralism,

> the party-state in post-Mao era has lost the enthusiasm and capacity to moralize the people, while some slogans such as "Learn from Lei Feng" (*Xue Lei Feng*) reappear periodically. . . . The political reform of China is believed to have to rely significantly on the "rule by law" (*fazhi*) rather than on pure mobilization and political means. The law will become a major means by which the state shapes and reshapes people's moral thinking about self, other, and society, as the film suggests.[29]

Obviously taking the side of rule by law, Li Bo, the intellectual protagonist in the novel *Divorce*, yearns to solve his personal problems by legalizing the boundary of the domestic sphere. Rather than stoking revolution or class struggle, his speaking bitterness calls for the institutionalization of legal regulations of emotional and ethical issues. Negating the historical legacy of political moralism, he detests state mediation of and communal intervention with his private matters of marriage and divorce. The very existence of an unofficial "moral court" (*daode fating*), a metaphor for public opinions on ethical issues, is compared to the anachronistic "big-character posters" (*dazi bao*) used to attack class enemies during the Cultural Revolution and regarded as a cultural deformation caused by the incomplete institutionalization of a legal system.[30]

Therefore, Li chooses to go to court to settle his divorce case. Interestingly, in real life, workers were more willing to go to court for divorces while intellectuals were more concerned with "saving face" and "unwilling to draw the state apparatus into their affairs."[31] Justifying his unusual decision in his diary, Li states that his action illustrates China's evolution from man-ruled to law-ruled, putting it on a par with Euro-American countries. Thus, the fictional divorce case, renarrativized in judicial terms, reproduces a binary structure of Western legalistic modernity and Chinese man-ruled tradition. Judicial reformation is deemed to be an essential means for China to modernize and to catch up with the West.

Li's view precisely reflects 1980s intellectuals' idealization of the Euro-American judicial system in which social justice and emotional authenticity were supposedly guaranteed by a practice based on laws. But in fact, instead of holding homogenous views toward the subtle relationships between legality and domesticity, different groups, divided along gender, age, race, and class lines in Euro-American societies, may have had diverse points of views. For instance, the American middle class tended to look down on those who bring "intimate, domestic problems to court" because they allow "everyone to see [their] personal affairs and to talk about them."[32] Deviating drastically from Li's fantasy of a homogeneously legalistic and individualist West, this "suburban morality" of the American middle class actually reinforces the conservative tendency of family ethics.

Rather than disputing the utopian vision of legalistic modernization, Li is inspired by the ideal of social justice in a Western law-ruled country that he has learned about from watching imported foreign films.[33] Accepting the transplantation of the sublime goal into Chinese soil, he starts writing a petition letter for his first prosecution of divorce. In this lengthy petition letter, Li reveals the details of his troubled love life to the state judicial apparatus. It begins with how he, Li Bo, and his wife, Zou Huixian, first met during the Cultural Revolution. Back in 1968, Li, a college student in the Department of Philosophy, joined a violent fight between two Red Guard factions. After being hit in the head with a brick, he was sent to a hospital where Zou worked as a nurse. During his stay in the hospital, Zou took good care of Li and developed a strong attachment to him, despite her parents' objections. Li did not harbor an equally strong passion for Zou, but her good looks, youthful vitality, and unreserved devotion to him touched his heart. They got married.

In retrospect, this male intellectual regards his "free marriage," forged against patriarchal authority, as a mistake made during the Cultural Revolution and wants it to be corrected in the post-revolutionary period by legal means. Justifying his petition for divorce by alluding to the post-revolutionary political rhetoric of "rectifying the aberration and setting things back in right order" (boluan fanzheng), he aligns his domestic affairs with the essential spirit of the time. However, Li's divorce request meets with constant frustration. The reason, according to the male intellectual, lies in the close association of excessive feminine sentiments with the destructive forces of history, or, literally, because the judge is a woman.

In Li's eyes, the middle-aged woman judge, Wu Lanzhen, is still bound by the "'traditional' bonds of moral sentiments" (renqing).[34] When Li follows the stringent legal procedure and states his reasons for initiating the divorce, Wu appears stern and aloof. However, once his wife starts to tell her side of story (in an irrational manner, as Li sees it), the judge constantly nods her head in approval and shows emotional support with her sympathetic eyes. Li's bitter reasoning is revealed in his diary entry: "At this moment, a woman can only help another woman." Moreover, he feels reluctant to rebut his wife with factual evidence that he could have gathered in their marital life because, in his opinion, this kind of evidence is too prosaic and insignificant to be persuasive. If he makes use of these trivial details from everyday life, he will not look like a masculine man anymore.[35]

In the end, the judge does not grant Li's request for divorce. Instead, she urges Li and Zou to work out a better division of household chores and to solve their domestic conflicts with more patience and self-criticism, because the "emotional foundation" (ganqing jichu) of their marriage is still stable.[36] Such a verdict is more in line with Maoist-mediated reconciliation (tiaojie hehao) than with fulfilling Li's desire for modern judicial practices. Li is disappointed by the outcome of the proceeding and blames the judge's "primitive" feminine sentiments, which he interprets as working against the establishment of an impartial legalistic rationality. Li's frustration implies that, despite her professional raison d'être, a woman always follows her instinctual compulsions because gender determines her way of thinking and structure of feeling. In other words, rule by law can be achieved only with rule by man, not rule by woman.

In the following weeks, Li Bo participates in a sociological research project about contemporary Chinese family life. After reading a stack of court dossiers of divorce cases, he finds that approximately 70 percent of divorce cases have been initiated by women.[37] Li does not do an in-depth analysis of the socioeconomic implications of this new phenomenon, nor does he speculate on a possible link between the high divorce rate and the Second Marriage Law or women's increasing financial independence. Rather, he rushes to a biased conclusion that more women have initiated divorce because men are more rational and have a stronger sense of responsibility. In his December 6 diary entry, he makes a highly sexist statement: "Women deal with divorce in a very different manner from men. Compared to men, women are more unreasonable, more whimsical, and more unscrupulous!"[38] Thus, the complexity and ambivalence of ethical issues and domestic affairs caught between emotionality (*qing*), rationality (*li*), and legality (*fa*) is reduced to a series of binary structures of masculine versus feminine, rational versus sentimental, and modern rule by law versus traditional rule by man.[39]

"WOMEN ARE WOLVES!"

After his high hopes for rule by law are dashed by the woman judge's ruling, Li feels disheartened. At this moment, he meets twenty-four-year-old Jin Dao, the poetry editor of a literary journal who displays great admiration for Li's sociological works. To Li, she looks like a wild girl from the countryside. Showing great interest in this young admirer's physical appearance, he describes his first impression of her: "She is medium-sized, suntanned, not very pretty, but full of vitality. In particular, her eyes, hidden behind her long lashes, are always burning with passion."[40]

Li's first impression of a wild woman filled with primitive passion is further enhanced by their lively conversation about Isadora Duncan when Li pays his first visit to Jin following their chance encounter. Showing Li a copy of *The Autobiography of Isadora Duncan*, Jin eagerly shares her reverence for this modern artist:

> Duncan is the mother of American, or more precisely, Western, modern dance as a whole. She devoted herself to her art, to her career! In her private life, she also defied traditional conventions in order to

live her life of her own free will! She fell in love with many people and had sex with many more. But I like her because she was true to herself![41]

Hearing these zealous words, Li is struck by the thought that the Chinese incarnation of Duncan is standing in front of him. From then on, they start developing an intimate relationship, embracing a new dating culture of leisure activities, physical intimacy, and sexual titillation. In his April 29 diary entry, Li describes his sensual experience of their first kiss:

> All of a sudden, I cannot control myself. Like crazy, I throw myself at her and hold her tightly in my arms.
> Then my kisses, like raindrops, fall on her eyes, cheeks, neck, and lips!
> Her lips are burning! She presses her burning lips tightly on mine. Then the whole world evaporates!
> My entire body twitches and trembles, electrified with an indescribable sensation that flows through every single part of my body, again and again and again. . . .
> Volcanic eruption? Earthquake? Tsunami? No! This sensation is much more groundbreaking than all those!
> It feels like the earth going out of its orbit! Like all the constellations reassembling! Like the universe returning to its primeval state of chaos!
> . . .
> This is the most passionate kiss in human history!
> With such a kiss, one would die with no regret![42]

Exclamation points and superlatives saturate this passage of sensual indulgence with a hyperbolic theatricality, which, not unlike May Fourth–style sentimental romanticism or Maoist revolutionary romanticism, emphasizes a strong sense of complete transformation and subjective assertion. The short paragraphs and rhythmic sentences further enhance the dramatic effect and the intensity of affective outburst. Analogous to the story "Flying Afar" (discussed in ch. 2), the narrative of romantic love also compares the explosive power of one's fervent yearnings, affective enjoyment, and physical sensation to a series of natural phenomena, celestial movements, and even the death and rebirth of the whole universe.

This boundless heteroerotic pleasure enjoyed by Li and Jin is further reinforced in a large illustration, one-third the size of a page, printed next to the passage. This black-and-white illustration (the only one in the main body of the literary text) depicts a man and a woman locked in an intimate embrace against the abstracted background of a cluster of skyscrapers, obviously a reference to urban modernity. Going along with the "human-centered" spirit of the 1980s, the two human figures are disproportionately large, exceeding the high-rise buildings in the background in size. In the center of the composition, a man passionately kisses a woman's neck. His right arm holds the barely clad woman close to his muscular torso, and his left hand grabs her protruding breasts in a possessive manner. Going along with the textual monologue focused on the male narrator's feelings, fantasies, and erotic pleasures, the visual image shows the man's sexual aggression and physical possession of the woman.

This human-centered, or, more precisely, male-centered, illustration provides readers with a concrete image of Jin's highly eroticized female body, which shatters Li's old world, absolves his existential angst resulting from his agonizing past, and rekindles his youthful passion. The lost ten years of this middle-aged man's youth have been retrieved and reintegrated and set back on the correct track of progressive temporality. However, this passionate romance does not lead to sexual abandon. Believing that a pure and appropriate sex life can be permitted only within the boundaries of a legally recognized home, Li refuses to make love to Jin, even when they spend the night in the same bed.

However, Li's optimistic belief in a better marriage based on the domestication of sexuality is seriously challenged when Jin tells him frankly that she has had quite a few impromptu intimate relationships with other men. The modern masculine subject built on a rational monitoring of his sexuality is undermined by Jin's refusal to be a passive object of male desire or domestication. As a result, Li's diary entries swing from the one extreme of eroticizing the female body to the other of demonizing its "dangerous pleasures." The Chinese Duncan morphs into a wanton vixen, a mythologized lascivious figure who controls the rhythm of romantic fantasy and exploits men's sexuality to maintain her perennial youth.

In his diary entry of June 6, 1983, Li cries out in bitterness: "Why did you tell me this? Why?! Don't you know that there is a sacred totem as high flying as a kite in every man's heart? Your honesty just destroyed this sublime totem!"[43] Obviously the lofty totem he mentions refers to Jin's chastity and unconditional fidelity to Li. Ironically, Li dismisses his appreciation of Duncan's unconventional lifestyle and his own critique of conservative familial morality. It appears that what the modern intellectual desires is really a reform of emotional and domestic interiority that leaves the patriarchal power intact.

While the femme fatale's seductively feminine figure compensates Li for the ten youthful years that he feels he lost during the Cultural Revolution, her transgressive sexuality threatens the male intellectual's self-image as the modern subject.[44] If a modern subject is constructed through the new fad of translated Freudian theories about individual sexuality in post-revolutionary China, then this subject at the core of sexual modernity has to be male. A femme fatale like Jin Dao can never be a "heroine of modernity."[45] Rather, she has to be punished and eradicated from the text of modernity composed by a male intellectual. One cannot help but wonder what this novel would have been like if it had been written by a woman writer and told from Jin Dao's point of view. As a Chinese admirer of Isadora Duncan, Jin refuses to be owned and domesticated by patriarchal heterosexual monogamy, which puts her on a par with earlier progressive yet decadent female figures such as Sophie in Ding Ling's famous story "Diary of Miss Sophie."

However, in this male-authored novel narrated as a male intellectual's monologue, such a femme fatale figure only serves as a catalyst to the forging of a homosocial male-male bonding established on a simultaneous common desire for and collective hostility toward women. Discussing Jin's promiscuity with Li, Nan Yang, a divorced man himself, concludes that the young woman's attitude toward intimacy and sex is "quasi-modern" (*wei xiandai*), fundamentally different from the authentic modernists, or "rational modernists" (*lixing de xiandai pai*), represented by male intellectuals such as themselves.[46] Actually, it should be regarded as a direct result of the ten turbulent years of the Cultural Revolution. Nan Yang continues his relentless attack on Jin Dao:

> Growing up in the wasteland of the Cultural Revolution, they [Jin's generation] have witnessed men's degeneration into wolves and too much violent fights among those wolves. As a result, they have developed their own life philosophy: Survival is everyone's top priority. There is no room to consider other people's welfare!

On hearing Nan Yang's analysis of the "new youth," Li laments: "Alas, I fell in love with a wolf!"[47] Similarly, Wang Laijun, Li's ally in his winding divorce procedure, utters the same condemnation of women whose dangerous sexuality threatens to devour their male prey. Wang tells his story to Li Bo with such fiery anger and hatred that "every word sounds as sharp as a dagger": He has an extra-marital affair and divorces his wife. Unexpectedly, his girlfriend then dumps him to go abroad. Associating female eroticism with carnivo-rous bestiality, Li and Wang proclaim: "Women are wolves!"[48]

Worth noting here is the male intellectuals' attribution of unruly feminine sexuality that unleashes chaos to the ten turbulent years of the Cultural Revolution. This link is not accidental: in his lengthy peti-tion for divorce, Li also associates his marriage closely with the vio-lence, bloodshed, and atrocities of the Cultural Revolution and calls it a "historic mistake to be corrected in a new age." Similar misogynist rhetoric can be found in the collective imagination of Jiang Qing as an ambitious vixen, a female usurper who manipulated Mao Zedong with her dangerous sexual charms and treacherous political machina-tions.[49] This popular imagination regards Jiang as the "femme fatale" (hongyan huoshui) who leads the Great Helmsman astray and brings the nation to the verge of collapse.

Such a collective ritual of feminizing the evil makes possible the charge that the revolutionary years were characterized by exces-sive ideology and have left a legacy of traumatic memories. In his essay "The Precondition of Women's Liberation Must Be Men's Lib-eration" (Funü jiefang zhi qianti dang wei nanren zhi jiefang), Wu Ruozeng particularly condemns Chinese women like Jiang Qing for their over-liberated and "masculine" practices such as putting on men's attire and doing men's jobs during the Cultural Revolution, which, he contends, degraded them into something "non-man, non-woman, non- human, and non-demon" (feinan feinü feiren feigui).[50] Thus, the political chaos caused by the ideological Other and the sex-ual chaos caused by the gendered Other are fused.

Believing that killing a lascivious woman like Jin Dao means achieving social justice for all the other men of the world, Li Bo is determined to punish the seductive she-wolf and expel the feminized specter of history. So he calls on Jin, bringing with him a sharpened knife. When he arrives he is astonished to see that her face and body have already been mutilated by sulfuric acid, the result of an attack by a vengeful middle-aged woman, most probably his wife. However, Li still cannot forgive Jin. Although his wife unexpectedly agrees to their divorce at his second hearing, Jin's betrayal destroys Li's hope for a better domestic life. Caught between his yearning for sexual modernity and his wish to preserve patriarchal morality, the split subject finally chooses to kill himself in order to repel the contaminating "feminine" force and preserve the purity of the masculine subject's inner world.

Embodying the oppressing *yin* force, Li's wife and mistress are represented as thoughtless bodies suffering from psychotic conditions of hysteria and neurosis. This reproduces the dualistic logic of the body/ exterior versus the soul/interior: "The soul is precisely what the body lacks; hence, the body presents itself as a signifying lack."[51] Such a binary structure projects the body/soul dichotomy onto sexual differences. Thus, fear and anxiety about the violent past and turbulent present are transposed to the images of "backward" or "quasi-modern" women who embody either the stifling banality of everyday routines confined within the domestic space or the dangerous corporeal pleasures that destabilize its boundary.

TURN TO NEOREALISM

Compared to Wu Ruozeng, Su Tong, along with his modernist cohorts Yu Hua, Ma Yuan, Gefei, and Sun Ganlu, is better known for a more self-reflective approach to the narration of history and modernization. In the second half of the 1980s, Su Tong emerged as a prominent avant-garde writer, highly regarded for his exploration of metafictional narratives. The publication of *Wives and Concubines* (Qiqie chengqun; 1989), which was adapted into the award-winning film *Raise the Red Lantern* (Dahong denglong gaogao gua; 1992) by Zhang Yimou, marked Su Tong's turn to "neorealism" (*xin xieshi zhuyi*). The term "neorealism" was coined to distinguish a literary style from critical realism and socialist realism. It was used to categorize the writings of contemporary Chinese writers such as Chi Li, Fang Fang, Liu Zhenyun, Zhou Meisen, and Su Tong (for his later works).

A majority of Su Tong's neorealist works focus on the issues of love, marriage, and divorce. They are included in various anthologies of contemporary Chinese literature including the influential ten-volume series *Literary Works on Love and Ethics in Contemporary China* (Zhongguo dangdai qing'ai lunli zhengming zuopin shuxi). Thanks to its enormous popularity, "A Divorce Handbook," combined with Su Tong's "A Married Man," was adapted into an eight-episode TV series in 1995, the first installment of the *Southern Writers' TV Series Masterpieces* (Nanfang zuojia dianshiju jingpin); however, it was poorly received due to its shoddy production.

Although Su Tong himself calls these writings about love and marriage his representative novellas, these neorealist pieces have received less critical attention mainly because of their focus on the "trivial" topic of mundane life.[52] Despite, or because of, their popularity, some critics even label these works "vulgar low-quality fiction."[53] This deep-rooted prejudice against literary forms on "feminine" topics is regrettable. This trend may be questioned through a thorough investigation of the intersections of gender, family, and intellectual discourse (or its disintegration) in 1990s Chinese society that are evident in Su Tong's critically overlooked piece "A Divorce Handbook."[54] While Su's earlier experiments with avant-garde bildungsroman highlight a fictional juvenile's point of view, "A Divorce Handbook" and many of his other neorealist texts focus on the existential experiences of a middle-aged man in the contemporary urban world.

In the preface to *Snapshots of Married Life*, a collection of his neorealist novellas, Su states:

"A Married Man" and "A Divorce Handbook" portray a man, a man called Yang Bo, in our everyday reality. These works mark a turning point in my literary career. I seek to zoom in on reality by depicting a man's struggle in marriage. As idealism is encroached upon by dull and dreary everyday reality, the man's difficult and lonesome situation is worth pondering. I try to depict how the feet, bodies, and even heads of men like Yang Bo are entrapped in the muddy swamp of the mundane world. . . . This type of fiction might sound fearsome, but this kind of reality is indeed fearsome.[55]

In this short passage, the word "reality" pops up four times, attesting to Su Tong's sharp turn away from avant-garde experimentation in an effort to grasp social reality. However, the metaphor of the swamp ironically indicates the male intellectual's loss of a firm footing in such a reality. The words "dull," "dreary," and "fearsome" accentuate a deepening sense of disorientation and immobilization at a time of overwhelming "social transformation" (*shehui zhuanxing*).

By examining the marital crisis of a male intellectual, "A Divorce Handbook" has a more focused story line than Wu Ruozeng's novel *Divorce*. Without intercutting the narration with lengthy sociological reflections on various divorce cases, as in Wu's novel, "A Divorce Handbook" focuses solely on the male narrator's everyday experience of his marital life in crisis. In this sense, Su's narrative style is more individualized and trivialized. This stylistic trademark of neorealist fiction tends to depoliticize history and emphasize the idea of eternal mundaneness.

In spite of formal differences, there are many parallels between the two male writers' divorce narratives. Su Tong's protagonist Yang Bo not only shares the same first name as Li Bo in *Divorce*; he also occupies the same social status—that of a well-educated urban intellectual. Furthermore, his yearlong struggle to obtain a divorce mirrors Li's experience. Finally, Su Tong's male-centered narrative also focuses on the sufferings and bitterness of the introspective narrator Yang Bo, who is represented as a solitary soldier fighting against the whole world to obtain liberation from the institution of marriage. Given the publication date (1991) of this novella, Yang's desperate struggle can easily be read as an implicit comment on the intellectual's pursuit of political liberation. A lengthy passage that describes Yang wandering around Tiananmen Square reinforces the political message of the seemingly personal account.

At the very beginning of "A Divorce Handbook," Yang Bo, a middle-aged married man—just like the male protagonist of *Divorce*—suddenly initiates a divorce proceeding for no apparent reason. Zhu Yun, his wife, dismisses it as a joke. However, Yang's stubborn insistence makes Zhu realize that he is, in fact, serious. To make things difficult for her husband, Zhu agrees to divorce on the condition that Yang pay her ¥20,000 (around $3,000), a huge amount of money for the average urban professional in early 1990s China. After Yang manages to borrow the money from a wealthy friend, Zhu unexpectedly refuses to grant the divorce after all and attempts suicide by taking sleeping pills. She is taken to the hospital by neighbors and her family. Deemed responsible for Zhu's act, Yang is not only verbally abused by his neighbors and coworkers but also suffers blows from his brothers-in-law's fists. In contrast to Li Bo's sublimated act of suicide, Zhu's failed suicide attempt is depicted in such a sarcastic tone that it appears to be more farcical than tragic.

Depressed by his futile efforts to get the divorce, Yang turns to Yu Qiong, his young girlfriend, for emotional support. However, this does not provide peace or happiness either. Rather it leads to a violent confrontation between Zhu and Yu. Overwhelmed by all the hysterical women and meaningless violence around him, Yang gives up the idea of divorce altogether. When spring comes, a weary and disheartened Yang puts an end to his extramarital affair and resumes the

typical routine of a middle-aged married man. A deep sense of deso-
lation that "belongs to the elderly" fills his heart.[56]

SENSING THE MIDLIFE CRISIS

"A Divorce Handbook" starts out with a description of Yang's home
from a highly subjective perspective. After a long sleepless night, on a
freezing winter morning, Yang Bo hears the north wind fiercely striking the windowpanes of the old apartment. The cramped room is suf-
fused with the "stagnant, acrid stink" of human bodies, the bedding,
and the enamel bedpan.[57] Lying motionless in bed, Yang feels as if
his head is swollen as a result of the night's insomnia and the endless
thoughts that roiled his mind. Images of swelling, rotting, and decay
are frequently found in the writings of Su Tong and other contemporary Chinese avant-garde writers such as Can Xue and Yu Hua. These
are often used to externalize and corporealize the fictional characters' fear and anxiety about an outside world that is overwhelmingly
chaotic and uncertain, posing a huge threat to the peace and purity
of their inner world. Furthermore, the words "old," "stagnant,"
"motionless," and "exhausted" set the basic tone of the narrative. A
strong sense of discontent and fatigue pervades the novella, enhancing
Yang's feeling of loss with the realization that he is no longer young.

When Zhu Yun makes her first appearance, she, too, is seen from
the same subjective perspective of the male narrator. Under the male
gaze, Zhu fulfills the role of the hysterical Other with her disheveled
hair and greenish thermal top ripped open at the armpit. Her fishy-
smelling breath and jaundiced face make Yang think of a mummified
woman's corpse he saw exhibited in a museum. Throughout the story,
grotesque images of death, decay, sickness, waste, and rot abound
and punctuate the male-centered narrative with intricate details of
Yang's physical and psychological wounds. For instance, when Zhu
goes to Yang's work unit to seek help in solving their domestic problems, Yang hides his face behind a newspaper. Then he rushes into
the men's room to escape the curious stares of his coworkers. There,
the awful stink of human excrement makes him feel suffocated by the
rotting oppressive world around him. Through the constant use of
"He sees . . . ," "He hears . . . ," "He feels . . . ," and so on, the continuous fluctuations of Yang's inner world are meticulously external-
ized and convey his sense of the outside world as an accumulation of
redundant and magnified images. All these tangible details are drawn

from the male protagonist's point of view and constitute allegorical signs of highly gendered body politics.

As in many other modernist works, however, the male subject is decentered and fragmented rather than coherent as it was in the 1980s Chinese literary works considered earlier. Unlike Li Bo, Wu's assertive first-person narrator, Yang is more of an indifferent observer who persistently gazes at the world around him while being gazed at by an invisible yet omniscient spectator, which sometimes merges with the social network of surveillance from his neighbors and colleagues. Tired of feeling scrutinized and examined by the crowd surrounding him, Yang takes a business trip to Beijing. Once there, he visits Tiananmen Square on a snowy night and tries to figure out what practical measures need to be taken in the handling of his divorce:

> Yang Bo did his utmost to imagine the great events of history which had occurred on this hallowed ground, but it was all useless. His mind lingered obstinately on various thoughts related to the divorce. He bowed his head and then measured out the steps between the Memorial to the People and the Tiananmen Gate, and as he walked he thought through the steps he would need to take in order to get a divorce. First—they would have to *come to an understanding*, in order to avoid violence and injury. Second—he would have to give Zhu Yun advantageous terms and make sacrifices when it came to the division of property and finances. Third—he would have to start looking for a new apartment so that he would at least have a roof over his head. Fourth—he would need to make preparations to remarry, for which he would need to confer with Yu Qiong.[58]

Here, the narrative is not limited to Yang's point of view. Rather, it swings back and forth between his interior monologue and a more detached and objective point of view, a disembodied gaze regarding Yang's trivialized body that is wandering aimlessly at the center stage of modern Chinese history. Then this disembodied gaze is gradually fused with the vigilant square guard's perspective. Following his gaze, readers can visualize Yang's tiny and insignificant body walking in endless circles around the vast and well-guarded public space. This ghostly figure brings back the haunting memories of 1989, the specter exiled from the official narrative of Chinese history. Su Tong uses spectrality as a literary device in many of his writings to draw readers' attention to the "ghost," or the suppressed, the exiled, the unspeakable of history.[59]

Though no specific dates are mentioned in this story (possibly a result of self-censorship), the choice of this historical site as the place where Yang plans a "domestic reform" should not be considered at all accidental. Yang's pacifist divorce plan harks back to the historic moment in early 1989 when students and intellectuals hoped to come to an understanding with the government, a hope that was heartlessly crushed by state violence. The security guard's gaze over the vast expanse of Tiananmen Square reminds readers of the historical significance of the particular year that the author avoids mentioning in this narrative about private matters.[60]

As a narrative device, the word "gaze" and the act of gazing are often used by Su Tong to establish the connection between space and time, the spatial signifier and the historical signified. Here, the silenced specter of 1989 sneaks back onto the stage of Tiananmen Square in the dark. The very presence of the military guard makes visible the ghostly memories of the nightmare and bloodshed of the Tiananmen Square Massacre that took place two years before the publication of the story. His watchful gaze is indicative of the omniscient and omnipotent presence of the state apparatus. The enormous power attached to this gaze of surveillance renders Yang's individual efforts at controlling his own life futile and meaningless. Yang's awareness of the gaze constantly interrupts his speculations about his private matters, which makes his comments about the freedom to take such a night tour of Tiananmen Square sound dubious and sarcastic.

This mode of double gazing appears again near the end of the story when all of Yang's well-conceived divorce plans have failed in the face of enormous social pressure. Out of a profound sense of resignation, Yang gives up his divorce attempt. As he takes his son to get some new releases at a local bookstore, he runs into Yu Qiong and her new boyfriend. Again, the perspective swings between Yang's gaze at Yu and an invisible spectator's gaze at Yang's mechanical acts of reading and chatting. Rendered powerless by such a detached yet omnipresent gaze, Yang reconciles with the normative order of everyday life that buries traces of memory, struggle, and trauma under its surface of continuity and prosperity.

LOSS OF THE HUMANIST SPIRIT

Su Tong's use of multiple perspectives shows readers different visions of the same fictional scenario or life situation. The coherence of the subject position is constantly undercut by the exposed gaps and discrepancies of representations from different angles. While Yang's divorce plan sounds highly reasonable and logical from his perspective, shifting to an objective, all-knowing point of view reveals the futility and absurdity of all his well-planned reasoning and calculation. This sense of absurdity is further exacerbated through Yang's encounters with his male friends who have chosen to plunge into the sea of business in order to thrive in a globalizing market economy.

Because Zhu asks for ¥20,000 as the condition for granting his request for divorce, Yang has no choice but to turn to Big Head for financial aid. Big Head is a wealthy businessman whom Yang looks down upon for being poorly educated. Aware of Yang's scorn, Big Head uses this opportunity to take revenge on the poor intellectual. To get the loan, Big Head tells Yang, "You have to bend down and let me vault over you."[61] Yang agrees to this condition, although he feels tremendously insulted. As he does so, he hears something breaking. What is broken is not only Yang's self-esteem but also the 1980s intellectuals' promise to carry on the sacred mission of enlightening the masses through an alliance of science and literature, as discussed in the previous chapter.

At this moment, Yang's interior monologue is replaced again by the omniscient spectator's perspective, which seems to identify with Big Head's sadistic point of view. From this perspective, readers get to see how Yang bends down, then stands up, his body shivering and a weird expression on his face. Here, the narrative's vantage point has been given to the wealthy businessman. Despite his lowbrow tastes and poor education, Big Head is a new hero for the new times. This sense of irony is further amplified when Yang quotes Schopenhauer's famous line "Money is the downfall of man" to belittle Big Head while begging for a loan. However, despite Yang's success in procuring a loan, money does not solve his problem. Zhu Yun breaks her promise and refuses to grant a divorce. Emblematic of the inertia of the repressive mundane life, the hysterical woman cannot be changed by either the logic of the marketplace or the Enlightenment rationale. Rather, she insists on clinging to Yang like a monstrous force from the abysmal depths of history.

Feeling enormously disappointed and depressed, Yang goes to Old Jin's place for advice. Old Jin is Yang's philosophy teacher from night school, a man who can recite lengthy passages from Hegel, Schopenhauer, Heidegger, and other Western thinkers whose names sound familiar to New Enlightenment intellectuals. To Yang's great disappointment, however, Old Jin has thrown all his philosophy books in the trash and taken to selling watermelons on the street. Responding to Yang's questions about love and life, Old Jin tells him that philosophical thoughts and theories are simply bullshit: all are empty and meaningless words, totally ineffective as solutions to any real-life problems.

The philosophy teacher's profound disillusionment with book knowledge and Western philosophy resonates with the cultural elites' heated discussion about the "loss of the humanist spirit" (ren-wen jingshen de shiluo) in the 1990s. A decade after the "culture fever" of the 1980s, 1992 marked another turning point in China's sociocultural climate: the Fourteenth CCP Congress endorsed a free market economy, and Deng Xiaoping made an inspection tour of southern China. Following Deng's milestone tour, accelerated mar-ketization and commercialization led to stunningly rapid growth of the national economy. At the same time, the tightening politi-cal control after the 1989 Tiananmen Square Massacre dampened the enthusiasm of public intellectuals for participating in political movements.

In 1993, Wang Xiaoming, professor of modern and contemporary Chinese literature at East China Normal University, published a poi-gnant article, "Ruins on the Open Field—Literature and the Crisis of the Humanist Spirit" (Kuangye shang de feixu—wenxue he renwen jingshen de weiji) in Shanghai Literature. This article whipped up a cultural storm, with, at its center, an animated debate about Chinese intellectuals' loss of the "humanist spirit." In the same year, Wang Meng, a well-known writer and the former minister of culture who was forced to resign after supporting the 1989 students' demonstra-tion, composed the provocative article "Stay Away from the Sublime" (Duobi chonggao), which drew even more intellectuals across various disciplines such as literature, history, philosophy, and economics into the already heated debate.

This nationwide grand-scale discussion about the crisis of the humanist spirit underlined the shifting historical roles that male-dominant intellectuals played in cultural discourses from the 1980s to the 1990s.[62] In modern Chinese history, from the May Fourth Movement in 1919 to the June Fourth Incident in 1989, Chinese intellectuals occupied center stage in the social and cultural spheres, established the general value system, molded the national charac-ter, and shouldered the moral responsibility for building the nation and saving the people. However, since the radical marketization and commercialization of the 1990s, the sense of superiority that arose from the spiritual transcendence and cultural reflections of male-dominant Chinese intellectuals has been shattered. The new set of market values flooded in and reshaped social values by prioritizing wealth over knowledge, utilitarianism over spirituality, and pop culture over high culture. Even the most intimate relationships, such as family and marriage, were often discussed as matters of financial transaction. The strong sense of angst among male intellectuals caught in such a dizzying transition was displaced into inward-turning gestures and attempts to escape from the life order of the material world. As the New Enlightenment intellectuals entered middle age, they found it difficult to reconcile themselves to a banal and paltry everyday life that seemed to kill all the hope, passion, and excitement of their idealistic youth.

ESCAPE FROM THE FEMINIZED DYSTOPIA

Placing "A Divorce Handbook" firmly in this context, it is clear that the spirit of pragmatism and scientific positivism implied in the word "handbook" (zhinan) captures the essence of the transitional times. However, in contrast to Shi Ping's case (discussed in ch. 2), in this 1990s account of divorce, scientific positivism fails to solve the personal problems of the featured male intellectual. Overwhelmed by an increasingly utilitarian Chinese society, the protagonist appears clumsy and powerless in the face of real-life problems, even those as trivial as buying a train ticket. From winter to spring, time passes and nothing changes. Like the cyclical temporal frame visualized in the film Raise the Red Lantern, history just repeats itself, and ordinary life remains unchanged no matter what, a trademark vision of temporality in neorealist fiction.

The oppressive force of the chaos, triviality, and dullness of daily routines are always projected onto the female body. In the male narrator's eyes, his wife in pinkish silk pajamas is like a brainless, lifeless heap of pink trash whose stink of decay envelops and suffocates him. She does nothing but occupy herself with household chores and watch "shitty" soap operas. She is depicted as a member of the unenlightened masses who is unreasonable and maddening because they lack "training in lucid philosophical or theoretical thought."[63] Yang finds such a degenerate female body with no interiority abhorrent and refuses to make love to his wife. Instead, he resorts to masturbation to maintain the autonomy of the desiring male subject that fears the containment of feminized family life.

Likewise, his mistress Yu Qiong is depicted as equally irrational and dangerous, despite the fact that she is well educated. When Yang goes over to Yu's place to discuss his divorce issues, Yu appears to be an unreasonable creature, yelling at her lover:

> My patience is wearing thin. Yu Qiong suddenly begins to scream. Then she slams the wavering door, shutting Yang Bo outside. He can hear her smash something inside. Disgusting. Her shouting reaches Yang Bo's ears. I hate your phony decency, and I hate hypocritical scruples. You chicken out now? You don't want a divorce anymore? Then fuck off. Get lost and never come back.
> What are you talking about? You totally misunderstood what I was trying to say. Utterly dejected, Yang Bo sat down on the ground, one hand stubbornly knocking on the door behind him. Kant, Nietzsche, Marx, please come to help me. Help me put clearly what I need to say.[64]

The deliberate omission of colons and quotation marks diminishes the speakers' agency and makes their highly emotional dialogue into an inseparable part of the detached narrative that mocks the male intellectual's futile summoning of Kant, Nietzsche, and Marx—three thinkers frequently cited in the 1980s discourse of New Enlightenment. Realizing the unbridgeable gap between language and meaning, between philosophy and real-life situations, Yang feels anxious and speechless. For him, women are unreasonable and mystifying destructive forces. To escape from these crazy women who constitute the destructive masses in their association with banality, degeneration, and sickness, Yang runs away from his own home. He spends a cold winter's night inside a cement conduit, curling his body into a fetal position. Ironically, his rejection of the feminized institution of the nuclear family only leads him to a symbolic return to the maternal womb.

Running and escaping are recurrent themes in Su Tong's stories, such as "Nineteen Thirty-four Escapes" (1934 nian de taowang; 1987), "Escapes" (Tao; 1989), and "Running Wild" (Kuangben; 1991). They indicate a poignant "anxiety to escape" felt by a generation growing up during the Cultural Revolution that "now finds itself at a loss in a monstrous and rapidly modernizing urban landscape."[65] More intriguingly, the anxiety to escape and the astounding fear of urban modernity are often translated into misogynist rhetoric in Su Tong's divorce narratives. The tightening political control and cultural censorship following the 1989 Tiananmen Massacre leave little room for intellectuals to continue participating effectively in public affairs and politics. At the same time, the accelerating development of the market economy and consumer culture further marginalizes intellectuals such as Yang Bo who indulge in philosophical speculation. For him, the overwhelming drabness of a bleak picture of material life manifests itself in the predictable future of a disastrous marriage with a monstrous woman.

This misogynist rhetoric expressed through a gesture of escape from the feminized dystopic future is even more conspicuous in Su Tong's "A Married Man,"[66] which was published slightly before "A Divorce Handbook." "A Married Man" is set in 1989, when "the whole world [became] fat and cumbersome due to some qualitative changes."[67] Though Su Tong never specifies what these "qualitative changes" are, the constant discussions of "plunging into the sea of business" and going to the "Special Economic Zones" anchor the personalized narrative in a larger sociopolitical context. The male protagonist, a married middle-aged intellectual also called Yang Bo, looks emaciated and lonely in the fat years, like a typical "dejected scholar in dire straits" (luopo caizi) in a "scholar and beauty" romance.

Totally out of sync with the radically changing world, the middle-aged intellectual's clothing is always out of season and his head is disproportionately large and heavy. He fails to manage either his company or his marriage well. Everything is dysfunctional, out of control, and meaningless to him. Unable to find his position in the new social order, Yang chooses to commit suicide. On New Year's Day, he throws himself off the balcony of his apartment. Compared to Li Bo's suicide in *Divorce*, Yang's death is almost anti-cathartic. Death does not make him a hero of the times. No philosophical speculation or emotional outburst elevates the deadly moment. No close friends like Nan Yang offer compassion or moral support. Rather, Yang's act of jumping to his death is described in an objective and detached tone. His plummeting figure, like a trivial dark spot, disappears into the bustling marketplace under the balcony, the most dispassionate scenario of everyday life, the one from which he tries desperately to escape. Yang's wife happens to witness his suicide as she is bargaining with a fruit vendor in the marketplace. Without revealing her response to this fatal incident, the story ends. Instead of acting as a symbol for the defeated scholar's emotional catharsis or romantic fantasy, the female figure is shown to be an indifferent witness absorbed into the frenzy of the market force that pushes Yang to his death.

This deconstructive narrative of the romantic individualism that bestows the modern masculine subject with inner depth and emotional authenticity is not unique to Su Tong. Chen Rong's novella "Too Lazy to Divorce" (Lande lihun; 1988) conveys a similar sense of ennui and resignation felt by a middle-aged couple in marital strife. Chi Li, a wildly popular female writer (see ch. 3), wrote "Apart from Love" (Butan aiqing) in 1988, which cast doubt on the utopian vision of romantic love of the May Fourth and New Enlightenment generations. "Classical Love" (Gudian aiqing; 1988), a fable by Yu Hua, another avant-garde writer, parodies a legendary love story with a detached and objective account of violence, murder, and cannibalism. Even Zhang Jie, arguably the godmother of the post-Mao literature of romantic love (see ch. 3), published a three-volume novel, *Wordless* (Wuzi), in the 1990s to deconstruct the myths of romantic individualism and revolutionary idealism and to mock her own canonical piece "Love Must Not Be Forgotten." Similarly, harmonious gender relationships marked by utopian love and intimacy are seldom found in the works of Sixth Generation filmmakers. Rather, misogynist and sexist rhetoric prevails. Women are often portrayed as "the sources of men's confusion, targets of men's desire, and victims of their own mutual jealousy."[68]

The ideology of romantic love, which was supported by the 1980s intellectuals' pursuit of classical humanism and liberal individualism, is undercut by the literary and cultural representations of irony and trauma that prevailed in 1990s Chinese (post)modernist works written in the face of the increasing commercialization of Chinese society and the decentering of the intellectual subject within the system of social classifications.

CONCLUSION

Through the central mechanism of speaking bitterness, Wu Ruozeng's divorce narrative, published in the midst of culture fever, expresses the desire to negate the Maoist past and reconnect with a new mode of modernity, which is epitomized by romantic love and legalistic individualism practiced in the domestic sphere.[69] Explaining his motivation for writing about a fictional divorce case, Wu suggests that the changing family is a microcosm of reform-era Chinese society and that the male intellectual protagonist represents the spirit of the rapidly changing times.[70] Just as the May Fourth generation's proposal for family reform was inspired by "universal economic trends—industrialization, the separation of home and work space, the need for a rational, independent workforce," the post-revolutionary Chinese intellectuals' quest for a companionate marriage and individual freedom is inseparable from the political and economic agenda of China's capitalization and marketization.[71]

Fighting against the hegemony of socialist collectivism, post-Mao Chinese intellectuals engaged in heated debates about individual subjectivity, which went along with the reform ideology of promoting personal responsibility and freeing individuals for the market. Not unlike the Maoist mode of speaking bitterness, Wu's literary representation of a divorce case bridges the gap between a grand narrative of historical teleology and everyday experiences depicted in a language abundant with ideologically loaded terms such as "individual," "freedom," "development," "rule by law," and so on. As the socialist revolution was understood by Chinese peasantry in terms of emancipation (*fanshen*) from the oppression of the "three mountains" (*sanzuo dashan*)—referring to feudalism, imperialism, and capitalism—so economic reform was translated into a developmentalist narrative structure centered on individual choice of modern lifestyle and freedom to divorce. In other words, the Dengist agenda of reform and modernization was not only rationalized but also humanized and sentimentalized through the literary mediation of the global currency of romantic love and domestic sentimentality.

However, less than a decade later, Chinese intellectuals found themselves facing a different historical trauma: a dystopic future of drastic marketization that strove to erase the traumatic memories of 1989. Mocking the 1980s intellectual discourse of reform and progress, Su Tong's deconstructionist narrative represents divorce as a nihilist allegory of male intellectuals' disillusionment and loss of historical agency. In Su Tong's neorealist divorce narratives, the sublime subject of the male intellectual is no longer coherent but exists in linguistic fragments of competing narratives. In "A Divorce Handbook," the frequent appearance of phrases and expressions such as "I don't know . . . ," "I cannot understand . . . ," and "I

cannot remember . . . " further questions the reliability of the narrator and enhances a sense of powerlessness and futility in remembering the past and envisioning the future. In place of a rational
modern subject, the middle-aged male intellectual is depicted as a
pathetic misfit marginalized in the market age.

Intriguingly, what stands out in both works is the misogynist
rhetoric that represents women characters as superficial, who either
embody the dangerous passion of youthful bodies for the troubled
male subject in midlife crisis or the everyday boredom that threatens
the spiritual transcendence of the enlightened male intellectual.

CHAPTER THREE

Utopia or Dystopia?

The Sisterhood of Divorced Women

Gender biopolitics has been reimagined in multiple ways through literary representations of divorced women's intersubjective sisterhood. On this topic, no literary critic can dismiss Zhang Jie's "The Ark."[1] Hailed as "touchstone fiction for feminists in the 1980s," this work has been read as a protest against "the profound alienation from sexual life and heterosexual norms" imposed by the Cultural Revolution.[2] What marks this novella's breakthrough is an audacious fantasy of a matriarchal commune composed of three middle-aged divorced women living together in a small apartment in 1980s Beijing.

A comparative reading of "The Ark" and Zhang's earlier work "Love Must Not Be Forgotten" will aid in better understanding the literary representation of the divorced women's utopia.[3] Both pieces are connected by a central issue: What does the sisterhood mean for divorced women in renegotiating their gender identities outside of the heterosexual matrix? Particularly worth noting is the deployment of the narrative mechanism of speaking bitterness, which, at the same time, sets limits for the ambivalent homosocial structure of feelings and intersubjective sisterly solidarity in Zhang's writings.

In the essay "Dare Not to Cry Together with You—to Zhang Jie (Bugan yu ni tongku—zhi Zhang Jie), written in 1994, Chi Li, a younger woman writer, talks about her awestruck reaction to the unprecedented portrayal of divorced women in Zhang Jie's "The Ark" when she first read the novella in 1982. Probably intended to be both a tribute to and a parody of Zhang's groundbreaking fiction, Chi Li's novella "Good Morning, Miss" (Xiaojie, nizao; 1998) is a

contemporary fairy tale about the sisterhood of a group of divorced
women allied against a newly rich man who commits adultery. The
novella was adapted into a TV serial, *Beyond Romance* (Chaoyue
qinggan). Chi Li then expanded the novella, using the series script as
an outline, and published *Good Morning, Miss* as a script novel (*ju-
qing xiaoshuo*) in 1999. The first 100,000 copies sold out quickly.
The original novella, which has been included in various anthologies
and collections of Chi's works, is analyzed in this chapter.

   In contrast to Zhang Jie's emphasis on women's yearnings for
romantic love and career success, "Good Morning, Miss" associates
women's essential identity with their reproductive power and maternal sentiments. Such an idealization of sentimental motherhood can
also be found in Chi Li's earlier works. In her 1990 story "Sunrise"
(Taiyang chushi), the last installment of her well-known Life Trilogy,
motherhood becomes the only sacred ideal that provides salvation in
an increasingly commercialized world. In such a mercantile society,
a good mother should make every possible emotional and financial
investment so that her only child can climb the evolutionary ladder
and grow up with "a first-class body and a first-class brain," which
will enable him or her to survive in the intensely competitive environment of post-revolutionary China.[4] All the conflicts and problems,
trials and tribulations of history depicted in Chi Li's Life Trilogy are
resolved not through state intervention or social movements but by
an idealized maternal figure who gives birth to the future generation
within a modern nuclear family.

   Although recent scholarship in Chinese literature and history has
paid increasing attention to the study of sisterhood,[5] few studies show
any critical concern for the alliance of divorced women within the
larger sociocultural context of post-revolutionary China. This chapter expands the critical scope of intersubjective sisterhood by drawing attention to this marginalized social group and discovers new
meaning in the female-female bond, a bond that opens up new possibilities of resistance against patriarchal hegemony and heterosexual
marriage. A series of important questions will be addressed: How do
women's divorce narratives wrestle with the misogynist rhetoric in
male writers' divorce narratives? How does the imagination of a utopian sisterhood of divorced women negotiate with the socialist legacy
of women's liberation and the emerging discourse of domestic interiority? What kind of spatiotemporal order and gendered biopolitics
are established, stretched, and contested in this historical process?

"LOVE MUST NOT BE FORGOTTEN"

Born in Beijing in 1937 and raised by a single mother, Zhang Jie is a highly controversial Chinese woman writer. Zhang started writing fiction in 1978 and won a national prize with her literary debut "The Music of the Forests" (Cong senlinli laide haizi), a short story depicting the adversities endured by Chinese intellectuals during the Cultural Revolution. This harsh critique of the immediate past is a major theme in her later works, which are more or less colored by her personal experiences. At a young age, Zhang divorced her husband after falling in love with a high-ranking CCP cadre, a married man who was not willing to sacrifice his political career to get a divorce. For years, Zhang Jie lived with her daughter and mother in a cramped apartment where she composed her fiction on a cutting board in the kitchen. She forged such a strong bond with her mother that she took her mother's family name—a practice that is rare not only in China but also worldwide. After her mother passed away in 1991, Zhang dedicated her most brilliant work, *Gone Is the One Who Held Me Dearest in the World* (Shishang zui teng wo de nage ren qu le), to her loving memories of this maternal figure.

One of Zhang Jie's most widely read stories is "Love Must Not Be Forgotten," which depicts Zhong Yu, a divorced woman writer, and her platonic relationship with a married high-ranking CCP official. Zhang Jie was harshly criticized for "undermining social morality" because she validated a divorced woman's yearnings for romantic affection. However, what has been overlooked by critics is the asymmetry in the two lovers' commitment to the platonic relationship and an implicit double standard. Zhong Yu is an intellectual middle-aged woman whose right to work has been ensured by the socialist women's liberation movement. She is well educated and independent. Even so, she lives a puritanical life after her divorce, thus preserving her emotional and physical chastity for her lover. Nevertheless—contrary to Lu Xun's prediction in his famous essay "What Happens After Nora Has Left Home" (Nala zouhou zenyang; 1923)—even financial self-sufficiency does not bring her true gender equality. Rather, it merely enables her to devote her love in its purest form to her lover.

At the same time, through the internalization of a male-centered sexual morality, the female character voluntarily suppresses her own desires in order to meet her lover's demand. Yet, despite her sexual abstinence and economic independence, she is still labeled the despicable "third party" (*disan zhe*) by some critics. Ironically, but not surprisingly, few condemn the married man who enjoys his lover's wholehearted devotion while maintaining his marriage and social status. Though revolutionary in celebrating women's right to free love, which is considered the basis of a companionate relationship, the story stumbles back to the clichéd narrative of a woman's sacrifice for and loyalty to a man.

Beyond heterosexual romance, another significant layer in the structure of feelings is the prototypical sisterhood forged between Zhong Yu and her daughter. Rather than being a "feudal" matriarch bent on obstructing the younger generation's pursuit of free love, the maternal figure in "Love Must Not Be Forgotten" is her daughter's best friend. After Zhong passes away, her daughter expresses the deepest feelings for her mother in the form of interior monologue:

> My thoughts constantly turn to her, not because she was such a strict
> mother that her ghost is still watching over me since her death. No,
> she was not just mother but my closest friend. I loved her so much
> that the thought of her leaving me makes my heart ache.[6]

Longing for a soul mate and a companionate marriage, Zhong's daughter chooses to remain single until she is thirty years old—an age well beyond a woman's tender youth in the conventional Chinese view. Admiring her mother's pursuit of romantic love, the daughter denounces the idea that marriage is a political alliance or a commercial transaction for fulfilling one's desires—whether for upward mobility, sexual pleasure, or material comfort.

Whenever Zhong's daughter faces discrimination against "old maids" (*daling nü qingnian*), she thinks of her late mother, the only one who understood and supported her decision to wait for Mr. Right. The mother-daughter bond is established not out of the younger generation's filial piety but through a mutual understanding and sisterly intimacy that places mother and daughter on equal footing. This sisterhood in a matrilineal family is particularly strong because it forges a formidable alliance between two socially marginalized individuals.

UTOPIAN OR DYSTOPIAN SISTERHOOD?

In 1982, Zhang Jie published what is arguably the first Chinese feminist novella, "The Ark." In the succeeding decades, it has been applauded for its criticism of women's "oppression legitimized by natural gender difference."[7] In this work, a more iconoclastic form of sisterhood beyond blood ties becomes the central thread of the narrative connecting the individual stories of three middle-aged women who live together in a two-bedroom apartment in Beijing. However, what accompanies this unconventional sisterhood of divorced women is a profound sense of paradise lost.

When they were young, these three girls attended the same grade school, enjoying a carefree life as an intimate group. Nonetheless, the promise of "eternal friendship" is cavalierly broken once the girls are involved in heterosexual romances. In this sense, girlhood friendship is drastically different from the bond of brotherhood that defines a man's essential subjectivity in a homosocial environment. Sisterhood is regarded instead merely as a temporary stage of development in a woman's life, or, occasionally, as an aberrant substitute for "normal" heterosexual relationships—a detour, as it were, on the road between girlhood and womanhood that is expected to lead directly to the naturalized feminine roles of wife and mother. A coherent and stable concept of *woman*, it seems to suggest, can be established only through her involvement in heterosexual romance and the matrimonial institution. The binary reference frame of the sexes undermines the potentially subversive multiplicity and ambivalence of alternative forms of intimacy and love.

Marginalized in such a heterosexual system, all three divorced women struggle day in and day out to maintain a "normal" life. Cao Jinghua, one of the main characters, is a theoretician who seeks to recover the forgotten meaning, or humanist dimension, of Marxism. Her pursuit reflects the 1980s nationwide intellectual debate about humanism.[8] The portrayal of Jinghua as an intellectual seeking humanist values is indicative of a revisionist effort to recast feminine models in the 1980s: the privileged class and gender subject has shifted from proletarian women to urban intellectuals. A similar trend can also be found in the works of contemporaneous women writers. For instance, Chen Rong's fictional model of the ideal woman shifts from the rural woman who prioritizes the revolutionary cause over family in "Springtime Forever" (Yongyuan shi chuntian; 1979) to urban intellectual females in "At Middle Age."[9]

As the story unfolds, readers discover that Cao was born into an intellectual family. During the years of the Cultural Revolution, her father was persecuted as a "counterrevolutionary authority." Yearning for political protection and financial security, Cao married a forestry worker. In order to save money to support her father and sister, Cao ended an unplanned pregnancy, and her husband then divorced her for "murdering their child." Abandoned rather than reeducated by the working-class hero, Cao returned to work in Beijing but could not find a place to live on her own due to the housing shortage in big cities at the time. This situation forced her to move in with Liang Qian and Liu Quan, her friends and fellow divorcees.

Also an ambitious professional woman, Liang Qian is determined to produce a new film. She invests all her time and energy in the film, cherishing it as if it were her own baby. Her situation is similar to Cao's: her professional aspirations have constantly been thwarted by numerous malicious men including Bai Fushan, her estranged husband whom she intends to divorce. However, Liang's father, a high-ranking bureaucrat, has brought her some privileges, such as the apartment that she and her two women friends occupy.

Liu Quan is the most helpless divorcee among the wretched trio. Liu's father studied in England and was denounced as a "foreign spy." During the Cultural Revolution, Liu raced around to get her father's name cleared. Having performed the duty of a filial daughter, she came home, longing to find shelter in her husband's strong arms. However, "[h]e would come home drunk and foul-tempered, and force her to make love."[10] To escape from her abusive husband, Liu left home and took her school-aged son with her. Though well educated and competent at work, she does not receive a deserved promotion from her supervisor, who has a proletarian background. In addition, his sexual harassment often irritates her. She looks, therefore, to her "sisters" to find a home and a job transfer permit.

As many critics have noted, family disintegration is depicted as the root cause of the problems and hardships that crush these three intellectual women. Without the help of men, they have to support themselves while shouldering the burden of household chores. Cooking, cleaning, making furniture, delivering coal—all these routines become daily drudgery for them. Furthermore, the absence of men in their lives also invites discrimination and unfair treatment. Divorce prevents their work units from providing Cao and Liu with housing, because in principle only married couples are eligible for the state-sponsored program of public housing assignments.

Living together in Liang's apartment, they have to put up with Bai's unannounced visits and voyeuristic peeking even at the most embarrassing moments. At work, the mere fact that she is a divorced woman makes Liu an easy target for sexual harassment. In short, they still live "in a culture that remains predominantly family-centered and looks upon divorcees with suspicion and hostility."[11] The conventional association of divorce with an ineluctable stigma condemns the divorced women to social isolation. Zhang Jie compares this stigma to the mortifying scarlet letter A pinned on Hester Prynne's chest in Nathaniel Hawthorne's *The Scarlet Letter*. Obviously, the message that Zhang is trying to convey is that divorcees are not victimized by divorce itself but by the smothering social norms that inform and regulate personal matters and feelings.

SPEAKING BITTERNESS: THE FEMALE VERSION

Facing such social isolation and discrimination, the three women in "The Ark" are social outcasts who cannot find support anywhere but among themselves. And so, a women's commune evolves within the confinement of the small apartment. Here the women provide one another with the kind of support psychotherapy might offer:

> Often in the evening the three of them would sit beneath the lamp-light, the remnants of the evening meals still scattered over the table, none of them feeling in the mood to clear it up. Two of them would usually listen, while the other explained her latest grievances, or raged about the way in which she had been treated, banging her fists on the arm of the sofa.[12]

Not unlike the middle-aged male intellectuals Li Bo, Wang Laijun, and Nan Yang in Wu Ruozeng's novel *Divorce*, the three professional women also mobilize the mechanism of speaking bitterness to build a network of mutual support and reconfirm their intersubjective solidarity. Repetition and exaggeration are two central devices of the speaking-bitterness mode that help to collect the residue of their scattered everyday experiences and sentimental memories of the past. Analogous to the male intellectuals' divorce narratives analyzed in chapter 2, "The Ark" abounds with condemnations and demeaning descriptions of the opposite sex. Their ex-husbands are depicted as rude, poorly educated, commercial minded, power seeking, and emotionally inept. In the speaking-bitterness narratives woven by these middle-aged women, their menfolk represent the degraded generation of Chinese men produced by the Cultural Revolution.

In addition to their ex-husbands, other male characters appear to be wicked as well. Liu's father still highly values woman's unconditional fidelity to her husband regardless of the modern-style education he received abroad. The orchestra members who work on Liang Qian's soundtrack look down on her because she is an obscure woman filmmaker. Driver Tie in Liu Quan's workplace insults her, and Manager Wei, her supervisor, is good for nothing but making obscene remarks about women. While talking to Liu, Manager Wei puts one leg over the armrest of the sofa, leaving "the buttons of his trousers undone to reveal the kind of colorful underpants usually worn only by women."[13] The "Knife-face," a narrow-minded and cowardly bureaucrat, gives Jinghua a sleeping pill instead of a painkiller to prevent her from engaging in a debate with an important CCP leader over her controversial articles on Marxist humanism.

All these negative images give readers the impression that all the men in this world conspire to establish a menacing patriarchal alliance to oppress the three vulnerable women. Compared to male intellectuals' divorce narratives that connect the enunciation of inner self with universal humanity, the female divorcee's practice of speaking bitterness claims to address gender-specific problems. As the epigraph declares: "You are particularly unfortunate, because you were born a woman. . . . "

Resonating with this melancholy tone, a strong sense of lack, loss, and incompleteness infuses the embittered narratives of the three divorced women. They regard their "masculinization" as the cause of their unfortunate situations. Cao is disgusted with her muscular arms, strengthened by manual labor during the Cultural Revolution. She considers women's loss of "feminine grace and beauty" a shame and the reason for the short supply of "good wives and wise mothers." in contemporary Chinese society. Zhang Jie is not alone in lamenting Chinese women's masculinization. Her contemporaneous women writers such as Zhang Xinxin and Huang Beijia also tend to connect women's marital strife with their "masculinized" mind and body. Even Li Xiaojiang, the founding mother of women's studies as an academic discipline in China, also blames the tumultuous ten years of the Cultural Revolution for a series of gender-related problems: women's masculinization (a similar problem can be found in the former Soviet Union, according to Li); men's feminization (reinforcing Sun Lung-kee's argument in his influential book *The Deep Structure of Chinese Culture*); the increasing number of "old maids;" and the overall lower quality (*suzhi di*) of Chinese women in comparison to their "better half" (men).[14] Their heated discussions about Chinese women's "masculinization" or men's "feminization" reveal an effort to reestablish the unsettled gender order caused by the Cultural Revolution. This effort is often read as an expression of liberal intellectuals' pursuit of individual rights and personal happiness. Ironically, it resonates with the Thatcherite and Reaganite politics of "authoritarian populism" that sought to "marry the gospel of free market liberalism" with a neoconservative political orientation and an endorsement of "Victorian" family values (particularly women's domestic virtues) and moral authority to counter the radical civil rights and feminist movements of the 1970s.[15]

This yearning to restore the "normal" order in the 1980s Anglophone world, surprisingly, finds concrete forms in Zhang Jie's 1982 novella. In addition to its harsh critique of sex role reversal, Zhang's speaking-bitterness narrative also seeks to rewrite the class narratives that were jumbled during the Cultural Revolution. In order to counter the social violence inflicted on the three divorcees, a linguistic violence emanating from the mechanism of speaking bitterness establishes a narrative hierarchy. Well-educated urban professionals such as these three intellectual women are endowed with a sense of moral and intellectual superiority over the proletarian characters in the novella.

Throughout the speaking-bitterness narrative of the urban professional women, characters of working-class background or with poorer educations are deprived of an introspective dimension. Instead, they are represented as flattened characters with no voices of their own. The working-class men are characterized as menacing predators with no psychic interiority. Readers are overwhelmed by the women's excessive complaints and bitterness. Thus, the universal subordination of women has been specified and historicized as the result of the mismatching of different classes during the chaotic years of the Cultural Revolution, which they posit as the root cause of the disharmony and misfortune in their married lives. For example, Liang Qian's estranged husband, Bai Fushan, is the son of a violin maker, a working-class artisan. Realizing that he cannot understand her romantic whims, such as listening to Debussy or watching floating clouds on top of Mount Huangshan, Liang is always wondering if it would have been better if Bai had married a wonton seller instead of her.

The narrative hierarchy not only emphasizes the differences between men and women; it also creates differences among women.

Qian Xiuying, a married woman with a poor education, is depicted as flirtatious and superficial. She likes to pick on Liu Quan for no reason. Mrs. Jia, a working-class woman who serves as the head of the neighborhood committee, often comes to the divorcees' apartment to see if she can sniff out any signs of moral transgression. There is no psychological depth to these stereotypical "villain" characters. It seems that introspective exploration of the inner world is a privilege enjoyed by the educated elites who have accumulated cultural capital and linguistic currency. As a result, intimate sisterhood and intersubjective solidarity can be achieved only among the three women, who share a similar educational background and social status.

Moreover, the frustrations and setbacks that the three intellectual women have been through are so similar that a potentially rich intersubjective narrative is reduced to a monotonous and self-referential repetition of identical bitterness experienced by the same subject position. The sociolinguistic blockage disrupts effective cross-class interactions and sisterly bonding and reinforces "*differences within women.*"[16]

The failure to relate to the diversity of women's social groups and daily lives outside of the ark of the small apartment weakens the grounds for intersubjectivity. Zhang's effort to construct the coherent subject of Woman, as the epigraph to the novella suggests, obscures the historically constituted multiplicity of gendered experiences, an important issue that is often overlooked by feminist critiques of this work.

REVOLUTIONARY STRUCTURE OF FEELING: REFORMATION AND CONTINUITY

Zhang Jie's "Love Must Not Be Forgotten" has been acclaimed as a literary depiction of romantic love "that has nothing to do with Maoist politics."[17] However, a closer analysis of her love stories reveals an intricate dialectic of reformation and continuity of a revolutionary structure of feeling. Zhong Yu, the maternal figure, tells her daughter that unless "she worship[s] a man, she [cannot] love him even for one day."[18] The traditional mind-set that accepts "men as the stronger and women as the weaker" (*nan qiang nü ruo*) is revived as the core value of their romantic relationship. Instead of falling for a man's physical strength or material wealth, Yu worships the man for "his firm political convictions, his narrow escapes from death in the revolution, his active brain, his drive at work, his well-cultivated mind."[19] All these "masculine" features that win her heart are in sync with the ideal image of male revolutionary heroes such as Hong Changqing in *The Red Detachment of Women* (Hongse niangzi jun; dir. Xie Jin; 1961) who turns out to be women's savior and political enlightener. Rather than bidding "farewell to the revolutionary rhetoric," Zhang Jie's fictional structure of feeling indicates a twisted continuity of socialist sublime aesthetics and its gendered power dynamics.[20]

At the same time, this fictional structure of feeling is also conditioned by the party-state's new political-economic project: delegitimizing the Cultural Revolution–style attacks of the CCP bureaucracy. When the Cultural Revolution ended, the post-Mao regime reconciled with political and cultural elites who were not only brought back to the center of political power but also became the heroic protagonists of literary and cultural representations. Compared to heroes in socialist realist literature and cinema, these protagonists were endowed with more humane qualities such as a yearning for romantic love and domestic bliss. The combined forces of a new ideological orientation, power structure, and cultural politics inform the literary narratives about whom to love and how to love.

Along with the construction of the new hero in romantic narratives, a new type of heroine is also taking shape. The narrator's mother is a perfect example. As a "talented woman" (*cainü*), she admires the old CCP cadre's achievements in the public sphere while seeking to reeducate him on romantic love. She takes the role of a loyal emotional creature who brings compassion and warmth while imparting literary knowledge—the token of their love is a collection of Chekov's works!—to the high-ranking cadre who immerses himself in state affairs. As the veteran revolutionary's marriage to his proletarian wife is considered a tragic mismatch, the intellectual woman provides the answer to the question of how to love and puts a human face on the male-dominated CCP bureaucracy. A new alliance, in the name of romantic love, between political elites and cultural elites is thus forged.

Similarly, in the few happy marriages depicted in Zhang's literary oeuvre, the husbands are always accomplished professionals or high-ranking cadres while their equally well-educated wives are not distinguished for their professional performance. In "The Ark," the commendable romance between Zhu Zhenxiang and his wife provides a utopian vision of conjugal paradise that stands out in this pungent piece of speaking bitterness. Zhu is the head of the Bureau of Foreign Affairs who helps with Liu Quan's job transfer. His wife is well-educated and kind-hearted and has a soft voice and cultured manners. She does not interfere with Zhu's work-related business— that belongs in the public sphere. Rather, she maintains a peaceful domestic interior and, as a gentle "virtuous internal aid" (*xian neizhu*), takes good care of Zhu's visitors.

This model of ideal femininity not only is different from the image of the three "masculinized" female protagonists but also bears little resemblance to the portrayal of Qian Xiuying, who tends to use her feminine beauty to manipulate men to her advantage. Interestingly, while Qian's loose behavior is seen as a result of her lack of education, Zhu's wife exemplifies a role model of domestically situated proper femininity as a result of her better education and higher social status. This representational strategy of associating proper femininity with social distinction reminds one of Maoist literary and cinematic works in which loose sexual practices usually serve to indicate the immorality of class enemies.

With great admiration for this new feminine figure, Liu believes that Zhu and his wife are so well suited that their married life must be blessed. The harmony of this enviable marriage is compared to the moon faithfully following of the sun. In this passage, Zhu's wife's roundish face is likened to the shiny moon that gleams so quietly and lovingly over their domestic haven. This type of natural image can be found in numerous gendered metaphors and similes throughout this novella. For instance, the broad chest of Liu's husband is compared to lush grassland where Liu dreams of seeking peace and protection. Cao's working-class husband is associated with the forests where he works: dark, savage, and unbearably bestial. The divorced women's lives are conceived as withered flowers, whose thin and yellow leaves are as feeble and hopeless as the fragile women themselves.

Such a heavily gendered rhetoric tends to naturalize sexual differences and heterosexual relationships as part of the unchangeable essence of universal human nature. In this regard, the divorced women are inadequate and unnatural. No matter how physically strong and professionally competent they are, they will always be lacking something considered fundamental and natural: they have lost their conjugal paradise. Their sisterhood, for all its camaraderie and emotional intimacy, simply cannot compensate for this essential loss. The spiritual affinity of the sisterhood can never fill the void left by the disintegration of heterosexual marriage. They can solve their problems only with the goodwill of powerful men, those high-ranking CCP cadres such as Liang's father, Zhu Zhenxiang, or Lao An, the Party branch secretary in Cao Jinghua's work unit. The idea of strength is assigned to the men, while weakness, both physical and mental, is often used to sum up the gendered "essence" of women.

This self-referential weakness as the root of women's essential gendered identity enhances the sexual power imbalance. In "The Ark," the Cultural Revolution's "ten years of turmoil" are blamed for masculinizing and denaturing women, depriving them of the right to be the weaker sex or be protected "from the ravages of everyday life" by a man's strong arms and broad chest.[21] The reversal of sex roles results in a high divorce rate, the author suggests, and goes on to contend that the only solution for this social problem is well-matched marriages.[22] Beneath the revolutionary guise, the traditional idea of "making a well-matched marriage within the same social class" (*men dang hu dui*) has been resurrected.

Ironically, though often praised as the first piece of feminist writing in post-revolutionary Chinese literature, this novella perpetuates the idea of a heterosexual matrix and the concomitant social discrimination against divorced women. The characterization of divorced women as incomplete and unnatural creatures chimes in with the male intellectuals' misogynist rhetoric labeling "masculinized" women as something "non-man, non-woman, non- human, and non-demon" (*feinan feinü feiren feigui*). The uncanny affinity between 1980s male and female writers highlights their shared class position and value system. The gender division within the same class seems much smaller than the wide gap between women of different educational backgrounds and social classes depicted in "The Ark."

TRIUMPHANT SISTERHOOD?

In contrast to Zhang Jie's speaking-bitterness narrative, Chi Li's novella "Good Morning, Miss" features a triumphant female-female bond among divorced women. Many critics applauded this piece as a feminist fable about the awakening gender consciousness of three Chinese Noras and their collective resistance to patriarchy.[23] Adding a critical reading of the novella to this heated debate centering on "gender consciousness"—a catchphrase in post-revolutionary Chinese feminist writings—can illuminate the ways in which the gendered positions of divorced women are reconstructed through the remapping of feminine biopolitics and the domestic interior.

Chi Li was born in Hubei in 1957. After a brief period of being sent down to the country, she attended college from 1976 to 1979, and then worked as a doctor in Wuhan. Since 1979, she has published numerous stories, novels, and essays. As one of the most prolific women writers in contemporary China, Chi Li has also achieved phenomenal popularity and commercial success with her literary works, many of which have been adapted (sometimes by the author herself) into award-winning films and TV dramas such as *To and Fro* (Lailai wangwang; 1998), *Lipstick* (Kouhong; 2000), and *The Life Show* (Shenghuo xiu; 2002). In 2003, she signed a contract with the Shiji Yingxiong Film Corp. to establish the Chi Li Film and Television Workshop. Due to her consistent focus on the everyday lives of city dwellers in Wuhan, Chi Li is often categorized, together with Fang Fang, He Dun, Liu Heng, Liu Zhenyun and others, as a writer of "new urbanite fiction" (*xin shimin xiaoshuo*), also dubbed "neorealist fiction."[24] From a devotee of pure literature to a successful writer of lucrative best sellers and television scripts, Chi Li's career trajectory mirrors China's transition to a market economy and its impact on literary production and cultural politics.[25]

Like "The Ark," "Good Morning, Miss" features three urban-based women who are either divorced or (self-)exiled from legally recognized marriages. Qi Runwu, the forty-five-year-old female protagonist, is an accomplished researcher at the Institute of Grain Storage of the Ministry of Domestic Trade. Wang Zili, her husband, is a newly rich entrepreneur who plunged into the sea of business in the early 1990s, a historical turning point marked by Deng Xiaoping's inspection trip to South China in 1992. As Qi loses her physical allure in middle age, Wang starts an affair with their *baomu*, a young domestic worker from the country. After Qi discovers his infidelity, Wang fires the *baomu* and brings home Li Kailing, his longtime employee, to work temporarily for them. Despite Li's careful maintenance of feminine manners and womanly virtues, her husband divorces her to marry a younger woman. Li and Qi, the two middle-aged "abandoned women," develop a deep empathy for each other as well as a common hatred toward the unfaithful opposite sex.

Later, at a social occasion, Qi meets Ai Yue, a pretty woman in her twenties, whose sexy body gives Qi the idea of using the time-honored "beauty strategy" to take revenge on her husband. Hence, the three women of different backgrounds and generations work together to retaliate against Wang, the embodiment of all "low-quality" newly rich Chinese men. This practice of women using feminine beauty as bait for accomplishing a vengeful agenda against man rewrites the gender politics of the "beauty strategy" in such male-oriented classics as *Romance of the Three Kingdoms* (Sanguo yanyi). The women's norm-bending conspiracy is celebrated as the triumph of Chinese women's awakened gender consciousness, as suggested by a line toward the end of the story: "In a word, the awakening of Chinese women's gender consciousness is a prevalent trend nowadays. Chinese men should behave themselves."[26]

However, a radical shift in the narrative tone and style merits scrutiny. The heavy-handed happy ending narrated as a tabloid story in the style of Ming "vernacular fiction" (*huaben*) highlights the unrealistic quality of the triumphant ending and directs readers' attention back to Chi's trademark realism in depicting "feminine details" throughout the novella.[27] It has been suggested that Chi Li's use of feminine details renounces the master narratives (enlightenment or revolution) of history with its "engagement with an intractable daily reality."[28] However, it is worth noting that rather than being pure, uncontaminated, unmediated, or apolitical, daily reality, with all its feminine details, is always tinged with the ideological forces of the bourgeois cultural imaginary. A critical inspection of the fictional feminine details as written by Chi will reveal the ways in which the imagination of the divorced women's sisterhood engages and negotiates with a discursive interplay of state-sanctioned eugenics, modern medical science, and emerging middle-class domesticity.

FROM IRON GIRL TO STRONG WOMAN

The formation of a redemptive sisterhood is pivotal to the radical transformation of the female protagonist's gender identity and biopolitics from a bodiless iron girl to a sentimental mother with a naturalized body. Having come of age during the Mao era, Qi, the middle-aged female intellectual, behaves like a typical socialist iron girl in post-socialist China. The term "iron girl" was first used during the Cultural Revolution to refer to a group of young women peasants who formed an iron-girl team under the leadership of Guo Fenglian in Dazhai village, Shanxi. Following the Dazhai model, iron-girl teams were established nationwide and "positively accepted at the grassroots level."[29] As Jin Yihong has observed:

> Women in single-sex groups demonstrated high levels of work performance because working together made it possible for them to acquire a gender-based identity rooted in increasing confidence in their own strength.[30]

Their public image of actively participating in collective labor and political campaigns exemplified the state-promoted gender equality model that put great value on social production and political engagement.

In post-revolutionary China, this concept has been associated with the de-glorified image of "over-liberated" and "masculinized" Chinese women who are strong and competent in the public sphere—a traditionally masculine domain. The divorcees in "The Ark" are good examples of this "problematic" group. Judging from the new femininity standards of sexual modernity, these iron girls have lost their feminine charm and often encounter problems in their love and marital lives. In the mid-1980s, the "personal problems" of these women were identified as a grave "social problem" by Hu Yaobang, the CCP general secretary at that time.[31]

After the "socialist" market economy took off, the term "strong woman" (*nü qiangren*) replaced "iron girl" as the essential signifier of women who are active in the public sphere, which is still considered a male-dominant domain. Compared to "iron girl," the concept of "strong woman" puts more emphasis on individual career success than on socialist collective spirit and political commitment. However, in post-revolutionary misogynist rhetoric, the idea of "strong woman" is often regarded as a continuation of the concept of "iron girl," as the disastrous outcome of women's liberation. As a result, "women are most afraid of being a strong woman," because it implies a loss of femininity.[32]

Such a cultural bias against iron girls and strong women prevails in post-revolutionary Chinese society. Many prominent Chinese writers, male and female, exhibit strong feelings against career women. For instance, in Chi Li's story "Brocade Beach" (Jinxiu shatan), Meizi, a successful career woman who refuses to play the role of "good wife and wise mother," is described as a "woman like iron and steel" (*rugang shitie de nüren*).[33] As a result, her disappointed husband has an extramarital affair. In Liang Xiaosheng's work *Women's Feelings* (Nüren xinqing), Xiao Jing, a typical modern white-collar woman, fails to embody ideal femininity, while Shun Sao, a woman from the countryside, embodies the ultimate healing power of "pure femininity and maternity" that transcends political vicissitudes and urban materialism.[34] The story "Fortune" (Yun) by Liu Liu, a popular woman writer, shows a similar bias against strong women. The nameless female protagonist is a highly accomplished, wealthy businesswoman; however, her professional achievements are more like a mysterious curse than a blessing and bring a series of misfortunes to her immediate family, including her husband, son, and mother-in-law.

In the novella "Good Morning, Miss," the character Qi is a perfect mix of socialist iron girl and post-socialist strong woman. She is an extraordinary professional woman, whose enormous contribution to grain storage research wins her the political honor of having her picture taken with the vice premier of China. Her professional aspirations are always her first priority, and she spends little on her appearance, her maternal duties, or her household chores. At one point in the narrative, she is so distressed by the discovery of her son's blood disorder that she bursts into tears from time to time when she is at work. To punish herself for these moments of weakness, she plasters a "big-character poster" of self-denunciation on the wall of the workplace cafeteria. Publicizing her violation of the work ethics brings her a great sense of shame and guilt. Through the therapy of this Cultural Revolution–style self-condemnation, Qi is able to brush aside her personal concerns and regain her working vigor. She not only performs relentless self-criticism but also uses socialist moral standard to criticize her colleagues and husband, lamenting their corruption and decadent bourgeois lifestyle. However, her husband's extramarital affair completely shatters her sense of self-fulfillment and moral superiority. For the first time, she realizes that her worldview and lifestyle are totally out of sync with the new urban culture. This huge shock creates a sense of urgency about reeducating herself about the "truth" of her position in such a rapidly changing world.

IRON GIRL REEDUCATED

In the process of forging a sisterly bond, Qi experiences two critical moments of epiphany that open her eyes to a new gender culture in post-revolutionary China. In this sense, "Good Morning, Miss" can be read as Qi's bildungsroman, a narrative of the socialist iron girl reeducated by her sisters who are more adapted to a global consumer culture. The first lesson in Qi's reeducation is taught by her substitute *baomu*, Li Kailing. Chi Li devotes many pages to meticulous descriptions of Li Kailing's womanly appearance and virtues from the moment she appears in the story: her graceful ballerina-style gait, her body-fitting Chinese-style coat and the dazzling diamond pin perched on its mandarin collar, and the way she carefully brushes her thick and shiny hair into a big chignon to expose her long, elegant neck.

Arriving at Qi's home, Li Kailing further displays her feminine merits by taking good care of Qi and her son. Being such a perfect woman embodying traditional feminine etiquette, this virtuous classical beauty disapproves of Qi's management of her personal appearance and domestic life. Through Li's critical eyes, readers get a less-than-flattering portrait of the middle-aged intellectual woman: wearing a sloppy, threadbare sweater over her wrinkled pajamas, Qi walks aimlessly through her cluttered two-bedroom apartment. The sweater makes her neck itch, so Qi scratches herself hard from time to time, making unbearably loud noises.

By tidying up Qi's messy apartment, Li restores the domestic order. She asks herself: "Why does this type of unwomanly woman exist in this world?"[35] Despite, or because of, her master's degree and successful career, Qi is seen as a complete failure as a woman. Her disorderly domestic interior and unkempt physical appearance expose her lack of a "feminine" psychic interior. This view associating personal hygiene with femininity reflects a Cartesian dualism of mind and body. Since the male is considered to be the more intelligent sex, or the mind of the human being, great scientists are often applauded for neglecting their bodily needs or domestic duties. It is said that Sir Isaac Newton was so occupied by his scientific research that he forgot to eat, "and William Hamilton left half empty plates accumulating for days as he worked."[36]

While men's failure to manage their everyday lives is regarded as evidence of their passion for the great cause of science, women like Qi are criticized for prioritizing career success. Li's harsh opinion of this anachronistic iron girl implies that a woman who uses her brain too much will fail in her "natural" wifely and reproductive duties and turn the men around her into brainless, degenerate, and ailing creatures.

In other words, Qi's professional knowledge guarantees her career advancement but cannot ensure her conjugal bliss in a domestic order reestablished by a new set of middle-class rules and standards. Representing the bodiless mind, she loses her essential identity as a woman and threatens male authority with excessive brainwork. Wang's betrayal of Qi is presented as legitimate punishment for her transgression of the boundaries of gender norms. His infatuation with the young *baomu*'s voluptuous body embitters Qi. Compared to Zhang Jie's sympathetic characterization of female intellectuals, Chi Li's caustic depiction establishes Qi as a subject not worthy of compassion or sympathy but in need of (self-)reform.

Unlike Zhang Jie, who demonstrates an awareness of class division based mainly on differences in people's educational background and social status, Chi Li depicts female characters who display their mastery of certain class markers through their degree of familiarity with an emerging consumer culture and its accompanying gender norms. Generational differences play a vital role here in determining the three women's gender identities, which are gauged by a new set of middle-class values and cultural standards. Belonging to an older generation than Qi, Li seems an embodiment of traditional femininity uncontaminated by the Maoist "masculinization" of Chinese women. Her well-maintained feminine etiquette and classical beauty reminds one of the Shanghai ladies of the 1930s reincarnated in a wave of nostalgia for the essential gendered signifier of cosmopolitan modernity. In contrast, Qi, though from Shanghai, fails to embody the gendered charm of urban civilization. This can be read as a severe critique of the alleged desexualization of the female body during the Mao era and the socialist transformation of Shanghai, a cultural icon of the feminized metropolis.

GENDERED "HYGIENIC MODERNITY"

In order to redeem herself from her transgressions and desexualization, Qi starts learning from Li how to re-feminize and re-naturalize her body. First of all, Li buys a packet of sanitary pads and instructs Qi to use these in place of the old-fashioned, homemade "menstruation belt" (*yuejing dai*) that Qi received from her mother a decade ago. This mass-produced and widely advertised sexual hygiene commodity gives Qi a fresh intimate experience with her own reproductive organs, which makes her feel like a "real" woman.[37] No longer a masculinized iron girl, the female intellectual is re-sexualized, as the essence of her being moves downward from mind to body, from the brain to the flesh and blood of her reproductive organs. As a result, commodified markers of "hygienic modernity" replace public work and intelligent activities in defining her core identity.[38] Instead of abject body parts associated with shame and inconvenience, the woman's reproductive organs are transformed into an invisible but essential part of her natural body, with all the curious pleasures enhanced by modern technology and media advertisements.

Quite similarly, the female protagonist Li Xiaolan in the above-mentioned story "Sunrise" is also initiated into "natural" womanhood through her exposure to an anatomical account of her reproductive organs during her first pregnancy check-up. Modern medical science miraculously awakens her maternal sentiments, presumably hidden deep down in the core of her reproductive anatomy. Surprising everyone, she abandons her original plan to abort her baby and launches instead a radical self-reform involving the improvement of her physical and mental qualities so as to be a better mother.[39] In a sense, the affiliation of modern scientific communities, institutions, and disciplines contributes to guaranteeing the stability and continuity of biological filiation reproduction.

The reeducation of Li in "Sunrise" and Qi in "Good Morning, Miss" through the use of modern medical science and feminine hygiene products, harks back to the "vernacular sociology" of 1920s Shanghai. "Vernacular sociology" refers to the means of self-expression created by the urban-based educated elites. Vernacular sociologists created a new image of the "natural woman" that appeared in transnational corporate advertisements of women's commodities such as Kotex, Modess, and Comfort pads.[40] The advertising campaign of the "scientifically produced" pads was reinforced by a large number of articles that linked women's personal hygiene to eugenics. As a result, "[m]enstruation possessed the ability to centrally define the social evolutionary capacity of every *natural* woman."[41]

As post-revolutionary China undergoes an all-encompassing transformation of class structure, gender politics, and domestic culture, socialist iron girls such as Qi must face the challenge of performing the new gendered role of "natural woman." Such a biologization of woman can be fulfilled, ironically, only through the deployment of industrial commodity aesthetics. Beginning with her first lesson with Li Kailing, Qi works hard to accomplish an extreme makeover. In addition to modern-style sanitary pads, she purchases expensive lingerie and cosmetic products to re-feminize her face and body. She also learns from Li how to choose high-quality dairy products to fulfill the middle-aged woman's need for supplementary calcium. Most interestingly, the image of Margaret Thatcher shows up in this story as it did in "The Ark"; here, Thatcher serves as a role model who carefully manages her physical appearance and consequently preserves her feminine essence.

Ironically, Li's own failed marriage does not make her or Qi question either her credibility as a qualified mentor or the prevailing gender norms. Rather, the two grudge-ridden "abandoned women" come to the consensus that Chinese men are totally unworthy and loathsome creatures. Hence, they strive to comply with the male-dominant rules of heterosexual romance while manipulating the romantic game toward their own ends.

CONCUBINE, COURTESAN, AND THE THIRD PARTY

At this critical moment, Qi experiences her second epiphany at an extravagant banquet hosted by Mr. Liu, a Hong Kong businessman. Here, Qi meets Ai Yue, Mr. Liu's soi-disant concubine. In spite of her ambiguous social status and transgressive sexual practices, Ai considers herself superior to Qi, as the latter finds herself constantly lost in urban crowds and the commodified spaces of luxury hotels and high-end restaurants. Obviously more well versed in the sweeping consumer culture, Ai confidently serves as a successful hostess at the classy banquet as well as a social behavioral mentor to Qi, teaching her how to order dishes, interact with other guests, deal with snobbish waitresses, and so on.

At one point, they find themselves alone in the restaurant's restroom. Then Ai confides to Qi that she sells her body as a pricey commodity without sullying the purity of her soul. Ai's honest comments about exchanging her youthful body, often compared to that of a young mare, for material gain provide Qi with an entirely fresh insight into the general laws of commodity exchange and monetary operations in an increasingly commercialized Chinese society. Later, commenting on Qi's marital crisis, Ai points to the changing meaning of marriage as justification for their retaliation against Wang: "A marriage certificate is a social contract. He must pay for your loss if he breaks this contract."[42] This cool-headed comment shows Ai's possession of what the socialist iron girl lacks: market rationale.

However, Ai never discusses her own sexual desires when confessing her concubine experience. Her display of excessive femininity is only used as "a mask . . . to hide the possession of masculinity," or her rich knowledge of the market economy.[43] This deliberate self-containment of the danger of transgressive sexuality makes Ai a bodiless chaste woman, whose "true self" is not tainted by her occupation. Furthermore, Ai's "business is business" attitude exemplifies the modern spatial segregation of living and labor as well as the psychological dichotomy between the inner and the outer worlds. Her professionalism in managing her own sexuality as an enterprise makes her a superb entrepreneur in the business of self-ownership. For these reasons, Qi feels confident in her decision to hire Ai as a third party in the plot to frame her unfaithful husband.

Interestingly, the characterization of a third party in this novella deviates dramatically from predominant public opinion. There are two third parties in "Good Morning, Miss": the young *baomu* who has an affair with Qi's husband and Ai, who has played multiple roles in Qi's reeducation. Rather than accusing the young *baomu* of breaking up the marriage, Qi blames her husband for his infidelity. According to Qi, her husband is just one of the degraded Chinese men who get rich overnight but lack the masculine essence of a real man. As Qi bickers with Wang on the street, she relentlessly exposes all of his physical deficiencies in public: "You armpits smell, even after two surgeries. Your rotten teeth also smell so badly that you chew gum nonstop. Your foreskin is way too long and filthy. So disgusting!"[44] What's even worse, Wang never told Qi about his family's genetic blood disorder, which their son has inherited.

According to Qi, his low-quality body not only has reproduced its flawed genes in their son but also indicates a common sickness afflicting many middle-aged Chinese men. When she visits the Madonna nightclub that Wang frequents, Qi sees all the men there as replications of Wang, the sick man of post-socialist China: They drink and smoke heavily. They spit anywhere. With their unrestrained indulgence in carnal pleasures, their bodies are degenerate and rotten. The low quality of their bodies is further exacerbated by their continuous consumption of the low-quality commodities and services provided by the nightclub, despite its glamorous facade and English name.[45] In Qi's eyes, these Chinese men are simply flawed imitators of the real masculine modernity that originated in Euro-America.

In order to punish her husband, the fictional emblem of the underdeveloped Chinese male gender, Qi hires Ai as a feigned third party. These avenging angels plot to deprive Wang of all his money and power and then "send him back to the 1970s hometown" or the pre-reform past of poverty and underdevelopment.[46] By alluding to the evolution of the male sex, the female intellectual naturalizes the progression from socialism to capitalism. This Darwinian narrative, penned by a woman writer, almost reproduces the earlier male-dominant intellectual discourse that connected developmentalist thinking and biological evolution at the turn of the twentieth century. When China was jostled into a head-to-head clash with the world capitalist system, the Chinese body, often gendered as male, was also reevaluated as occupying an inferior and sometimes even infantile position in a developmentalist teleology determined by a "racialized hierarchy of the modern interstate system."[47]

The depiction of male devolution in "Good Morning, Miss" justifies the act of female revenge. Rather than being a victimizer as in the conventional view of a third party, Ai serves as an ally, empowering the abandoned wife to turn the tables and strike out in the name of defending her rights and eliminating the denegerate male body. This unusual characterization of Ai alludes to several archetypes in the Chinese literary tradition: the lustful femme fatale (e.g., Pan Jinlian in *Plum in the Golden Vase*), the famous courtesan (e.g., Li Xiangjun in *The Peach Blossom Fan*), and the woman warrior (e.g., Shisan Mei in *The Tale of Heroic Sons and Daughters*). As a sexy young woman, Ai is good at playing the game of seduction and conquest with rich men. Like other famous courtesans accounted for in the "unofficial history" (*yeshi*), she makes a living by entertaining male clients with the beauty of her voluptuous body and her quick wit. What distinguishes Ai from legendary courtesans such as Li Xiangjun is her unabashed pursuit of consumer privileges and material wealth rather than "sublime passion" or national loyalty.[48]

Embracing a hedonistic lifestyle, she openly declares her steadfast belief in the power of money. In this sense, she is more aligned with some of the images of Shanghai courtesans from the demimonde novels of the late nineteenth century that draw a picture of an emerging commercial culture and urban modernity. At the same time, however, she retains her moral integrity and emotional authenticity when it comes to women's problems. Outraged by the injustice that Wang has done to Qi, Ai determines to help her carry out her plan against him. Playing the roles of both femme fatale and woman warrior, she seduces Wang and then steals his assets before faxing evidence of his past economic crimes to the authorities.

Though clearly an outgrowth of various premodern Chinese literary traditions, this distinctive character of the modern libertine
woman demonstrates signs of gender self-creation. Ai is particularly familiar with the new set of gender norms of post-revolutionary
China and voluntarily conforms to them in order to move beyond the
limits that the patriarchal power structure has set for women. She
manipulates men's desires and exploits their wealth toward her own
ends. Taking advantage of the rules of value exchange in the male-
dominated market economy, she obtains power and agency through
her active participation in the commercial transaction instead of the
"virtuous transaction," or a woman's self-sacrifice made in exchange
for social respectability in a patriarchal system.[49] As an alternative to
passively supplying an object for the satisfaction of the male gaze and
for commodification, she refuses to play the role of good prostitute.
Instead, Ai's performance and manipulation of a certain gender identity pertain to the idea of performativity. As Judith Butler puts it, gender is "*a corporeal style*, an 'act,' as it were, which is both intentional
and performative, where '*performative*' suggests a dramatic and contingent construction of meaning."[50]

Rather than associating a fixed essential meaning with her corporeal performance of "femininity," Ai reenacts and appropriates the
gender roles that have been socially recognized and legally sanctioned.
The unique image of Ai suggests new possibilities of performative
womanhood activated by new forces of market individualism, gender
ideology, and cultural politics. Performative womanhood here refers
to the performance of a fluid and unstable gender identity (a courtesan, a concubine, a third party, a sworn sister, or a woman warrior)
that cannot be fixed in a singular expression of essential meaning or
ultimate value based on a sexual core. Rather, through the repetition, appropriation, and reenactment of gender consciousness, it constantly transgresses the boundaries of gender norms and cultural politics, plays fluid roles within the parameters of different sociopolitical
spaces, and adjusts itself to various female traditions and strategies in
dealing with specific gender-related problems and crises.

SENTIMENTAL MOTHERHOOD

The contingent nature and subversive potential of performative
womanhood is seriously undermined by the climactic catharsis of
"Good Morning, Miss." At Qi's place, Ai meets Wang Zhuang, Qi's

fifteen-year-old son, who has suffered from a blood disorder since birth. Holding the boy to her bosom, Ai bursts into tears, crying sorrowfully: "I want my Beibi! I want my Beibi!" It turns out that Beibi (from the English word "baby") is her three-year-old illegitimate son. This modern femme fatale had sent the child to a remote rural area to hide the dark secrets of the past. Deeply touched by Ai's overflowing tears, Li and Qi come to her side. The three women hold one another and have a good cathartic cry.

This unexpected revelation exposes the hidden brutality of Ai's life as a concubine—a role that in mainstream media is often associated with affluence and sexual abandon. The immediate identification of Ai as a suffering mother does not lead to any discussion of uneven capital accumulation and distribution along gender, class, and regional lines. Rather, it simply exempts her from moral condemnation and makes her a sublime figure with the ability to transcend "dirty" sex-money transactions. Ai's deliberate overstepping of the bounds of domesticity is also redeemed by her maternal instinct, which distinguishes her as a woman from a man who is viewed largely as an autonomous agent unabashedly pursuing sexual pleasures within and outside of a domestic sphere.

Ai's exhibition of maternal love not only catapults her back into the spheres of acceptable social norms and gender ideology but also builds up strong intersubjective connections between the three women, who are all marginalized by the institution of marriage. Motherhood brings them together across class and generation lines and redefines their seemingly prediscursive and prelinguistic corporeal experiences. As Chi Li puts it, they share a secret code beyond any human language, which is inscribed on women's reproductive bodies that exude blood, sweat, milk, and tears. This naturalized bond between *mothers* rather than sisters enables "each of them get to know the inner self" that is "as truthful as the origin of life."[51] Thus, both the iron girl and the femme fatale are properly domesticated and humanized with authentic interiority.

In contrast to the commercial transactions made with men, the intersubjective connections within the women's community are built through sentimental motherhood. Maternal goodness, with its invincible affective power, transcends class divisions, generational differences, and hierarchical gender positions redefined by an emerging consumer culture. The purity of the soul that Ai strives to preserve now manifests itself through the abundant tears that externalize the

powerful instinct of Mother Nature. The fatal flaw of Qi's unwoman-
liness, brought about through her fierce competition with men, is also
redeemed. All the effusive tears are channeled to remap "real" and
"natural" bodies for these "bodiless" women. The exclusive emphasis on feminine fluids brings readers' attention to Qi's given name,
Runwu, which literally means "nourishing or moistening things."
Often used to describe life-nurturing rain and water, the name Runwu
suggests the mystified link between women's bodily fluids and the
organic fluids and wetness of Mother Nature.[52] In an earlier passage,
Li's instructive words about women's diligent maintenance of feminine virtues are also compared to falling raindrops that nurture Qi's
new gender consciousness and worldview.[53]

This reclaimed feminine body of "blood and tears" establishes the
divorced women's shared identity as sentimental mothers and defines
the internalized domestic space as a women's affective sphere separate
from the masculinized outside marked by the heartless market economy. In the place of homosocial sisterhood beyond the heterosexual
matrix, the reproductive body and maternal sentimentality define the
core of the female identity situated in the middle-class domestic interior. This feminized domestic interior anchors women's sexualized
bodies and maternal sentiments. While this reproductive sexuality is
morally acceptable and "economically useful" (in terms of reproducing both labor capacity and social relations), other forms of sexual
behavior aimed at pure "fruitless pleasures" are rendered as men's
pursuit of "dirty" desires in "dangerous" places beyond the domestic
sphere.[54] Set in contrast to the urban-based male intellectuals who are
struggling with their crisis of interiority as discussed in the previous
chapter, women secure their interior world and moral superiority by
celebrating an outburst of their feminine fluids.

The emphasis on bodily fluids is found again in Chi Li's 2007
bestseller, *Therefore* (Suoyi), which features Ye Zi, a twice-divorced
woman who reinvents her gender identity not as a wife but as a
mother by dedicating all her financial resources to nurturing her only
son. She makes use of "scientific data" to confirm the "natural" superiority of maternal love over paternal love. According to Ye Zi, science has shown that every single male ejaculation releases 200 million
"little worms" (*xiao chongchong*; referring to sperm), while woman
can release only a single egg at a time. She interprets this to show that
maternal love is more focused and single-minded while paternal love
is dispersed and negligible.[55] The scientific data of bodily fluids play

an important role again in the naturalization of maternal sentiments and gendered division of labor. Moreover, an allusion to the economic principle that rarity enhances value attaches different market values to the movement and worth of gender-specific bodily fluids.

One of Chi Li's earliest works, "Look at My Eyes" (Kanzhe wo de yanjing; 1982), strikes a sharp contrast with her turn to "sentimental motherhood" after the 1990s. This short story highlights a woman worker's dilemma in balancing her work demands and her maternal duties and questions the gendered division of labor. However, in her later writings—and in works by many other women writers of the same period—these issues are made invisible. Rather, the gendered division of labor is often naturalized through a detailed account of the anatomical, biological, and, consequently, psychological, quintessential differences between the two sexes.

At the heart of these "body narratives" lies a fundamental ideology of sexual difference that prescribes the ways in which a body of signs is encoded and deciphered in an institutionalized system that regulates women's bodies and reproduction. Rather than resisting the official ideology, this eulogizing and naturalizing of women's maternal role plays back into the hands of Chinese mainstream eugenic discourse, which has been celebrated by educated elites since the May Fourth movement and was sanctioned by state policies. Scholars have noted that reform-era Chinese government has further sublimated women's reproductive function: "[t]he role of women in promoting spiritual civilization is enhanced by the primary tasks they take on in childcare and family education.[56]

Therefore, the sisterly intersubjectivity in the aforementioned divorce narratives fails to transcend the male/female dichotomy endorsed by the heterosexual matrix. In contrast to the male brotherhood that aims to overcome "the finality and contingency of biological reproduction," the "secret code" of woman's maternal instinct and reproductive duty provides an imagined utopia for sisterly intersubjectivity.[57] This affirmation of women's reproduction and physicality can be read as a critical effort to override the cultural stigma related to women's genitals. It is an invitation for women to reimagine their own bodies in an assertive way and thus create a reverse discourse that bestows positive cultural connotations on expressions of women's corporeality and sexuality.

Nevertheless, we should also be wary of the essentialist tendency in the naturalization of the maternal body and bear in mind Judith

Butler's criticism of Julia Kristeva's assumption of a prediscursive maternal body. Butler contends that the maternal body "would be understood, rather, as an effect or consequence of a system of sexuality in which the female body is required to assume maternity as the essence of its self and the law of its desire."[58] In this critical light, we can see that the claim on women's enhanced gender consciousness in contemporary Chinese women's literature has been closely associated with woman's corporeal functions and maternal roles. The exclusive emphasis on a woman's motherhood reduces the heterogeneity of female subjectivity to a singular mode of expression, which reproduces the binary structures of man/mind versus woman/body and consequently situates women back in the enclosed and naturalized domestic space.

This trend of casting sentimental motherhood is particularly striking if we consider the role of children in male writers' divorce narratives. In comparison, children in Su Tong's works "A Divorce Handbook" and "A Married Man" are never touted as the only anchor for male identity. Rather, embodying the meaningless continuity of prosaic everyday life, their very existence constantly reminds their fathers of the heavy burden of maintaining a middle-class lifestyle in an increasingly competitive modern society.

FEMALE EDUCATION, MALE SPORT

Quite similar to the ending of "The Ark," disillusioned divorced women put their hopes for the emergence of real men in the male offspring of the next generation. After Ai gets Wang's assets, she goes abroad and runs a clothing company in which both Qi and Li hold a sizable amount of stock. Enjoying a wealthy middle-class life together, Qi and Li purchase a spacious apartment and bring Beibi to live with them. Sending Beibi to play soccer, *the* symbol of global masculinity in Chinese mainstream media (think football in the United States), the three maternal figures hold the hope that he will become China's Ronaldo Luiz Nazario de Lima, the Brazilian soccer star, and lead the Chinese soccer team to the World Cup. They lament that Chinese soccer players are so disappointing that Chinese women can find not one man among them to love. Therefore, they decide to cultivate a new generation of good men if they can find none in China.[59]

Chi Li also devotes a lengthy discussion to this sport in many of her writings. For example, in her essay "Real Life" (Zhenshi de rizi), the woman writer confesses to readers her obsession with televised soccer games, particularly those with European superstars. Eroticizing her passion for soccer, she comes to the conclusion: "How can a woman dislike watching men play soccer? The best male qualities can be found in soccer games!"[60] In another essay, "Liaotian" (Chitchat), she traces the origin of soccer to ancient China and mourns China's failure to keep up with the modern development of the sport due to Chinese male soccer players' lack of "internationally universal beauty," that is, the spectacular display of speed, power, and physical strength.[61]

Interestingly, Chi never mentions Chinese women soccer players who have performed much better than their male counterparts in international games. This uneven treatment of male and female sports reveals a gendered desire for a better man. Compared to Zhang Jie's heroes, who are still more or less invested in sublime revolutionary aesthetics, Chi Li's imagination of a better man is rooted in the popular image of the ideal sportsman whose male stamina and athletic body are put in the spotlight of a global media culture. In this sense, what the triumphant sisterhood in "Good Morning, Miss" desires is identical to the desire of the cynical divorced women in "The Ark": a real man with better qualities who can restore the ideal heterosexual relationship in relation to which a woman can securely define her female identity as a wife and a mother.

Rather than deconstructing the "myth of the mother,"[62] Chi Li construes a new utopia of sentimental motherhood and domestic interiority mediated by market individualism, global biopolitics, and mother-son romance. In place of a revolution of the heart, a revolution of the womb, or an innovative way of reimagining women's reproductive organs through the new lenses of modern medical science and literary sentimentalism, she romanticizes and sublimates the maternal body. This romanticized motherhood stands in sharp contrast to the de-romanticization and de-sublimation of political idealism and heterosexual love in Chi Li's writings. However, one essential link between the utopian maternal interior and the dystopian male world is money, which "is at once excluded and ubiquitous, absent and present."[63] In other words, the seemingly self-sufficient maternal utopia will fall apart without, ironically, the wealth that Ai steals from the spurned "low-quality" man.

Eschewing this inconvenient link with the "dirty" marketplace, Chi Li highlights the spirituality of the maternal utopia by emphasizing the importance of investing in proper quality education. It is not only about Beibi training on a boys' soccer team for a stronger male body but also touches on the central piece of women's liberation: female education. Rather than compete against men using her higher education and intelligence, the middle-aged intellectual Qi puts her knowledge to use to ensure a better and more gender-appropriate physical education for the next generation. Female education has often been an important issue at critical moments in the history of modern China.[64] As Harriet T. Zurndorfer has noted:

> Education for girls and women formed part of a general reformist view that women should contribute to the productive power of the Chinese state by becoming "erudite" mothers who in turn would produce better-informed sons and thereby a stronger body-politic.[65]

More than simply fulfilling the need to "strengthen the Chinese race and defend the nation" (*qiangzhong baoguo*), a better-educated mother in a post-revolutionary age is expected to nurture a better man whose ideal image is no longer invested in a nation-building intellectual discourse or a socialist revolutionary cause. Rather, through gender-appropriate educational affiliations, the mission of the new mother is to reproduce the filiation of the post-socialist new man—a cosmopolitan individual living up to the global standard of biopolitical masculinity.

CONCLUSION

The sisterhood of divorced women in Zhang Jie's and Chi Li's literary works embodies women's collective efforts to challenge prevailing gender norms and social ethics. It frees women's imagination of a utopian homosocial space in which they can establish intersubjective solidarity against patriarchal hegemony. However, this type of fantasy is influenced by the dominant imagery of contemporary women's literature on romantic love and gender sexuality.

This women's commune provides an ambivalent utopian vision of a romanticized sisterhood, yet these economically independent and professionally capable female intellectuals are represented as women who are still lacking an essential without the presence of newer and better men. In 1932–33, Ding Ling published her well-known novel *Mother* (Muqin), which depicts "a reinvented, politically defined, female identity" in place of the universal female identity defined on the anatomical basis of "sexual differentiation and sexual categories."[66] Compared to such a "political sisterhood," the female-female bond between divorced women in post-revolutionary feminist writings, ironically, reaffirms well-established gender norms and the cultural imagination of the proper domestic scenario.

Seeking to undo "the Party's politicization of personal space," Chinese women scholars and writers embark on an alternative path to individual fulfillment that is, ironically, marked by an unabashed enchantment with "the privacy and sanctity of feminine domesticity."[67] This trend of feminizing the domestic even in feminist writers' works can be better understood if we consider that the development of Chinese liberal feminism as an indispensable part of the marketization of contemporary Chinese society in general and the commercialization of women's writing in particular. Fighting against the hegemony of socialist collectivism, the post-revolutionary Chinese intelligentsia has engaged in heated debates about individual subjectivity, which complements the reform ideology of promoting personal responsibility and freeing individuals for the market. As a part of the intellectual discourse about market individualism, post-revolutionary Chinese liberal feminism criticizes the allegedly gender-erasing and desexualizing state feminism.

The overemphasis on individual gendered identity based on anatomical differences and biological traits associate women's nature with managing interpersonal relationships. This lends a ready excuse to the naturalization of a gendered division of labor and consequently acts as a prelude to a postfeminist discourse that seeks to coax women back to the domestic interior to relearn wifely "quality" (suzhi).

CHAPTER FOUR

What Quality Do Chinese Wives Lack?

Performing Middle-Classness in Chinese-Style Divorce

Wang Hailing's megahit television serial *Chinese-Style Divorce* (Zhongguo shi lihun), of 2004, focuses on urging women to cultivate feminine qualities demanded for middle-class domestic bliss.[1] In contrast to Chi Li's works in which money is an "absent presence," in *Chinese-Style Divorce* it is omnipresent and omnipotent, "becoming the only tangible value by which an individual's worth is measured."[2] In comparison to women writers' divorce narratives that still emphasize relationships between woman and woman, as well as mother and child, *Chinese-Style Divorce* highlights the reconfiguring relationship between woman and market, that is, how a middle-aged woman should readjust her gender role and resituate the family in an expanding market economy as China turns to authoritarian neoliberalism.[3]

Going with a global trend, China has become increasingly media-saturated since the 1990s. More and more prominent writers, particularly women writers, are involved in scripting television melodramas about family, marriage, and divorce. Among a recent deluge of narratives about divorce, the most popular has been the best-selling novel *Chinese-Style Divorce* by Wang Hailing, who has been called "the best writer on marriage."[4] Combining the clichéd victim narrative and the neoliberal rhetoric of self-development, the television serial adapted from the best seller was also phenomenally popular. This show has a structure akin to those of many other recent family melodramas: the wife is confronted with a midlife crisis and tries desperately to save her marriage when her husband joins the rising group of nouveaux riches in contemporary China and becomes alienated from her. This scenario is often characterized as a typical case of Chinese middle-class divorce, a result of the rampant marital crisis in contemporary China. Going through a series of pedagogical lessons in her cultivation of feminine qualities, the female lead learns from both younger-generation cosmopolitan women and her mother, a traditional "good wife and wise mother" figure.

This formulaic serial is distinguished from similar divorce narratives, such as "Good Morning, Miss," by its constant emphasis on the female protagonist's lack of quality, capacity (*nengli*), and self (*ziwo*), which is deemed to be the root cause of her marital failure. This explicit self-development rhetoric resonates with the sweeping popularity of various how-to marriage guidebooks such as *Wife's Art of War* (Qizi bingfa), *How to Make a Man to Love You for a Lifetime* (Ruhe rang nanren ai ni yisheng), and the Chinese translation of *Divorce Is Not the Answer: A Change of Heart Will Save Your Marriage* (Lihun wuji yushi: Ruhe tiaozheng yu wanjiu hunyin). This type of self-help manual, advice literature, and television drama, as well as mushrooming "perfect women" clubs, indicate a new trend of industrialization and marketization of gendered self-development and middle-class identity.

The enthusiastic reception of all these self-help cultural products, including *Chinese-Style Divorce*, invites the question: How does a state-sanctioned and market-informed self-governing rhetoric composed of ideologically tinged terms like "quality," "self," and "capacity" regulate the representation of gendered subject and domestic space in a neoliberalizing China? A close investigation of the televised representation of changing family values, intimate relationships, and gender dynamics that has developed in parallel with China's neoliberal turn may shed new light on this important issue.

A MIDDLE-AGED WOMAN IN TRANSIT

First aired during evening prime time in 2004, the twenty-three-part serial drama *Chinese-Style Divorce* immediately became the megahit of the year. According to data from Nielsen Media Research, the average viewer ratings were 10.2 percent in Beijing, 15 percent in Chengdu, and 20 percent in Chongqing.[5] At the end of the year, it received multiple awards for TV Drama of the Year, Best Female Lead, Best Male Lead, and Best Supporting Actress. Together with "harmonious society" and other phrases, "Chinese-style divorce" topped an official list of "the hottest Chinese keywords" in 2004. The term was so influential that the state-owned Central China Television (CCTV) News Channel produced two episodes of *Social Record* (Shehui jilu) special programs called "Chinese-Style Divorce." Since 2004, numerous reruns of the series have been broadcast on CCTV and local television stations. It is reported that many college students viewed this TV show as a textbook on married life in urban settings.[6]

Since *Chinese-Style Divorce* first aired in 2004, Lin Xiaofeng, the middle-aged female lead, has been widely recognized as representative of the "old-fashioned" wife in need of self-reformation. Compared to her husband, Song Jianping, a well-educated urban professional, Lin is a middle-aged woman with no special professional training in the growing middle-class occupations (e.g., lawyers, physicians, and other market-oriented knowledge workers). She belongs to the vulnerable low-income group who cannot take advantage of the freedom to job-hop in search of a better salary and often face the risk of being laid off. Horrified by her marginal position in the market economy of contemporary Chinese society, Lin particularly needs to protect herself with what the marital relationship could provide. To highlight this radical sense of transition, audiences witness a fairly dramatic scene at the beginning of the serial: In the hospital cafeteria, Lin runs into the retired head of the state-owned hospital in which her husband works. Insulted by the cafeteria cashier for his persistent bargaining over food prices, the senior cadre has a sudden heart attack and passes away.

Lin is dumbfounded by what has transpired before her eyes. She is glued to the spot, staring blankly at the motionless body in front of her. Her mouth is agape, pallid lips twitching in sadness and shock. At a loss, she blindly follows the crowd to the gate of the cafeteria and sees the ambulance carrying away the corpse. Accompanied by the rhythmic percussion of bass drums, the shaky jump cuts enhance the sense of panic and commotion in this scene, which forms a sharp contrast with Lin's solitary, rigid body, which appears helpless and fragile in a time of unexpected change and crisis. The emotional intensity of this highly allegorical event is particularly compelling to Chinese audiences who have witnessed the collapse of the old system on the screen and experienced it in their real lives.

Lin rushes back home and breaks the news to her husband, which triggers a face-to-face confrontation. Wearing an oversized apron, Lin impatiently does the dishes in the small kitchen while shouting indignantly at Song: "We cannot afford a decent life with your meager wages—two or three thousand *yuan* [approximately $400 to $500] a month! You don't even have a tiny bit of courage to try competing out there!" In the following weeks, Lin tries to persuade Song to find a better-paid job so that he will not repeat the former hospital head's fatal mistake, that is, to stay in an underpaid position in the state-owned hospital. She constantly reminds Song that Dangdang, their six-year-old son, is their only hope and deserves a much better (read: more expensive) education to succeed in an increasingly competitive society. Lin tries every possible means to push Song into action. She even refuses to make love to him as a way of punishing him for his failure to realize his self-value, or entrepreneurial masculinity, in the market economy. Finally, Song follows her advice to take advantage of the expanding privatization of the medical and health care system. He resigns his job in the state-owned hospital and goes to work in the Pacific International Hospital, a private institution with U.S. investors, and receives a generous raise in salary.

A NEW TYPE OF WORK UNIT

When Song accumulates economic capital and upward mobility as a well-paid surgeon and later a vice president at the hospital, Lin develops an even stronger sense of insecurity triggered, now, by her aging body and the prevailing practice of "adopting a concubine" (*bao ernai*) among newly rich Chinese males. As a middle-aged woman, she no longer seems to be an appropriate match for her husband. While economic and social capital is being redistributed between husband and wife in the domestic space, divorce means very different things for each of them. Due to this power imbalance, Lin loses self-confidence and feels neglected. Signs of her husband's intimacy with other women easily irritate her. Unable to stand Lin's bad temper and nearly paranoid suspicion of his infidelity, Song initiates a divorce, which Lin refuses to accept. Hence, incessant bouts of domestic conflict, cold war, verbal abuse, and physical violence bombard the audience of the serial drama.

In *Chinese-Style Divorce*, Lin often acts like an old-fashioned abandoned woman by resorting to collectivist countermeasures and public opinion to deal with her domestic issues. For example, she chooses to go public with her personal grievances by turning to her husband's workplace for moral support. However, she is rebuffed by the American hospital director, and becomes a laughingstock because she has made the anachronistic mistake of mixing the "public and private affairs" (*bufen gongsi*). Unlike the socialist version, this new type of work unit is built on the spatial separation of the private/feminine and public/masculine spheres.

Lin's and Song's conflicting views of the domestic problem climax in a scene of violent confrontation. After a war of words the previous night, Lin intrudes into Song's office without notice. When Song sees her, he says coldly to his colleagues: "Please expel this person. She interferes with my work." Bathed in bright light, Song and his fellow doctors in white lab coats exhibit the professional authority and rational order of the public space aligned with the "universal" modern science and healthcare system.

Lin, however, refuses to retreat from a place where she neither belongs nor has any power. Rather, in the old-fashioned manner of appealing for collective moral support, she insists on publicizing their conjugal problems in front of Song's colleagues. Song heaves a heavy sigh and turns to exit the room. All of a sudden, a deafening sound of glass cracking draws him back to his office, where Lin has broken the window and threatens to jump out of it. With her back toward the people in the room and audiences in front of their television screens, Lin, in a bulky black overcoat, appears to be a faceless monstrous force that not only causes her man to lose his masculine authority in public but also transgresses the public/private boundaries. Looking up at Lin's backlit figure, Song slowly kneels down.[7] Following his low-angle point of view, the camera stretches Lin's body to a towering height. A two-minute close-up of his distorted face twitching in pain and bowing his head in silent endurance displays this male figure in a more sympathetic light. The contrasting spatial positioning of the male and female bodies disrupts the normative order of the public space in which the male professional exercises his power and authority.

Chinese rural women once employed this type of "old-fashioned" and vociferous behavior of airing dirty laundry, or publicizing one's domestic problems, as an effective political strategy in their collective struggle for gender equality and marriage reform.[8] Based on the solid moral ground of political sisterhood, they participated in various kinds of mass mobilizations. This not only provided Chinese women with a vehicle for mobilizing mass support but also gave voice to their emotions, identities, and political agency in the 1950s campaign of "revolutionizing the family." However, in the urban centers of contemporary Chinese society, few venues outside the domestic are available for women who seek affective satisfaction and moral support by establishing alternative modes of sociality. Without recourse to a legitimate language or social mobilization for bringing family issues into the public sphere, the same gender strategies have lost their political significance and are viewed as a middle-aged woman's neurotic symptoms that should be diagnosed and cured through proper private means.

Instead of tackling this gender- and age-related social problem, the author Wang Hailing, a middle-aged divorced woman herself, uses words such as "low-quality" (suzhi di), "irrationality," and "postmenopausal symptoms" to pathologize her female protagonist. According to her analysis, Lin fails to keep up with the rising living standards and emotional demands of China's urban middle-class lifestyle. Then Wang proposes self-development as the solution to Lin's marital problems.[9] Concurring with Wang, many critics regard the lack of self as the root cause of Lin's marital crisis.[10] Commenting on the sexual dynamics represented in this show, Liu Siqian, a Chinese feminist critic, has criticized the implicit patriarchal double standard in the serial; however, she has also emphasized that Lin's biggest mistake is overlooking the "material foundation" of the marriage, or the man's desire for the woman's body.[11]

Viewers of the divorce melodrama also express similar views on numerous online forums hosted by entertainment websites and in print media. For example, Sina.com, one of the largest Chinese commercial portals, provides a special section where viewers may discuss Chinese-Style Divorce, which lists 742 comments. Many of the commenters regard the television drama as a faithful rendition of rampant domestic problems and refer to Lin as a crazy "yellow-faced old hag" (huanglian po) who cannot find her own self. Though some self-identified female viewers show sympathy toward Lin, they also suggest that Lin hire a baomu for household chores so that she can spend more time on learning marriage management skills and making herself look younger and more attractive. A baomu could serve as a mentor for an intellectual woman in "Good Morning, Miss," but in Chinese-Style Divorce, the image of the baomu only reinforces social stratification and class distinctions.

The critical response to the serial shows that the recent trend in professionalizing and marketizing domestic labor does not change the unequal nature of gendered division of labor but works as a catalyst in the formation of a gendered middle-class identity. On the one hand, the "low-quality" work (household chores such as cleaning and cooking) domestic laborers perform allows their middle-class employers to enjoy a "high-quality" domestic life in which the "curse of labor" is made invisible.[12] On the other hand, hiring these "low-quality" laborers enable middle-class housewives to engage in a more sophisticated form of gendered affective labor: cultivating their feminine qualities and boosting their sexual and emotional appeal within domestic boundaries.

Improving her gendered qualities and individualized self has become a precondition for a woman's success in the modern heterosexual nuclear family, and divorce is narrated as a central mechanism that does not simply break up a romantic relationship but propels women to engage in a self-development campaign. Lin's precarious position as a deficient wife is analogous to that of middle-aged women factory workers confronted with the threat of massive layoffs. For both groups, the prescribed solution is self-improvement and realization of self-worth through constant adjustment and transformation in order to meet the demands of the reconstituted political economy and cultural politics. Nonetheless, while female factory workers improve their capacity through their performance in a public sphere of industrial production, the demand for Lin's self-development becomes particularly urgent after her return to a privatizing domestic sphere.

RETREAT TO THE DOMESTIC INTERIOR

In the first few episodes of *Chinese-Style Divorce*, Lin works as a Chinese-language teacher in a public elementary school. She often complains to her colleagues that such teachers are underpaid and worthless (*yiwu suoyou*, in her own words) in the market economy. This is not her individual problem but reflects the declining status and low income of grade school teachers in post-revolutionary China. Yet despite all her laments, she is enthusiastic and conscientious, obtaining a strong sense of fulfillment from her professional accomplishments and interactions with her students.

At the very beginning of the serial, following an establishing shot that shows Song reading patients' medical records and walking in the hallway of a busy hospital, the subsequent long take shows a similar visual image: Lin is walking slowly from the back of a well-lit and quiet classroom toward the front. Holding a Chinese textbook, she reads aloud a poetic passage along with a group of young students:

> Little grasses are green,
> And wheat seedlings are green.
> I live in the countryside,
> So my dream is green too.

Then she pauses, smiling at her students. The golden rays of the sun shine through clean windowpanes, lighting up her face.

However, the serene pastoral aura soon fades out, as the seemingly perfect balance of the husband's and wife's professional labor is disrupted by a new domestic demand that calls for differential gender roles. When Lin is about to take the school's comprehensive exams, their son falls ill. As her husband is occupied with his professional obligations, she single-handedly takes care of the sick child while studying a huge pile of textbooks. Finally, the ailing son recovers, but Lin passes out in the middle of the exam.

When this middle-aged woman struggles with her double burden, what appears to be at stake is not a social problem but a personal choice to be made by an essentially gendered being. In order to ensure her son's "quality education" (*suzhi jiaoyu*), Lin resigns from her job and becomes a full-time housewife. This decision precisely reflects the reconfigured family structure and its changing relationship with one's work unit in contemporary China. On the one hand, the modernized new kinds of work units, like Song's hospital, do not provide support for employees' domestic needs and draw a clear line between private and public life. On the other hand, transformed from an extension of the socialist work-unit system into a privatized space, the nuclear family in contemporary Chinese society is now responsible for vast financial investments in health care, housing, and children's education as a result of the dismantling of the socialist welfare system. And most of the time, it is a woman's responsibility to nurture the next generation and devote her time and labor to helping her husband build up his intangible assets (education, professional training, and career development) by giving up or putting off her own education and career.[13]

As the market-oriented economy drives contemporary China toward greater self-reliance and individual development, children's quality education has become the priority in the domestic economy of urban middle-class families. In her study of quality education, Ann Anagnost argues that *suzhi* "defines the middle-class family as a theater of neoliberal subject project production."[14] As a "value-coding" discourse, *suzhi* plays a key role in constructing the urban middle-class culture and shaping gender politics in post-revolutionary China.[15] However, the highly gendered division of labor within the domestic sphere has not been discussed much.

In her reading of *Chinese-Style Divorce*, Xueping Zhong suggests that Lin Xiaofeng's marital crisis is a result of her "unreasoned pursuit of happiness."[16] It should be noted, however, that Lin urges her husband to pursue career development (read: better income) not so much for her own happiness as for their son's quality education. As shown on television, Lin shoulders the reproductive duties of a self-sacrificing mother alone. Her return to the domestic site severs her close ties to public life as a social subject and transforms her identity from Teacher Lin (Lin Laoshi) to Mrs. Song (Song Taitai). Busy with her domestic chores, Lin seems to find more pleasure in her reproductive role of nurturing a high-quality child than in the middle-class privileges of conspicuous consumption. However, her performance of virtuous womanhood in the domestic space does not earn her social recognition or affective attention from her husband but simply lowers her from a middle-class *taitai* to a working-class *baomu* who knows only how to do "low-quality" gendered labor—household chores.

IN SEARCH OF MIDDLE-CLASS CONSUM(ER)ABILITY

Totally out of sync with the fashionable middle-class lifestyle, Lin fails to meet the newer expectations spurred by the development of a consumer-oriented economy. For instance, she cannot understand why Song has to buy two cars for their nuclear family. She is also puzzled when Juanzi, a younger woman in her early twenties, flies from Beijing to Shanghai merely for a Broadway musical. She struggles to learn how to use a cell phone, how to send text messages, and how to purchase luxurious lingerie with which to seduce her husband. Her home interior looks plain and lacks taste, with none of the trendy decorations featured in popular home remodeling advertisements and magazines.

In short, she is not a desirable middle-class wife because she does not consume in a classy way that would distinguish her as a high-quality middle-class wife. The variety of glamorous commodities and services advertised in mass media and targeted at young female consumers do not offer Lin pleasure but trigger anxiety about aging. As class values determined by one's capacity to consume commodities appropriately are displaced into gender identities, Lin's old-fashioned lifestyle is coupled with her undesirability as an object of male sexual consumption. While Lin tries desperately to please her newly rich husband by way of sex, Song makes every possible excuse (even including a fake diagnosis of erectile dysfunction) to reject his wife. The term "consum(er)ability" may be used to designate this dual quality that Lin lacks.

To represent this lack of corporeal consum(er)ability extracted and transferred from the consumability of commodities, Jiang Wenli, a prominent Chinese actress in her forties, appears in the serial without makeup in order to create the impression of a jealous, hysterical, and fatigued middle-aged housewife. Lin's coarse skin, unkempt dry hair, and out-of-shape figure are matched by her loose-fitting, monochromatic, and unfashionable clothes. Shot in grayish lighting, her desexualized laboring body is constantly staged within the domestic setting, where she is shown busily cooking in the kitchen, cleaning the apartment, and taking care of her husband's and son's daily needs. Her exaggerated body language, high-pitched yelling, redundant complaints, and volatile temper all enhance the cultural stereotype of the middle-aged shrew (*pofu*). In sharp contrast, Xiao Li and Juanzi, two younger women characters, have delicate makeup and chic clothing and are shot in bright, soft lighting, often framed in a sequence of close-up shots from Song's point of view.

Particularly noteworthy is the fact that *Chinese-Style Divorce* is not the first (and obviously not the last) popular narrative defining consum(er)ability as feminine quality. Instead of being invisible, like men's ageing bodies, the middle-aged female body is often represented in recent cultural productions as an indication of women's physical degradation and mental disorder. Such a narrative convention assigns the root of the middle-aged woman's anxiety to the biological, the corporeal. In China's paradigmatic shift, age has become an index of the repositioning of different social strata and the accumulation of gender-divided capital.

Foreign Babes in Beijing and *To and Fro* are perfect examples of this type of popular melodrama produced at the turn of the century. *To and Fro* is a television serial adapted from Chi Li's best seller, in which Duan Lina, the middle-aged protagonist, is also represented as a woman from the past who fails to fit into the domestic order of the present.

Born and brought up during the Mao era, Duan is informed by the gender values and moral code developed along the line of women's liberation and revolutionary tradition. She prefers Maoist terms like "comrade" (*tongzhi*) and "the loved one" (*airen*) to the title "madam" (*taitai*), often used to refer to wives of officials and bourgeoisie, which was always associated with the colonial modernity of treaty ports such as Shanghai and thus was undesirable for both the May Fourth–style new woman and the Maoist revolutionary.[17]

After Kang Weiye, her husband, "plunges into the sea of business," she continues to work in the the Municipal Women's Federation of Wuhan. This sexual division of professional labor is a typical practice of "one family, two systems" (*yijia liangzhi*), a spin-off from the famous Dengist policy of "one country, two systems" (*yiguo liangzhi*), meaning that the husband ventures into the private (capitalist) sectors of the market economy for higher income while the wife sticks to her job in the state-owned (socialist) work unit for financial and social security.[18] Again, this practice of "one family, two systems" is built on an implicit double standard and gender inequality: woman is obligated to stick to the old system in order to guard domestic stability and economic security, while man is encouraged to pursue his career potential and develop his intangible assets in the new economy, supported by his wife, who provides affection and domestic labor. In this sense, Kang's new adventure in "the sea of business" should be viewed as a "two-person career."[19]

Their "cooperative effort" and "mutual investments" make Kang's career transition quite successful.[20] However, after Kang becomes a newly rich entrepreneur with the power of transnational capital, Duan cannot adapt to a high-quality middle-class life. Her refusal "to subjugate herself to consumer culture" leads Kang to conclude that his wife still belongs to the Maoist generation that "has always been poor, is used to being poor, and is proud of being poor."[21] Duan "internal poverty" and her lack of capacity to consume are transcoded into her lack of corporeal consumability, similar to what happened to Lin in *Chinese-Style Divorce*. In both divorce narratives, while the man's gendered capital (entrepreneurial masculinity) has been enhanced by the accumulation of his intangible assets, the woman is considered to be a loser in the race to keep up with the new trend of middle-class femininity.

To and Fro depicts Duan's lack of consum(er)ability in the eyes of her entrepreneur husband in graphic detail: "Her chest was no longer full and the skin of her neck was flabby." Furthermore, in sharp contrast to the commodity aesthetics reified by her husband's Rolex watch, Montague leather belt, and English air-cushion leather shoes, the blouse Duan wears is "a mass-produced one without style" that erases her individuality.[22] As a result of her essential lack of feminine quality, Duan loses her husband to a woman of a younger generation who can speak fluent English, enjoy red wine at a candlelight dinner, and seduce Kang with her eroticized body half submerged in a rosebud-strewn bathtub.[23]

This middle-class fantasy is more explicitly internationalized by a cross-cultural, interracial romance narrated in the TV melodrama *Foreign Babes in Beijing*. Viewed by 600 million Chinese, this prime-time hit has not only been rerun numerous times in Beijing but has even penetrated the remote border area of Tibet.[24] The twenty-part soap opera, with its "hot depiction of sex, wealth, and success," unfolds an interracial extramarital romance.[25] Jiexi (played by Rachel DeWoskin) falls in love with Tianming (played by Wang Ling), a successful Chinese entrepreneur, and "ruthlessly chases and seduces him" despite the fact that he is married and has a young son.[26] At the end of the serial, Tianming divorces Qin Fen, his virtuous, hardworking, but old-fashioned Chinese wife, and goes to the United States with Jiexi.

Commenting on this soap opera, Sheldon H. Lu contends:

> In terms of gender representation in popular culture, the rivalry between nations and economies turns into a libidinal economy. The reassertion of Chinese masculinity takes the form of transnational fantasy, the wish fulfillment of competing with foreigners for the possession of capital and women.[27]

In addition to this new paradigm of constructing phantasmagoric Chinese masculinity in a transnational "libidinal economy," the highly eroticized body of Jiexi crystallizes a new femininity imaginary. In keeping with Chinese audiences' fantasies about American culture, Jiexi is portrayed as the perfect embodiment of imported sexual modernity, an exotic woman who appears far sexier, more romantic, and more open-minded (*kaifang*) than Qin Fen, the Liu Huifang–style Chinese wife. DeWoskin recalls that when they were shooting the episodes, the director always asked her to perform with more enthusiasm (*reqing*), or act in a sexier and more passionate way in order to accentuate the "American-style" femininity of her role.[28]

A sequence of montages presents the contrastive female bodies, a highly eroticized and thus consumable body versus a laboring body bearing the double burden of work and domestic duties, as DeWoskin describes in her book:

> All of my writhing, naked love scenes with Tian Ming are juxtaposed to scenes of his wife doing virtuous things—walking down rows and rows of the factory, working overtime, and patiently teaching their baby how to read. She breaks her back in a factory and then runs home to cook beautiful dinners for the family.[29]

Following the wide circulation of this serial, Chinese audiences enthusiastically embraced a new femininity model. Overall, this divorce melodrama was consumed by Chinese audiences not only as a celebration of Chinese-style entrepreneurial masculinity, as Lu has suggested, but also as a triumph of an eroticized femininity over the "old-fashioned" (be it socialist or traditionalist) labor aesthetics. Rather than being condemned by traditional Chinese family ethics, the imagined American version of feminine qualities displayed by the third party was admired and mimicked by Chinese audiences. DeWoskin recollects that after the soap opera aired, many young girls followed her through stores, marketplaces, and shopping centers to purchase whatever she bought so that they could become "more like Jiexi."[30] This collective act of imitating the cultural Other to acquire new feminine qualities tells a story about how the constructed racial difference is translated into a measurement of differential gendered quality.

These melodramas make a statement about how women can manipulate their corporeal capital to achieve social mobility, domestic bliss, and personal value, which exemplifies the neoliberal logic of "self-ownership."[31] Marking the boundaries of the individual body, self-ownership is predicated on autonomous possession and management of one's bodily capacity that can be traded for market value and a high-quality life. Grounded in the resexualized individual body, self-ownership underscores the fetishization of gender differences in the formation of selfhood. While the transnational imaginary portrays high-quality men conquering women with economic capital, for women, gendered quality cultivation involves accumulation and control of one's sexuality as an enterprise.

This new femininity ideal promoted in television representations resonates with a new wave of imported curricula for training Chinese women to develop wifely quality. A report titled "Producing Perfect Women for Successful Husbands" (Wei chenggong zhangfu dazao wanmei nüren) describes an example of this thriving industry.[32] The report introduces Nie Yelan who, after getting a PhD degree in Australia, returned to China, where she witnessed a good number of broken middle-class marriages, due, in her opinion, to the wives' "low quality." To remedy this situation, she opened a Perfect Woman club to teach Chinese middle-aged wives how to cultivate the wifely quality necessary to preserve their marriages. Based in Guangzhou, where "concubine villages" (*ernai cun*) have mushroomed, this club sold a weeklong package consisting of two parts: "Comprehensive Training of Perfect Wifely Quality" (Wanmei furen zonghe suzhi xunlian) and "Extravagant Consumption" (Zongqing xiaofei), which included classes on physical fitness, facial care, social skills, dining etiquette, shopping advice, and so on.

Transcoding commodity aesthetics to corporeal consum(er)ability, the wifely quality training curriculum renders the woman's laboring body invisible while fetishizing and resexualizing it on the basis of biological gender differences and global middle-class cultural norms. Enmeshed in the consumerist culture, Chinese women are thus redefined as both the consumer and the consumed, joining the universal rank of *nüxing*, the sexualized individual as "*nanxing*'s (man's) other," instead of the Maoist *funü*, a politicized national subject.[33]

On the one hand, this group of middle-aged full-time housewives such as Lin must take on household and reproductive duties and are often confronted with the problems of financial dependence and social isolation. On the other hand, the value of their unpaid reproductive and affective labor is not recognized. They have often been criticized as old-fashioned women bound by a set of traditional values generated within the confines of the domestic sphere. With little community support or political resources, they are left with only their individualized bodies as a resource for self-improvement. Therefore, the suggested solution for this gendered dilemma is to rebuild connections with the outside world through the very means of consumption. Consum(er)ability thus becomes the tangible measurement of gendered capacity in conducting self-discipline and management of the body and making constant self-improvements and adaptations to changing feminine ideals.

CONSUM(ER)ABILITY: SELF-DEVELOPMENT PROJECT OF BODY AND SOUL

Gendered self-development does not simply dwell on the corporeal surface of women's bodies in the serial but is further romanticized and sublimated by a revisionist characterization of a female Maoist cadre. In his examination of "the transnational politics of visuality, sexuality and masculinity," Sheldon H. Lu argues that the marginalization of the traditional self-sacrificing Chinese woman goes hand in hand with middle-class Chinese men's empowerment through economic ascendancy.[34] In *Chinese-Style Divorce*, however, this trend in gender representations has been revised to cash in on the most recent nationalist sentiments about the revival of Confucian family ethics. In the serial, Lin's mother plays the important role of assigning "Chinese characteristics" to the new vision of wifely quality.

Toward the end of *Chinese-Style Divorce*, when Lin's escalating conflicts with her husband cause her to neglect her household duties and maternal role, her mother furiously chastises her, slaps her on the face, and has a heart attack. After her mother passes away, her father reveals that he had an extramarital affair and Lin is his illegitimate daughter. Although his wife knew about this, she still lavished love on her husband and reared Lin as her own daughter. This most unexpected melodramatic twist turns out to be a vital lesson in Lin's "gendered quality education." She spends a sleepless night on a bench by the sea, gazing into the distance. The wide and calm sea, enveloped in grayish twilight, dominates two-thirds of the frame, dwarfing Lin, who becomes an insignificantly tiny figure.

The next day, Song's hospital holds a combination farewell party and American-style Thanksgiving party for Song, who has decided to work in Tibet for two years in order to obtain a legally valid separation and eventual divorce. To everyone's surprise, Lin shows up in the well-decorated banquet hall, determined to display her reformed self to Song and all his colleagues. For the first time, viewers get to see a feminine and elegant image of the middle-aged woman. She wears a well-fitting short jacket, a figure-flattering skirt, and a pair of stylish boots, and her light makeup evens out her skin tone and covers her freckles and the sagging skin under her eyes. Enhancing this carefully groomed image of an understanding and attractive well-educated woman (*zhixing nüren*), Lin's body movements also appear more controlled and graceful than usual.

Stepping up on the platform, Lin tearfully makes a lengthy self-criticism. Her voice is gentle and full of emotion. She begins this heart-wrenching public confession with a well-known fable about the science of romance: On the eve of the wedding ceremony, a young girl asks her mother how to maintain a happy marriage. Her mother tells her that love is like a handful of sand. The harder you clench your fist, the faster the sand will slip away between your fingers. Then Lin scolds herself for trying so hard to keep a firm hand on her marriage that she loses herself, which destroys the relationship. She concludes, "Love is a kind of capacity" (ai shi yizhong nengli), a capacity to manage one's marriage wisely and artfully so that one is able to be loved.

As this pedagogical story about love unfolds, the camera cuts back and forth between Lin's figure and the banquet guests. Prolonged close-ups linger on the faces of a few young women who listen to Lin attentively and are moved to tears. Empowered by these "transparent" and "universal" images of women's sentimental faces, the intense emotional communication reenacts the apprentice structure of the sand story, which seems to identify Lin with the mother who teaches a lesson and female audiences with the daughter who needs to be enlightened and disciplined. Song, too, appears to be deeply moved by Lin's public confession and extreme self-reform. On such a sentimental note, the serial drama ends with a close-up of Song kissing his wife lovingly. Audiences are left wondering whether or not they will divorce.

Lin's self-denunciation, which softens her husband's heart, turns the divorce melodrama into, paradoxically, a highly gendered narrative of self-development in which each woman plays the role of producer of consumable romantic fantasy within the domestic sphere. In order to realize the exchange value of the romance, the wife is individually responsible for developing her lovability, measured ultimately by the criterion of consum(er)ability. A new wifely subject is established through performing radical self-improvement and reform and subsequently subjecting herself to male desire. Thus, the divorce melodrama is transformed into a guidebook on courtship and marriage, which reduces the complexity of marital conflicts and structural inequities into a standard model of a depoliticized and free individual's artful management of risks, gains, desires, and pleasures derived from one's love life. Paradoxically, this type of self-help romance exhibits the glamour of "consum(er)able" female figures and publicizes personal matters as consumable commodities while returning gender-related problems to the private domain.[35]

WHO HAS THE RIGHT TO "FREE LOVE"?

In this narrative of calculating the self-management of one's romantic life, the younger generation displays the cosmopolitan consum(er)able

surface of the highly self-disciplined body, while Lin's mother's generation embodies traditional feminine virtues of loyalty and self-sacrifice that grant the ethical ground and affective value of the gendered
self-development discourse. What is most intriguing about this self-
sacrificing mother figure is her conspicuous association with revolutionary iconography, which taps into the recent trend of consuming
commodified collective memories of the Mao era.[36] As retired Communist cadres, Lin's parents join the chorus singing revolutionary
songs. Often dressed in a Red Army uniform during the performance,
the maternal figure gestures toward a subtle compromise between a
traditional "good wife and wise mother" image and nostalgia for the
Mao era, as well as between cosmopolitan femininity (global) and
traditional feminine virtues (local).

In an article on woman's essential gender quality, author Wang
Hailing reveals that the inspiration for the maternal figure in this
drama comes from her own mother. Having lived through the tumultuous years of the Mao era, Wang's mother remains devoted to her
husband and always positions the maintenance of domestic bliss
above politics.[37] On the surface, the virtuous image of the moth-
erly figure resembles the character of Liu Huifang, the female lead of
Yearnings (Kewang), arguably China's first soap opera, which aired
in 1991. Under closer scrutiny, however, the two apparently similar
figures of "good wife and wise mother" yield a remarkable difference.
Liu's working-class background makes her self-sacrificing behavior
relevant to "the iconization of the model socialist citizen Lei Feng."[38]
In other words, the redeeming power of Liu's image retains close ties
with vestiges of socialist labor aesthetics.

Compared to Liu's, the characterization of Lin's mother is premised
on a revisionist rewriting of Maoist memories through a "romantic
love" narrative with "Chinese characteristics." In the serial, Lin's
mother chooses to make a lifelong sacrifice because of her whole-
hearted true love for Lin's father. She is represented as a genteel, loving, and well-bred lady who gains her personal value from her unconditional dedication to the maintenance of a happy and harmonious
marriage. Rather than stirring any relevant memories of the historic
specifics, the characterization of the elderly Maoist cadre is completely
depoliticized and re-gendered as "a televised object," a simulacrum
that situates moral and affective values not so much in the revolutionary tradition but more in "a network of incessant, unreal circulation"
of the signs of a transnational imaginary of undying romantic love.[39]

The value of consumability is attached not only to the female figure in the divorce narrative but also to the revolutionary legacy that has been romanticized and feminized in order to cater to contemporary Chinese audiences.

This type of Chinese-style romance narrative has been warmly received and has resonated with contemporary Chinese intellectuals' efforts to de-revolutionize Maoist gender politics. It is worth noting that women writers' works have played a central role in promoting and circulating the imaginary of romantic love since the 1980s. Zhang Jie's widely read short story "Love Must Not Be Forgotten" launched the post-revolutionary literary tradition of depicting women's yearnings for romantic love and liberal individualism.

To rewrite the asexual and bodiless revolutionary subjects, a new account of gendered individualism is couched in terms of inner feelings, the (re-)sexualized body, and heterosexual romantic love. All are crucial ingredients of contemporary Chinese family melodramas as well as imported Euro-American, Japanese, Korean, Hong Kong, and Taiwanese romance fiction and films, in which the gendered interior world of innermost human feelings and desires is usually reified through the externalization of details of middle-class material life. The gendered division of labor is also crystallized and naturalized through the circulation of a transnational imaginary manifested in popular gender representations since the 1990s.

Discussing the ways in which desire and intimacy rewrite the politics of interpersonal relationships in everyday life in modern society, Anthony Giddens contends that in marriage and other intimate relationships, "egalitarian communication" serves as a mechanism by which to pursue interpersonal equality and democracy.[40] However, this interpersonal democracy turns out to be limited and vulnerable when confronted with the formidable alliance of the expanding neoliberal economy and a revived patriarchy. In *Chinese-Style Divorce*, while Song's attraction to a fashionable middle-class woman testifies only to his wife's lack of feminine charm, Lin's search for interpersonal democracy through the pursuit of intimate relationships is ridiculed and even punished.

After resigning from her job, Lin is socially isolated and financially dependent. Meanwhile, the value of her domestic labor is unrecognized, although her husband's and son's everyday lives heavily depend on it. Commenting on her "stark poverty," Song says, "She has nothing but me." Haunted by a strong sense of loss, Lin pleads for emotional support from Song, but her yearnings for affection and communication are totally dismissed. Rather, Song resorts to purchasing expensive things such as a sleek new car to mollify his wife and steer her attention and energy toward the realm of consumption. Commodities become the token of love that translates interpersonal democracy based on egalitarian communication into the "democracy of consumption," the illusionary equality of everyone having ready access to the privilege of commodity consumption.[41]

Driven by her yearning for interpersonal communication on an equal footing, Lin turns to online chatting to vent her anger and search for virtual intimacy. Coincidentally, a male friend of Song's spots her online. He tells Song about this, and the two men conspire to set Lin up via the use of QQ, a type of instant messaging popular among Chinese youth. In order to obtain evidence of Lin's disloyalty to Song, they decide to ask her out for a date. At the agreed time, Lin paces back and forth anxiously, facing the wide sea rolling in the burning light of the setting sun. Song shows up, walking slowly toward Lin. Following his point of view, the viewer is placed in a position of power, watching Lin's back coming closer and closer, like the trapped prey of the camera's predatory male gaze. Then Song stops, calling out Lin's Internet name, Blossoming Peach (Taohua Shengkai). Lin turns her head, looking startled, disappointed, and then fearful.

The next sequence cuts to the domestic interior of their home. Its dim lighting contrasts sharply with the splendid sunset in the vast open space. In the cramped living room, Song stands firmly against the wall, reading aloud the evidence of Lin's "extramarital affair," the line-by-line record of Lin's online chatting. Lin curls up in an armchair, bowing her head, disheveled hair covering her face. This contrastive spatial positioning renders the man morally superior and the woman powerless and invisible. All of a sudden, Lin pulls herself up and breaks the windowpanes that mark the boundary of a claustrophobic domestic interior. She then continues to smash everything in sight. Her fierce movements, glaring eyes, swelling nostrils, and clenched teeth, magnified in a series of slow-motion frames, externalize her mixed feelings of shame, anger, and frustration at having lost control of a life situation mired in the patriarchal power networks. Song, however, views all of this simply as symptoms of an incomprehensible spell of hysteria in a stereotypical middle-aged shrew. Disgusted, he shakes his head and closes his eyes.

The explosive sounds wake up their young son, who is sleeping in his bedroom. He comes out of his room, finds a small knife, and cuts his hand in an effort to get his mother's attention. Lin rushes him to the hospital, crying out repeatedly, "I am sorry! I am so sorry!" Thus, Lin's violation of the domestic order is finally ended by the demands of her maternal role. Her initial attempt to negotiate for egalitarian communication and interpersonal intimacy is shattered by the reinvented traditional family ethics that impose a double standard for women and men. Ironically, the expanding technological revolution weaves a more totalitarian network of surveillance rather than bringing a greater degree of freedom to the desiring female subject. This frustrating outcome deviates radically from the 1980s feminist assertion of romantic love and women's agency. This shift in gender politics bears the significant imprints of recent state ideological regulation and cultural policies.

THE DEMOCRACY OF CONSUMPTION IN A "HARMONIOUS SOCIETY"

Since the late 1980s, the Chinese government has promoted the "socialist mainstream melody" (*zhu xuanlü*) mass culture to produce politically correct and morally conservative films and TV dramas that focus on portraying positive images of contemporary China.[42] In 2000, the State Administration of Radio, Film and Television and the Chinese Propaganda Bureau joined the effort to regulate TV culture. They severely criticized popular domestic dramas such as *Love Rules* (Rang ai zuozhu; 2000) that were regarded as too "Westernized," disturbing the socialist morality with excessive depictions of "unhealthy male-female relationships" and extramarital affairs.[43]

The increasingly tightened control of media broadcasting and cultural products is a result of the current "harmonious society" campaign, which prioritizes the maintenance of a stable and proper domestic order and places great value on traditional family ethics.[44] Responding to the state's call, a recent TV serial, *Golden Anniversary* (Jinhun; 2007), starring Jiang Wenli, the actress from *Chinese-Style Divorce*, even advertises itself as "a humanist epic advocating Chairman Hu Jintao's important ideas of 'building a harmonious socialist society'."[45]

Aiming to provide social stability for further economic development, this political project also encourages the "democracy of consumption" of both commodities and pop culture in order to divert attention from struggles for gender equality and social justice. As the middle-class family has become a basic unit of contemporary Chinese consumerist society, wives are remodeled to be the primary agents of the democracy of consumption. At the 2001 conventions of the National People's Congress (NPC) and Chinese People's Political Consultative Conference (CPPCC), Wang Xiancai, a member of the CPPCC, proposed that women should go back to the domestic space, as gendered labor division is an indicator of social progression that contributes to economic development.[46] The government's promotion of women's domesticity exposes its strategy in manipulating traditional family ethics to support the neoliberal development mentality of post-revolutionary China.

As the "harmonious society" project is sanctioned by the state as a warranty for desirable social conditions and economic development, familial harmony is scientized as an essential tool in improving social production efficiency. For example, the majority of the informants in one survey considered a high-quality family life indispensable for social development because of its direct effect on boosting their workers' efficiency and competitiveness.[47] A British report distinguishes itself with "well-tested" data proving that men with virtuous wives make more money.[48] These "scientific" theories support the prevailing view that a high-quality (*suzhi gao*) wife should maintain the proper middle-class domesticity so that her husband can fulfill his self-value in a market competition of individual bodily capacity.

Notably, urban elite women have contributed greatly to this new scientized political discourse. In 2005, the Beijing Women's Federation organized a series of debate contests and seminars for female college students to articulate the connection between building a harmonious family and a harmonious society. Yu Dan, a woman professor at Beijing Normal University, has led a surge in the adaptation of traditional classics into self-help handbooks that allegedly guide people to cultivate inner harmony and build a harmonious society.[49] By the same token, the Qiong Yao–style romance fiction and TV melodramas are considered vehicles for realizing feminism with "Chinese characteristics" that strives to achieve the lofty goal of the "harmony of both sexes" (*shuangxing hexie*).[50]

Soap operas highlighting the theme of romantic love with "Chinese characteristics"—many produced by well-known female authors, including *The Days of Burning Passion* (Jiqing ranshao de suiyue; 2001), *Eldest Brother* (Dage; 2002), *Married for Ten Years* (Jiehun shinian; 2002), *Romantic Stories* (Langman de shi; 2003), *Eldest Sister* (Dajie; 2004), and *Mother-in-Law* (Popo; 2004)—have flooded Chinese TV screens and won high viewer ratings. As Shuyu Kong has noted in her study of recent family melodramas, "Filial duties, in-law relationships, parental responsibilities, and maintenance of family harmony in an extended family are constantly recurring themes." Audiences turn to melodramas that emphasize harmony and stability in order to assuage the enormous emotional anxiety caused by "an increasingly aggressive and individualistic society where morals and family values, whether traditional or socialist, have collapsed."[51]

Compared to the Mao era, when the family served as a primary unit for both genders as they participated in social production and political activities, the urban middle-class family in contemporary China is a product of the depoliticization and privatization of domestic space.[52] The once-blurred boundary between the public and the private has been redrawn. Cut off from an outside world that is marked by relentless competition, exploitation, and the dismantling of the socialist cradle-to-grave welfare system, the middle-class family is represented as a harmonious haven, soothing the pain of radical social change, or as a site where the quality of life is materialized through consuming high-quality commodities including feminine sexualities and romantic fantasies. As a result, the converging forces of a transnational middle-class culture and an indigenous "harmonious society" campaign reshape women's role to be the administrator of domestic consumption as well as the repository of romanticized traditional feminine virtues.

Paradoxically, this imaginary harmonious middle-class interiority follows the same logic as the market-oriented self-development discourse. This discourse not only inscribes a differential value to various professions (e.g., Lin as an elementary school teacher vs. Song as a surgeon in American-financed hospital) and a hierarchy of gendered division of labor (productive vs. reproductive, paid vs. domestic) but also fosters fierce competition between women on the basis of their corporeal and emotional consum(er)ability. As traffic in women becomes a crucial indicator of male entrepreneurs' masculinity, the prevailing practice of adopting concubines contributes directly to the skyrocketing divorce rate and many middle-aged women's deep sense of anxiety.[53] In this sense, the state's reinvention of Confucian family ethics and gender conservatism evokes memories of the ancient concubinage system, a practice that is rarely represented in television narratives, probably as a result of self-censorship by media workers.[54]

CONCLUSION

As the neoliberal governmentality of contemporary China turns to "the art of exercising power in the form of economy," the population is managed with the political rationale supported by institutional power, scientific statistics, disciplinary knowledge, cultural reproduction, and nationalist sentiments.[55] Rather than merely counting on the enforcement of laws and legal codes, the state also governs through each individual's capacity to manage herself or himself. As Li Zhang has noted, "Self-cultivation and self-control is touted as the emblem of the superior *suzhi* of modern middle-class Chinese citizens."[56] Popular cultural products, including domestic fiction, women's magazines, advertisements, how-to marriage guidebooks, and TV shows, turn the family into an educational institution, enlightening middle-class women with the art of self-cultivation: how to manage affective labor and how to accrue the symbolic capital of consum(er)ability in order to accomplish a certain quality of domestic life and sense of self-fulfillment.

Read in this context, *Chinese-Style Divorce*, among many other family melodramas penned by renowned women writers, has played a dominant role in promoting a formula that combines transnational middle-class culture and traditional family ethics with "Chinese characteristics." In place of interpersonal interactions and egalitarian communication, love is redefined as a highly gendered interior quality that an individualized woman is expected to achieve through meticulous management and control of her own mind and body.

The neoliberal validation of individual freedom and self-reliance has not yet been fully addressed by Chinese feminists. Rather, quality, self-development, and individualism are often keywords of postrevolutionary Chinese "market feminism" and activities sponsored by the All China Women's Federation.[57] Meanwhile, contemporary male intellectuals disavow the historic legacy of women's liberation by suggesting that, in a postfeminist era, the challenge is to tame and re-gender the "over-liberated" Chinese woman within the domestic sphere.[58] Their criticism of socialist revolution often takes the form of "an implicit revival of the Confucian patriarchy by means of misogynistic discourse" and consequently cancels out serious discussion of structural inequities along class, gender, age, ethnic, and regional divisions.[59]

CHAPTER FIVE

Seeking Second Chances in a Risk Society

The Cinema of Divorce in the New Millennium

Partly as a result of the simplified divorce procedures stipulated in the 2001 amendment to the Second Marriage Law and its 2003 modification, China's divorce rate has spiked in the new millennium,[1]and in response to this social phenomenon, cultural representations of broken marriages and dysfunctional families have flooded the media. One genre is the cinema of divorce, including films that center on the cinematic representation of marital strife and family crisis. Within this genre, two new trends of cinematic innovation can be identified.

First, instead of narrating infidelity as a fable of social transformation and liberation of private desires,[2] a sense of nostalgia prevails in recent films about divorce. Second, compared to the more conventional (or male-dominant) gender politics depicted in earlier works such as *Mr. Zhao* (Zhao Xiansheng; 1998) or *I Love Beijing* (Xiari nuan yangyang; 2001),[3] the cinema of divorce in the new millennium often casts border-crossing women characters who take the initiative in filing for divorce, reshaping family relationships, and redefining the form and meaning of marriage. Deviating from stereotypical female figures, these women are represented as more freely able to navigate both private and public spaces, traverse the boundaries of the rural and the urban, and actively negotiate with male desire. Overshadowed by these strong women, their male counterparts appear weak or even emasculated. Does this new trend in gender politics indicate women's acquisition of more power and agency in reconfiguring marital relationship and domestic space? Or can we read it as a cinematic projection of the formation of a new (feminized?) affective economy and moral fabric in the face of domestic and social chaos? How does this new cultural imagination of domestic affects engage with the prevailing sense of nostalgia for earlier (pre-capitalist) modes of life?

CINEMA OF DIVORCE

Persevering female protagonists who continue to perform their maternal duties in a broken home are featured prominently in Chinese films about divorce and marital strife. Sun Zhou's *Breaking the Silence* (Piaoliang mama [literally "Pretty Mom"]; 2000) depicts a divorced woman (played by Gong Li) who is also a laid-off worker yet is single-handedly raising her deaf son. This sentimental melodrama evades the social problem of the massive layoffs of women workers, a result of industrial restructuring and sexual discrimination. Instead, it glorifies one pretty mother's individual struggle and self-sacrifice in what she believes to be the best interest of the next generation.

Similarly, *Shanghai Women* (Jiazhuang mei ganjue; 2002), directed by Peng Xiaolian, one of the few Fifth Generation woman filmmakers, also features a middle-aged divorced woman as the person who is solely responsible for child-rearing duties. The first installment of Peng's *Shanghai Trilogy*, *Shanghai Women* remaps the everyday space of Shanghai. It bears witness to the female protagonist's (played by Lü Liping) bitter experiences of a series of broken marriages and her moves from one household to another.[4] In the end, she gives up the plan of getting remarried once again in exchange for the physical space of a home or housing unit that she cannot afford to purchase, given the recent boom in real estate in Shanghai. Rather, she chooses to start a new life with her teenage daughter in a small rented apartment. This unexpected ending guides audience to speculate on the idea of a matriarchal commune, which harks back to the depiction of cross-generational sisterhood in Zhang Jie's story "Love Must Not Be Forgotten."

Ning Ying is another Fifth Generation woman director. Her low-budget film *Perpetual Motion* (Wuqiong dong), which premiered on International Women's Day (March 8, 2006), also portrays an imaginary sisterhood, this time, of four middle-aged women who are either divorced or estranged from their husbands. Seemingly a response to criticism about the lack of female perspective in her previous neorealist films such as *I Love Beijing*, this film explores middle-aged women's libidinal agitation within an enclosed spatiotemporal framework.[5]

The women's disillusionment with the present and their individual memories of the past reveal a gendered nostalgia for the idealistic "Golden Era" of the 1980s, when the authenticity of interpersonal feelings could still be imagined.[6] Such a strong sense of nostalgia is also manifest in many other divorce films, including Feng Xiaogang's *Cell Phone* (Shouji; 2003), Lu Xuechang's *Under One Roof* (Liangge ren de fangjian; 2008), and Zhang Meng's *The Piano in a Factory* (Gang de qin; 2010).

Compared to contemporaneous filmmakers such as Zhang Yimou and Chen Kaige, Feng Xiaogang always zooms in on slices of everyday life in a dynamic urban milieu. His 2000 film *A Sigh* (Yisheng tanxi) dramatizes the moral quandary and emotional crisis of a middle-aged writer, a perfect representative of the adulterous "successful personage" caught between his wife and his mistress. Echoing the suspenseful ending of *A Sigh*, in which the writer's superficial familial harmony is cracked open by a mysterious call on his cell phone, Feng's 2003 "new year's film" (*hesui pian*) *Cell Phone* further explores the perplexing relationships between modern technology, male desire, and urban middle-class domesticity. Instead of fulfilling its promise to weave a close-knit social network, the widely used high-tech telecommunication device succeeds only in generating a profound sense of insecurity and distrust, leading ultimately to the disruption of marital relationships.

Striking a sharp contrast with the bleak picture of moral uncertainty and emotional estrangement in a market age, the film's opening sequence takes viewers back to a coal mine in 1969. Lü Guihua, a mine worker's wife, goes a long way to the town post office to call her husband Niu Sanjin, asking him if he will be coming home soon. Because the whole mine shares one telephone, the receptionist has to broadcast Lü's message through a loudspeaker to every corner of the mine. The following montage shows the smiling faces of various mine workers' as they hear this message, accompanied by an extra-diegetic male voice repeating Lü's question over and over to the tune of a folk song. The simple but lyrical melody evokes a collective fantasy of a glorified socialist era that is set as contrastive to contemporary urban China, which is marked by advanced telecommunication technology and strained interpersonal relationships. In light of such nostalgia, the absence of modern telecommunication technology offers people more space for transparent and trustworthy communication.

The "Sixth Generation filmmaker Lu Xuechang's *Under One Roof* not only stars the same cast, Zhu Shimao and Cong Shan, as the Fourth Generation filmmaker Xie Jin's canonical film *The Herdsman* (Muma ren; 1982) but also intercuts some classic sequences from the latter. Presumably, this 2008 film is intended to be a sequel to *The Herdsman*. Produced and well received in the days after the Cultural Revolution, the 1982 film is a typical Xie Jin–style political melodrama that acts as "the nexus between public and private life."[7] It tells the highly idealistic story of a sent-down intellectual's unwavering love for his rural wife and "backward" motherland. In comparison, Lu's sequel presents a dystopian vision of the couple's wealthy but unfulfilling family life in today's China.

The dissipation of revolutionary idealism in contemporary urban China has been a haunting theme in Lu's cinematic oeuvre since his highly acclaimed directorial debut, *The Making of Steel* (Zhangda chengren; 1997). In *Under One Roof*, the filmmaker shows his audience the loss of idealistic youth through an on-screen representation of midlife crisis. Drastically different from the famous Xie Jin model that connects the public and the private, the political and the emotional, Lu's sequel retreats into the typical setting of the middle-class domestic interior. The film's title, which literally means "a room of two people" in Chinese, refers to a trend toward privatizing home ownership as well as domestic sentiments.

Having survived the tumultuous Maoist political campaigns, the nomadic couple moves to a big city and thrives there. Ironically, while the political turmoil of the past era brought the man and woman together, their new affluent material life drives the herders-turned-yuppies apart. Rather than strengthening their emotional ties, the privatization of wealth and desire causes a loss of passion and trust. Toward the end of the film, when they are preparing for their divorce, the two cannot find their marriage certificate. Often represented as emblematic of the strict state control of private life (as in Huang Jianxin's dark comedy *The Marriage Certificate* [Shei shuo wo bu zaihu; 2001]), the marriage certificate turns out to be the last bit of emotional security in a postmodern world where everything once solid melts into thin air.

Mixing various genres such as the melodrama, slapstick comedy, and the musical, Zhang Meng's new film *The Piano in a Factory* is also such a visual display of rupture and nostalgia, innovation and destruction, erasure and reconstruction of collective memories. Set in

Anshan, the central locus of China's rust belt, *The Piano in a Factory* unfolds its narrative around a divorce between Cao Guilin (played by Wang Qianyuan) and his wife. Cao Guilin is a laid-off worker who struggles to make a living by playing the accordion, an obvious indicator of the Soviet influence on his generation, in an amateur local band. His wife plunges into the sea of business in South China. After getting rich by selling fake medicine, she returns to Anshan to ask for a divorce. Fighting for his daughter's custody, Cao needs to get a piano in order to prove that he can afford a respectable life and contribute financially to his child's "quality education" (*suzhi jiaoyu*).[8] In desperation, he mobilizes his old friends, former coworkers in the steel factory, to build a piano from scratch.

This story of a single father's bitter struggle reminds one of *The Pursuit of Happyness*, a 2006 American blockbuster starring Will Smith and his son Jaden Smith. However, unlike the latter's Hollywood-style narrative of individual struggle and accumulation of private wealth, *The Piano in a Factory* emphasizes collectivist sentiments and communal bonding. The piano (*gangqin*), the fetishized marker of a global middle-class lifestyle, is reinvented by members of the former Chinese working class as a steel instrument (*gang de qin*), an anachronistic icon of utopian labor aesthetics during the heyday of Anshan's socialist industrialization.

This new revolutionary cause of making the impossible possible brings the laid-off workers back to the bankrupt steel factory. After a series of action-packed twists and turns, the mission impossible is miraculously accomplished in the postindustrial ruins of Anshan. However, the grand steel piano fails to keep the younger generation from fleeing the rust belt to seek a better future in China's sun belt, the special economic zone along the southeast coast. In the end, Cao's daughter follows her mother to the south, the new direction of massive migration in the midst of China's drastic transformation, leaving the failed father figure in post-socialist Anshan, where memories of its collective past are mourned under the camera's lingering gaze.

In all these post-socialist divorce films, the idealization of a utopian past, be it 1980s "culture fever" or the earlier socialist revolution, suggests an implied critique of China's metamorphosis into an authoritarian capitalist society. The unparalleled paradigmatic shift from high socialism to high capitalism effects epochal changes in all aspects of the social fabric of contemporary China, including the most private spheres of everyday life.

RISK SOCIETY, SECOND CHANCES

In their influential sociological work *Second Chances: Men, Women, and Children a Decade after Divorce*, Judith S. Wallerstein and Sandra Blakeslee examine the long-term effects of divorce on sixty families. According to Wallerstein and Blakeslee, a broken marriage brings emotional turmoil and profound anxieties to family members. At the same time, they suggest that divorce and remarriage can also bring the estranged couple and their children the chance to "grow emotionally, establish new competence and pride; and to strengthen intimate relationships far beyond earlier capacities."[9] Such elaboration on disruption and reconstruction of interpersonal relationships sheds new light on our understanding of divorce. However, it also runs the risk of collapsing social and economic inequalities back into the private sphere of domestic sentimentality. In the face of pervasive social uncertainty and financial pressure, for Chinese families, divorce, and remarriage, often go beyond a domestic melodrama centering on the emotional growth of husband and wife, parents and children. Rather, a second marriage often serves as the last recourse, particularly for middle-aged women with little professional expertise, to seek second chances to survive the perils and contingencies of a risk society.

Examining personal relationships and crises in the midst of the radical spatiotemporal transformation of late capitalism, Anthony Giddens and Ulrich Beck both use the concept "risk society" to characterize today's world. Beck suggests that risks in modern social life "are a *wholesale* product of industrialization, and are systematically intensified as it becomes global."[10] Concurring with Beck, Giddens defines a risk society as "a society where we increasingly live on a high technological frontier which absolutely no one completely understands and which generates a diversity of possible futures."[11] In direct contrast to the claims of the 1980s Chinese intellectual discourse of scientism, the unprecedented development of modern science and technology does not bring ultimate truth and rational progression. The consolidation of an "unstable and complex framework of scientific claims and counterclaims" (wine is toxic . . . or not, is one of Giddens's classic examples) generates more and more questions, fears, doubts, and uncertainties about all aspects of our everyday lives.[12]

Transcending the strict sense of the word in academia, the term "science" in modern social life refers to the institutionalized disciplinary knowledge and professional expertise that inform our life decisions and consumption choices as trivial as drinking red wine, using the microwave, choosing a certain brand of bottled water, or opening a bank account. "The risk society is in this sense also the *science, media and information* society."[13] Such a totalitarian restructuring of the everyday world through institutional knowledge, mass media, and human intervention causes two major transformations: "*the end of nature*" and "*the end of tradition*."[14] Under such new social conditions, people count on individual mastery of professional knowledge in place of interpersonal trust built on traditional social networks such as familial relationships and local communities to conduct everyday life and fulfill self-values.[15]

A trend similar to what Ulrich Beck calls "individualization" in a risk society can also be found in contemporary Chinese society. Seeking to catch up with the global trend of developing a knowledge economy in an information age, the neoliberal China combines "economic rationalism" and "governmental authoritarianism."[16] As a result of this unparalleled historical transformation, contemporary Chinese society has changed from a socialist country to a post-natural and post-ethical "risk society" in which "the state reforms governmental institutions to redirect responsibilities and redistribute risks to the individuals."[17] In addition to modern science and technology, uneven developments along regional, gender, ethnicity, and age lines in contemporary China exacerbate the conditions of social fragmentation and class polarization and produce a more profound sense of financial insecurity, moral uncertainty, and emotional and ethical crises. Surviving in such a risk society demands "a calculative attitude to the open possibilities of action, positive and negative, with which, as individuals and globally, we are continuously confronted in our contemporary social existence."[18]

The two divorce films discussed here engage with different aspects of this global risk society. In the first one, *The Postmodern Life of My Aunt* (Yima de hou xiandai sheng huo; 2006), a profound sense of emotional and financial insecurity in a perilous modern society is particularly intensified by the middle-aged divorced woman's chance encounters with numerous strangers in metropolitan Shanghai, which frequently disrupt and redefine familial relationships and communal space. In *Tuya's Marriage* (Tuya de hunshi; 2006), the biggest risk facing a Mongolian divorced woman and her home(land) is the desertification of the Inner Mongolian grassland, one of the grave environmental problems in the Third World.

In both films, the middle-aged divorced women, living at the margins of contemporary Chinese society, are left with limited resources and denied access to the new means of self-fulfillment in a knowledge economy. In order to explore new horizons and tame the unknown future, they struggle to calculate risks, make "free" choices, and optimize possible benefits (upward mobility, emotional fulfillment, and domestic bliss) by reorganizing gender and class relationships in their experiences of divorce and (re)marriage.

GETTING REMARRIED TO SHANGHAI

Adapted from the novel by the mainland Chinese woman writer Yan Yan, the film *The Postmodern Life of My Aunt* (2006) is directed by Ann Hui (also known as Xu Anhua), a veteran Hong Kong filmmaker. This film was well received by the public and garnered awards for Best Picture, Best Female Lead, and Best Director at various national and international film festivals. Once a prominent figure in Hong Kong New Wave cinema, Ann Hui has tried her hand at a wide range of commercial and art-house genres such as political epics, ghost stories, crime thrillers, gangster films, love stories, family melodramas, light-hearted comedies, and frantic farces. Traces of many of these genres find their way into *The Postmodern Life of My Aunt*.

This is not the first film Hui has shot in Shanghai. Her earlier works *My American Grandson* (Shanghai jiaqi; 1992) and *Eighteen Springs* (Bansheng yuan; 1997) were also set in Shanghai, in the early 1990s and the 1930s respectively. Particularly adept at capturing the lives of ordinary people, Hui, with her unique cinematic aesthetics and strong concern for social underdogs, visualizes the often-overlooked faces and niches hidden behind the glamorous facades of the urban space. In her words, Shanghai is "an extreme representation of all the fast-moving cities in the world, and the fate of all those people who cannot catch up, those who can, and the marginalized."[19]

This film both brings to the screen the devastating impact of China's neoliberalism on women[20] and goes beyond that victim narrative in reproducing a space in which a middle-aged divorced woman functions as an active agent connecting historical memories and quotidian experiences. Following the woman's perspective, Hui's moving camera maps out an alternate mode of looking, re-presenting, and remembering the often suppressed, erased, and forgotten desires, memories, voices, and faces of a disappearing local history. This gendered contemplative gaze at earlier modes of existence offers an alternative ethos of living outside the masculinized universe of instrumental rationality. Negotiating with residual legacies, the cinematic representation of the woman and the city challenge the new social order of spatial segregation and an emerging discourse of middle-class domesticity.

Ye Rutang (played by Inner Mongolian actress Siqin Gaowa), the title character of the film, was born in 1947, the same year as Ann Hui. Ye has lived through all the political movements and transitional moments in a "new China." Having benefited from the socialist campaign of women's liberation, she has received a higher education and achieved financial independence. During the Cultural Revolution, she was sent down from Shanghai to Anshan, an industrial city located on the northeast frontier (Manchuria), which just happens to be Hui's birthplace.[21] As the center of the industrial base first colonized by Japan (1932–45) and then further developed as the center of steel production during the heyday of socialist industrialization, Anshan is laden with multiple historical legacies of colonial and socialist modernities.[22]

During her Anshan years, Ye married a factory worker and had a daughter with him. In the post-Mao era, Shanghai reemerges as the center of a spatialized imaginary of global modernity, while the state-owned enterprises in Manchuria collapse under the mounting pressure of marketization and privatization. After divorcing her husband and abandoning her daughter, Ye relocates to Shanghai to seek a "second spring" in her life. Her migration is not revealed to audiences until later in the film. It is only through the retrospective narration of her daughter, Liu Dafan (played by Zhao Wei), that we find out about Ye's past. Liu's bitter recollection of her mother's abandonment, is accompanied by a flashback showing a lonely woman carrying a large suitcase, hurrying away from the camera and finally out of the frame. The socialist past from which Ye breaks away is reified as a grayish cluster of standardized Soviet-style dormitory buildings. In contrast to the gloomy cold tones of the monotonous cement buildings standing silently in Manchuria's wintry weather, Ye's crimson scarf and suitcase brighten the whole frame, externalizing her awakened hope and desire for a better tomorrow as promised by the renewed lure of post-revolutionary Shanghai.

However, her passionate pursuit of a new life is a betrayal to the family she leaves behind in Manchuria. This long shot of her escape from a socialist past is obviously taken from her daughter's and/ or husband's point of view. Full of resentment of Ye's self-centered choice, her daughter problematizes the message of hope and optimism suggested by the vibrant red color. In a sarcastic and bitter tone, Liu recollects: "When you were thrown into destitution, you married my father. As soon as it became possible to return to Shanghai, you divorced my father. To you, Shanghai is far dearer than us. . . . I still remember the day you left my father and me. Without shedding a tear, without turning back to look at us even once, you left for Shanghai so resolutely and so happily, as if going on a date [*xiangqin*]."

The metaphor of *xiangqin* eroticizes Ye's passionate relationship with the city, the ultimate object of a rekindled passion for post-socialist urban modernity. Leaving her family and youthful idealism behind in the post-socialist industrial city, Ye throws herself into the embrace of Shanghai, like many other former sent-down youths of the reform era.[23] Nonetheless, like her first marriage, inspired (or coerced) by Maoist revolutionary idealism, her second "free love" romance with post-revolutionary Shanghai does not work out either. Far from being the ideal object of her desire, Shanghai, with all its cosmopolitan allure and seemingly boundless opportunities for a better tomorrow, acts more as the agent of history that perpetually generates and regulates desires with an alienating new market rationale that Ye fails to grasp. This profound sense of estrangement prevails in this "second marriage" and is made manifest through various chance encounters with strangers as she navigates the dark corners of the urban space and different planes of individual and historical legacies.

DANGEROUS STRANGERS IN A RISK SOCIETY

Though visual and verbal reenactments of the past situate the film in a broad sociohistoric framework spanning several decades and various locations, the main section of the film is set in urban Shanghai during the first decade of the new millennium. In place of a coherent central storyline, the filmic narrative is composed of non-sequential segments of urban experience revolving around Ye's random interactions with an assortment of strangers of different class and educational backgrounds. The people she meets speak various dialects and occupy physical spaces that range from colonial-style buildings, to Soviet-style apartment complexes, to run-down Shanghai vernacular architecture, the stone-gate alleyway houses (*shikumen*) in the old section of the city, which may soon be demolished in a new round of urban renewal.

The sociology of modernity often focuses on strangers because "[t]he modern city was, concomitantly, the world as experienced by the strangers, and the experience of a world populated by strangers."[24] As metropolitan cities become physical and representational centers of a globalized network of production, exchange, and consumption, the modern monetary system exemplifies the agency of strangers in urban social life: "The desirable party for financial transactions—in which, as it has been said quite correctly, business is business—is the person completely indifferent to us, engaged neither for nor against us."[25] Thanks to its unprecedentedly high social mobility, upward and downward, metropolitan China has been described as such a "strangers' society."[26] Analogous to the segregation of urban spaces with different functions—residential, commercial, pleasure, and professional—interpersonal relationships, particularly one's constant interactions with numerous strangers, also operate within the same logic of functional efficiency, rationalization, and standardization.

In the beginning of *The Postmodern Life of My Aunt*, Ye Rutang seems to perform as a rational self-governing subject who carefully calculates the risks involved in dealing with strangers. In the opening sequence, she goes to the train station to pick up her twelve-year-old nephew, Kuankuan, who has hurt his leg in an accident. Having no access to modern telecommunications such as a cell phone, Ye has to shout out her nephew's name at the top of her lungs. Her loud voice startles an elderly man nearby who suddenly passes out. Ye's first response to this unnerving happening is "None of my business! None of my business!" uttered in the Shanghai dialect, a linguistic marker of the cultural stereotype of selfish and stingy Shanghai urbanites. Unable to tell if the sick man is a person truly in need of help or a predatory swindler, Ye chooses to protect herself from dangerous strangers and potential financial risk. Aspiring to join the emerging Shanghai middle class, she adopts risk-management strategies in order to survive in post-revolutionary Shanghai, a complicated urban world (with a huge population of 20 million and unprecedented social mobility) full of uncertainties, traps, scams, and gray areas between traditional morality and modern legality.

The following day, Ye goes to an interview for an English tutor job. She brings her nephew with her. In a sequence of bird's-eye-view shots, the moving figures of Ye and Kuankuan, the latter limping along on crutches, appear as two colorful small dots that are swallowed up by the urban tumult: crowds of pedestrians, bustling traffic, and row upon row of rooftops of residential compounds dominate the composition. Then the camera drops to eye level, following Kuankuan's point of view, cruising the streetscape, taking in vegetable vendors, the fish market, food stalls, and finally a quiet young girl sitting on the back of a tricycle and staring curiously at her surroundings. Starting with Kuankuan's exploratory gaze, the sequence comes full circle to end with the young girl's act of watching. This pattern of merging male and female spectators' visions repeats itself in other sections of the film.

Accompanied by a lively tune, a swirl of diegetic sounds, colors, and images of busy laboring figures highlights the vitality of daily life in a typical Shanghai back alley. An homage to canonical city films such as Walter Ruttman's *Berlin: Symphony of a Great City* (1927), Ann Hui's emphasis on the mundane details of the life of an ordinary community also harks back to a similar market scene in her semiautobiographical film *Song of the Exile* (Ke tu qiu hen; 1990). Connecting the domestic and the communal, Hui's representation of a dynamic street world opens up a heterogeneous space where people of different ages, genders, ethnicities, occupations, and social backgrounds come into close contact with one another.

Linking all these sporadic street shots, Ye's loud and confident voice is heard above (and in contrast to) the cacophonous background of urban life. She proudly announces to her nephew: "Taking you to my job interview is my strategy. If we can work out an acceptable contract, then I'll take the job. If not, then I'll use you as an excuse to get out of there. You know, living in Shanghai, you really need strategies to survive."[27] The gap between the disjointed visual (the aunt's trivialized figure) and the audio (her self-important and rational voice) not only creates a comical effect but also implies that her effort is doomed to failure.

As expected, Ye's "primitive" kinship-based strategy of making calculated and risk-controlling decisions does not fool her employer, who is apparently a member of the newly rich residing in a luxurious gated community. The English education experts whom he hires to monitor Ye's teaching deem her unqualified because she speaks English with a British accent when the pupil she is teaching is headed for the United States. Trying desperately to counter this linguistic-spatial hierarchy and sell her language skills to the pupil's wealthy father, Ye defends herself: "But, you know, the British accent is the classiest." The man responds scornfully: "Yes, classical Chinese is also classy. But who speaks it nowadays?"

Calling her Teacher Ye (Ye Laoshi) instead of "aunt" (ayi), the wealthy man adopts a professional attitude that establishes the lines between kinship and business, family and work. Closing the door in her face, he expels her from the exquisitely decorated and well-guarded middle-class domestic interior, a privatized space in which the younger generation acquires the cosmopolitan tastes and language skills that, it is hoped, will secure them a central place in a hierarchical global imaginary.

EVERYONE'S AUNT BEYOND THE DOMESTIC

Straddling different moral universes ranging from traditional kinship network, to residual socialist legacy, and, finally, to the post-socialist regime of entrepreneurship, Ye has failed to convert her cultural capital into economic capital. Aware of her marginal position in a new social order, she constantly reverts to an anachronistic structure of feeling shaped by "earlier modes of life" to seek a sense of self-fulfillment and emotional warmth that she cannot find in her hollowed-out domestic interior.[28] The way in which people address Ye best exemplifies this ambiguous interpersonal relationship. Kuankuan, her nephew, calls her yima, and strangers call her ayi, both of which can be translated as "aunt"—either one's mother's sister or any woman of a mother's generation.

The term "aunt' in this context indicates not a well-defined modern gender role like that of a mother or a wife situated safely in domestic interior but traditional community ethics: the whole society is viewed as a big family and an elderly woman is not just one's mother's sister but everyone's aunt, a maternal nurturing figure who provides comfort to the downtrodden and the wounded. This filmic focus on a hybridized domestic-social space inhabited by different social groups can be traced back to the cinematic tradition of visualizing a heterogeneous grassroots community in canonical Old Shanghai films such as Lights in Thousands of Families (Wanjia denghuo; 1948), Crows and Sparrows (Wuya yu maque; 1949), and The House of 72 Tenants (Qishier jia fangke; 1963). Due to its enormous popularity, the latter was remade in 1973 by the Hong Kong–based Shaw Brothers Studio and adapted for several Hong Kong stage plays. Its influence can still be found in recent Hong Kong blockbusters such as *Kung fu Hustle* (Gongfu; 2004), Stephen Chow's (also known as Zhou Xingchi) action comedy, which portrays collective resistance against gangster assaults by residents of a 1940s Shanghai slum led by a middle-aged *ayi*-turned-kung-fu-master.

Situated in such a cinematic tradition of community reimagination, the middle-aged divorced woman, who is also a failed mother *in The Postmodern Life of My Aunt*, evokes the ethical sense of "aunt." Rather than simply perform the role of everyone's aunt, or accept the status of a maternal nurturing figure positioned both inside and outside the domestic space, Ye constantly engages with strangers, attempting to maintain public order and cure the social ills that she finds in different corners of the bustling city. This sense of mission, along with her frequent evocation of her past glory of being a model worker during the socialist years, can be viewed as her critique of the new social order in which she struggles to find a position.

Ye's perceived identity as everyone's aunt, instead of an elderly woman's socially recognized gender role of wife or mother, blurs the boundaries between public and private space. Rather than an enclosed and claustrophobic middle-class domestic interior, her home in a Soviet-style apartment complex is an extension of the socialist institution of the work unit. Obviously, Ye cannot afford to purchase commodity housing given the skyrocketing cost of private housing in Shanghai. Instead, she lives in a state-subsidized apartment on a meager retirement pension, both of which are legacies of the socialist cradle-to-grave welfare system. In this tight community, a quasi-village located in the old section of the city, people develop close interpersonal relationships. The door of Ye's home is often wide open. Neighbors come and go, functioning as an intimate network of both surveillance and mutual support.

However, this neighborhood linkage becomes more and more fragile as radical social stratification starts to institutionalize a spatial hierarchy within the residential complex. Ye's neighbor Mrs. Shui (played by Lu Yan, a Hollywood veteran), empowered by her ready access to consumer culture and ability to travel overseas, feels superior to Ye. Attempting to find her place in this new spatial imaginary, Ye tells everyone that her daughter lives in Los Angeles, while in reality her impoverished family resides in China's rust belt.

Living a frugal and lonely life, with a fantasy overseas family and a household that consists of dozens of parrots and goldfish, the aunt often opens her door to neighbors and strangers. Her home provides shelter not only for her nephew Kuankuan but also to Jin Yonghua, a migrant worker who is forced to become a con artist to pay the mounting medical bills for her ailing daughter. Later, at Kuankuan's request, Ye approaches his teenage friend Feifei and plays the role of a kind *ayi*. Moreover, she brings home another stranger, Pan Zhichang, to pursue her second chance at finding interpersonal intimacy and financial security.

FAILED SECOND (LAST) CHANCE

Ye meets Pan when she is practicing tai chi swordplay in a park. Attracted by a disembodied voice singing music from the Peking opera *The Capricorn Purse* (Suolin nang), which is about remedying social injustice through cross-class sisterhood and emotional bonding, she stops her swordplay to find the source of the singing. A slow 360-degree panning shot follows Ye's point of view and then turns to zoom in on the opera performer. While Ye listens attentively to his singing, a disembodied gaze lingers on his face in a close-up shot. The performer's name, we are told later, is Pan Zhichang (played by Chow Yun-fat), a middle-aged man twice divorced (see figure 1).

Wearing a Mao suit, Pan is standing in the middle of a small community of male opera fans and instrumentalists, singing the role of the female character Xue Xiangling. Typically, this kind of point-of-view shot stands in for a male gaze, particularly in film noirs when the femme fatale appears on-screen for the first time. Here, conversely, the owner of the gaze is female and the object of desire is male. After Pan is finished singing, Ye performs as Yu Ji, a pretty warrior woman from the opera *Farewell My Concubine* (Bawang bieji), transforming herself from an observing spectator to the center of the male community's attention. As Pan and Ye switch their roles of performer and spectator, the gender of the gaze owner is also changing rather than fixed. Echoing the earlier marketplace scene with Ye and Kuankuan, the Peking opera sequence reenacts the pattern of merging male and female visions.

In her seminal article "Is the Gaze Male?" E. Ann Kaplan points out that the female bearer of the gaze is masculinized by simply reproducing the masculine role of domination.[29] The performative gender identity highlighted in this opera scene seems to transcend the binary structures of male/female, active/passive, and dominant/submissive.

Figure 1. Pan sings "The Capricorn Purse." (Source: *The Postmodern Life of My Aunt*)

Furthermore, multiple allusions to cultural archetypes make the establishment of female spectatorship even more complex and intriguing. While *The Capricorn Purse* is about female-female bonding, Ye's fascination with Pan's performance of a feminized moral fable reveals not simply sexual desire; the above-mentioned disjuncture between the disembodied gaze and Ye's point of view highlights her aural rather than visual pleasure. This emphasis on the aural alludes more to the legendary figure of the *zhiyin* than the object of visual desire in the modern cinematic apparatus. The term *zhiyin* is roughly equivalent to "soul mate." Literally, it refers to *the* one who knows how to appreciate music, alluding back to the legendary cross-class male-male friendship between the musician Yu Boya and woodchopper Zhong Ziqi in the Spring and Autumn Period (770–476 BCE).

Although audiences see later that this lyrical scene actually is the point of origin of a contrived scam, this sequence shot in bright outdoor lighting amid beautiful autumn scenery is the most memorable one in the film. It highlights Ye's heartfelt delight in finding a *zhiyin* in an alienating modern world and casts the character of Pan in a more ambiguous light: he's not just a male version of the femme fatale. In contrast to both the gray-toned domestic interior of Ye's home and the hustle and bustle of city life, the quasi-natural park serves as an emotional and aesthetic space where spiritual fulfillment, operatic fantasies, traditional morality, and a sense of community are anchored

Figure 2. Ye and Pan put on Peking Opera costumes and take pictures of each other. (Source: *The Postmodern Life of My Aunt*)

and grounded together. The operatic mode of attraction and fantasy sets the basic tone of Ye's interactions with Pan, a stranger seemingly emerging from the city's murky past.

Pan is a middle-aged man with a heavy Hong Kong accent. His talent with traditional Chinese literature and art immediately wins Ye's admiration. In the emotional climax of their romance, Ye and Pan put on Peking Opera costumes and take pictures of each other. In this scene, the operatic practice sutures the sexual fantasy in the domestic interior and the public socialization in the park. More interestingly, both don women characters' costumes and act out an ambiguous sexual fantasy playing with homosocial sisterhood and heterosexual desire at the same time (see fig. 2). Here operatic performance and cross-dressing transcend not only the boundaries between the private and the public and the traditional and the modern but also the binary structure of male versus female. In discussing Huang Shuqin's film *Woman, Demon, Human* (Ren gui qing; 1987), Haiyan Lee notes, "Theatrical cross-dressing has the potential to destabilize gender identity by introducing the thrill of imagining other, indeterminate or transgressive forms of identity and belonging."[30] This ambiguous gendered space is even more intriguing considering the fact that Chow Yun-fat is famous for playing "tough guy" characters in John Woo's gangster films, which celebrate masculine violence and brotherhood. Deprived of his guns this time, Chow is feminized through the operatic costume and performance.

Figure 3. Pan reveals his past to Ye. (Source: *The Postmodern Life of My Aunt*)

Invested in this cultural space of grassroots sociality and traditional aesthetics, their romantic relationship is, however, constantly interrupted by financial concerns. At one point, Ye stops inviting Pan over because plying him with delicacies becomes a financial burden for this elderly woman living on a meager retirement pension. Soon after that, Pan proposes a plan for investing in a cemetery, an alternative form of real estate investment popular among average urbanites bent on becoming rich overnight. Instead of playing his usual role of a loyal brother, this time the Hong Kong star seems to reenact the idealized female role in the Peking Opera *The Capricorn Purse* who provides timely financial aid to her poor working-class sister and receives a karmic reward for her moral virtues.

However, this utopian fantasy of emotional comfort and intimate sisterhood is overshadowed by Pan's strong ties with Old Shanghai, a "complicated and deceptive cosmopolitan world."[31] The divorced middle-aged man lives in a colonial-style apartment building, a far cry from Ye's Soviet-style housing complex. Walking on an overpass with Ye, he points to a newly built apartment complex with Gothic-style rooftops, saying nostalgically: "My family used to live there. Now everything is gone." Then he reveals to Ye that his mother is the second concubine of a silk merchant, a typical female icon common in fiction and films set in Republican Shanghai (see fig. 3).

Pan's nostalgic comment can be read as a critique of the fast-paced, widespread renovation of the cityscape as well as an evocation of a reincarnated Old Shanghai that is often represented as a combination of glamorous facade and subterranean sin, crime, and fraud. In addition to this highlighted diegetic connection, on an intertextual level, the star image of Chow Yun-fat is also closely associated with a collective memory of Old Shanghai. He became famous overnight in mainland China as the character Hui Man-keung (also known as Xu Wenqiang) in the Hong Kong TVB series *The Bund* (Shanghai tan; 1980). Narrated as a tale of three cities, 1930s Shanghai is portrayed as a city of gangsters, crimes, risky enterprises, and foreign power encroachments, in contrast to Beijing, the center of national politics and student movements, and Hong Kong, an escapist haven with its rural setting and idyllic lifestyle at the time.

These textual and intertextual links make Pan the perfect embodiment of the risky world of Old Shanghai. His ambiguous background contrasts with Ye's past as a socialist model worker and creates a strong sense of suspense. One day, after she follows Pan's instructions on investing in a cemetery, Ye discovers that the whole plan is a scam and that her life's savings have evaporated into thin air. Her effort has failed to create the hoped-for bright future "through the mobilizing of risk."[32] The imagined trustworthy subject in a performative sisterhood turns out to be a con artist, an embodiment of the seductive danger and financial risk of post-revolutionary Shanghai. The failed emotional and financial investment devastates Ye; it seems to be a punishment not only for the divorced woman's violation of the proper domestic order but also for her mixing of business and personal relationships that are supposed to operate in two separate spaces of urban modernity.

Unaware of this rationale of spatial segregation, Ye fails to perform as the neoliberal subject of a *homo economicus* who is supposed to adopt a "business is business" attitude in financial transactions and achieve upward mobility and financial autonomy through rational self-governance and risk calculation. As the modern world stops operating according to the cast-iron moral code of rewarding the good and punishing the bad (*shan you shan bao, e you e bao*) in an idealized Peking Opera universe, free-floating individuals often become easy prey to the affective and economic exploitation of illicit commercial transactions and capital accumulation if they fail to practice effective self-care and self-protection. In such a modern risk society, access to knowledge, instead of wealth, makes a successful entrepreneurial subject. No wonder then, that "knowledge capitalists" (*zhiben jia*) have replaced capitalists (*ziben jia*) as the most successful entrepreneurs in contemporary Chinese society. Failure to perform the new role of knowledge capitalist marks the end of Ye's second and, most probably, last chance, given her age and health.

LOVE AT LAST SIGHT/SOUND

Devastated by the fatal blow of failed emotional and financial investment, Ye loses her mobility, physical and social, in an accident. Having explored in vain her second chance with the city and the man, Ye is resigned to her fate, realizing that she has no other place to go but Anshan. Taking a taxi to the Shanghai train station where the audience first saw her, Ye sticks her head out the window for a last look at the nighttime landscape of the "sleepless city" (*buye cheng*). Drastically different from the visuals of the grassroots community shown in earlier parts of the film, this farewell sequence displays the urban splendor of Shanghai. Following Ye's point of view, the camera takes a panoramic panning shot of the street scenes, lovingly caressing the vibrant surface of the neon-lit maze of wide highways, weblike overpasses, postmodern high-rises, colorful lights, streaming cars, and huge billboards advertising international brand products in the bustling New World (Xin Tiandi) commercial district. Although Ye walked out on her first marriage without a backward glance, her "break-up" with Shanghai ends with a last lingering look at the city and carries with it a poignant yearning for and sorrow over the lost love.

Her sense of pain and loss is not relieved when she arrives home at Anshan. Instead of redemptive domestic comfort or emotional warmth, what await her are dysfunctional and alienated interpersonal (mother and daughter, husband and wife) relationships in the postindustrial ruins of the frontier city. Due to the housing shortage, Ye, her grown-up daughter, and ex-husband have to live together in a small apartment. Her ex-husband, like thousands of other factory workers, has been laid off in a round of restructuring and privatization of state-owned enterprises. Symbolically castrated by the market economy, the laid-off worker still struggles to hold on to his patriarchal power within the crumbling domestic world. Such a vulnerable father figure is reminiscent of the father Li Yaojie in Zhang Yuan's film *Erzi* (Sons; 1996) who continues to live with his wife after their divorce, covering up his aging and loss of power by exercising his residual patriarchal authority.

Figure 4. Ye sits in an open-air marketplace, staring blankly into space.
(Source: *The Postmodern Life of My Aunt*)

Eking out a meager living, Ye and her ex-husband have to get up
early every morning, even on the bitterest days of the dreary winter,
to sell cheap shoes in an open-air marketplace. Clad in an old-fashioned dark bluish coat, Ye chews her breakfast—cold steamed buns
with pickles—mechanically and almost chokes. The green colors
(train, Ye's umbrella, and skirt) of summer and the golden color (park
scenery) of fall in Shanghai are replaced by the cold tones of winter
in Anshan (run-down factory buildings, gray industrial ruins, frozen
fish for sale in the marketplace, Ye's gray hair and scarf, white snow
and ice). The film ends on this melancholic note with an anticlimactic
closing shot of Ye staring blankly into the air (see fig. 4). This uneasy
moment of indeterminacy is a tribute to the iconic freeze-frame shot
of the child "gazing out across an endless ocean, an uncertain future
ahead" at the end of François Truffaut's *The 400 Blows* (1959) and
Ann Hui's own 1982 film *Boat People* (Touben nu hai).[33]

Such a pessimistic portrayal of Ye's homecoming rewrites the postfeminist "going home" myth that regards home as the ultimate therapeutic site for ambitious career women who have been wounded
by fast-paced urban life.[34] The above-mentioned film *Cell Phone*
reproduces a binary structure of the therapeutic hometown versus
the risky metropolis. In *The Postmodern Life of My Aunt*, director
Hui subverts such a rigid dichotomy. Instead, the film demonstrates
the ways in which the market logic of commodity exchange, capital

accumulation, and coolheaded calculation penetrates every corner of contemporary Chinese society, including postindustrial Manchuria.

In such a risk society, Hui seems to suggest, the only outlet is a cross-class moral sisterhood performed in the traditional operatic mode. In the last scene of the film, sitting in the open-air market, Ye hears the faint sound of a radio broadcasting the Peking Opera *The Capricorn Purse*, which reminds her and the film's audience of Pan's performance at the chance encounter in Shanghai. The sound of the opera revives Ye's lost love and affection for Pan. Mediated through the technologized mode of acousticity, the personal memory of that moment of intimacy brings a last fleeting feeling of interpersonal warmth, which is slowly devoured by the melancholy notes of the swelling nondiegetic music composed by the internationally renowned musician Joe Hisaishi. This contrast between the emotional warmth, no matter how transient or phantasmagoric, brought by strangers in a disappearing community, and the estrangement of mother and daughter as well as husband and wife in a post-socialist nuclear family challenges the audience's concept of what proper domestic space, moral values, and gender identities truly are.

DIVORCED TO RETURN HOME

Unlike external dangers and hazards that threaten certain individuals in a preindustrial society, risks in modern society (e.g., pollution, death of forests, land expropriation, uneven development, nuclear fission and radioactivity) are "the *implicit* consequence of industrialization."[35] These man-made global problems pose "the threat of self-destruction of all life on Earth."[36] *The Postmodern Life of My Aunt* shows that such a systematic risk culture not only prevails in the metropolitan space of Shanghai but also pierces the fabric of the everyday life of a dysfunctional family on the remote frontier of postindustrial Manchuria.

Wang Quan'an's film *Tuya's Marriage*, which also features a woman's border-crossing trips through divorce and remarriage, shows the ways in which such a risk culture effects change in another frontier area of North China, the vast steppe of Inner Mongolia. Following Zhang Yimou's *Red Sorghum* (Hong gaoliang; 1987) and Xie Fei's *Women from the Lake of Scented Souls* (Xiang hun nü; 1993), *Tuya's Marriage* is the third Chinese film to win the Golden Bear Award, the highest honor given at the Berlin International Festival. Coincidentally or not, all three of these films, directed by male filmmakers of three generations, focus on the daily struggles of rural women in flawed marriages.

Wang Quan'an is a Han Chinese born in Yan'an, Shaanxi, in 1965. A 1991 graduate of the Beijing Film Academy, Wang is regarded as a prominent figure of the Sixth Generation, or Urban Generation, to use Zhang Zhen's term, the group of "young filmmakers who emerged in the shadow of both the international fame of the Fifth Generation directors and the suppressed democracy movement in 1989."[37] However, unlike other Urban Generation filmmakers such as Zhang Yuan and Lou Ye, Wang Quan'an does not limit the scope of his creative vision to the urban landscape. Rather, drawing on his personal experiences of traveling frequently across regional and national borderlines, Wang's films visualize the expanding social mobility, upward or downward, in urban and rural China. Starting with his directorial debut, *Lunar Eclipse* (Yueshi; 2000), his camera has followed the migrating female figures who try to make sense of their intimate relationships and family lives in a world in constant flux.

All the haunting motifs of Wang Quan'an's oeuvre can be found in *Tuya's Marriage*, his fourth feature film: agitated female desire and deep-seated anguish, border-crossing mobility (or the lack thereof), and strained gender and familial relationships. Set in a remote herding community in the Inner Mongolian Autonomous Region, the film bears witness to the daily ordeals of a dysfunctional Mongolian family. Bater (played by Bater), a middle-aged Mongolian shepherd, is paralyzed as a result of an accident during the digging of a well for his family. As a result, Tuya (played by Yu Nan, a Han actress), his wife and the mother of his two young children, struggles to feed their family and has to shoulder the heavy burden of household duties alone. Due to the increasing desertification of the Inner Mongolian prairie, the majority of the local herdsmen have migrated to the city. Among her daily chores, Tuya has to go a long way to fetch water every day. In addition to the strenuous task of tending a large flock of sheep, this task strains her back and finally brings her down. Suffering from a serious lumbar vertebral injury, Tuya also faces the risk of deprivation of physical (and social) mobility for the rest of her life.

Threatened by this grim vision of the future, Tuya makes an unusual decision that shocks everyone: she decides to divorce her husband in order to find a man who is willing to support her, her disabled first husband, and their two children. It is the only way she can think of to keep her family from falling to pieces. This unusual proposal for a polyandrist family structure reminds viewers of the 1988 film *A Woman for Two* (Chuntao; dir. Ling Zifeng), which was adapted from Xu Dishan's (under his pen name Luo Huasheng) story of the same title. Set in 1930s Beijing, that film also features a strong woman character, Chuntao (played by Liu Xiaoqing), who chooses to cohabit with Liu Xianggao (played by Jiang Wen) when she receives the news that her husband Li Mao (played by Cao Qianming) has been killed in the Sino-Japanese War. One day, Li Mao unexpectedly returns home, his legs having been broken by Japanese troops. Refusing to allow either man to control her fate, Chuntao struggles to maintain a precarious balance between moral ethos, emotional needs, and daily livelihood within the impoverished polyandrist family afloat in the midst of the wartime terror and turmoil.

Compared to Chuntao, Tuya is bound by less rigid ethical demands, partly due to the fact that the Mongolian community is more removed, geographically and culturally, from the center of Confucian civilization. Instead of arousing shame and a sense of guilt, Tuya's bold decision to divorce for the purpose of having a second chance gains her a reputation as a virtuous wife and consequently attracts a parade of Mongolian suitors from near and far, from rural and urban areas, who woo her with promises of wealth, spacious housing, urban residency, and a good education for her children. In the end, Tuya decides to marry Senge (played by Senge), who lives nearby, because he promises to dig a well so that the isolated small village can survive desertification. Instead of uprooting Tuya and her family, her second marriage actually situates her in her home(land) and seeks to restore affective and ethical ties among the local nomadic community.

Deviating from his previous exploration of cinematic aesthetics marked by "fission, nonlinear narrative, jostling camera movement, jump cuts, discontinuous editing, and noir-style lighting and mise-en-scène," *Tuya's Marriage* creates a semidocumentary feel with the use of a nonprofessional cast (Yu Nan is the only professional in the film), location shooting, realistic lighting, and diegetic sound.[38] The barren, harsh landscape of the diminishing Inner Mongolian grassland is presented in Bazinian long shot and deep-focus cinematography. Foregrounding the grim reality of Tuya's literally backbreaking chores and her family's everyday life in the vanishing local community, this film can hardly be categorized as a conventional "ethnic minority film" (*shaoshu minzu dianying*).

In earlier PRC cinema, ethnic minorities were usually portrayed as the exotic Other who provides visual and acoustic pleasure. In emphasizing their cultural differences, these films cast ethnic minority people as a group that is always wearing colorful costumes and "flashy ornaments" while happily singing, dancing, and engaging in romantic affairs.[39] At first glance, the Mongolian herders in *Tuya's Marriage* are exoticized and eroticized, not through the filmmaker's indulgent display of romantic songs and eroticized dances, but through an ethnographic treatment of a marital custom that is unacceptable in a society that sets the heterosexual, monogamous, nuclear family as the norm.[40] However, the filmic narrative stresses moral dilemmas and the emotional turmoil caused by uneven regional development and environmental crisis. The "reality effect" achieved through the faithful recording of everyday concerns makes the seemingly primitive matriarchal practice of polyandry more understandable for viewers.

Such a dialectic between the familiar "us" and the strange "them" can also be perceived in the soundscape and camerawork of *Tuya's Marriage*, which is also de-exoticizing yet at the same time consolidates local cultural identity. The most distinctive feature of the cinematic diegetics is that all the characters speak standard Chinese (Mandarin) with a heavy Alashan accent. While standard Chinese brings Han audiences closer to the everyday reality of the diegetic world, the distinct Alashan accent—complementary to the Mongolian "long tunes" (*changdiao*; *urtiin duu* in Mongolian), with no translation of the song lyrics is provided throughout the film—reasserts the cultural identity of the Mongolian community.[41]

In a similar manner, the deep-focus and wide-angle long shots of barren landscapes bring spectators to an unfamiliar world far from the security and comfort of everyday life at the center of urban modernity. A portrait of Genghis Khan hung in the center of a wall in Tuya's home marks the distinctive cultural and ethnic identity of the small Mongolian community. At the same time, the cinematic language marked by Bazinian realism further enhances this demystifying effect and brings to audiences, be they Mongolian or Han, domestic or overseas, "an ever-intensified engagement with the real" and makes a general comment on the risk and deep-seated anxiety that prevails in the wider world.[42]

In an interview conducted after the Golden Bear Awards ceremony, Wang Quan'an stated that the film expresses a profound sense of irretrievable loss in the wake of China's economic revolution:

> Although the film tells a story about the shepherds and the industrial-
> ization they are facing, Wang said, the situation in the film is actually
> what all of China is going through. "Perhaps this is the last glimpse
> of the herders of the Inner Mongolia region," he said. "Ultimately
> they are going to disappear into cities."[43]

Wang's distressing observation on rapid urbanization and the culture
of disappearance reminds one of Walter Benjamin's famous Angel of
History, "who is blown backward by the wind of the modern age
toward the future while facing the debris of the past."[44] Rather than
an imagined nostalgia toward a utopian past, what a backward-gaz-
ing Angel of History reveals is a shadow of doubt about the rosy
future promised by production-oriented industrial modernity. As
visualized in *Tuya's Marriage*, "the debris of the past," or the damage
done to a disappearing tradition in the name of modernization, is represented as a global threat to locally grounded masculinity.

THE PREVAILING RISK OF CASTRATION

During the culture fever of the 1980s, Fifth Generation cinematic
practices represented ethnic minority people on horseback (e.g.,
Mongolians in Tian Zhuangzhuang's 1985 film *On the Hunting
Ground* and Tibetans in his 1986 film *Horse Thief*) as embodi-
ments of hypermasculinity superior to Han men, who allegedly are
emasculated by the mainstream culture (be it party-state ideology
or Confucian tradition in the loose sense of this word). In the new
millennium, however, even the male virility of nomads is threatened
and destroyed when risk culture penetrates into the most remote
corner of modern society.

Tuya's Marriage paints a grim picture of the devastation and dissipation of the nomadic mode of life in the Mongolian community.
Its emphasis on disintegrating family ethics and community bonds is
crystallized through the visualization of an unsettled gendered spa-
tiality. Traditionally, in Mongolian herdsman communities, there is
a strict gendered division of labor, with men working outdoors and
women indoors. Furthermore, in the domestic milieu, there is stringent gender segregation of the space and household chores: "Women
should not enter the male section, usually the north-west end of the
tent, and men should not enter the women's cooking area (the south-
eastern part). . . . Men are also forbidden to sew, make beds or wash
clothes."[45]

Figure 5. Sitting in bed, Bater mechanically rocks a wooden horse that their young daughter rides. (Source: *Tuya's Marriage*)

In *Tuya's Marriage*, this strict gendered division of labor and spaces is completely overridden. The opening sequence shows Tuya riding a horse and doing a man's work--herding a flock of sheep alone against the background of barren mountains and rugged steppe. Meanwhile, Bater, her invalid husband, is confined within the domestic interior. Sitting in a corner of the *kang*, a traditional-style heatable brick bed widely used in north China, he mechanically rocks a wooden horse that their young daughter is riding (see fig. 5). This overturning of the traditional patriarchal order is further accentuated by the fact that Bater has lost his physical mobility, and, presumably, his sexual vitality, as a result of his paralysis. Like a woman or a young child, he stays at home, doing a woman's job and counting on his wife to survive in the risky modern world.

In her blog, Yu Nan, the actress who plays Tuya, reveals that the real-life situation of the amateur actor Bater resembles that of the male character he plays in the film. The actor Bater used to be a well-known horseman who always won the highest prize in horse racing and wrestling games in his hometown. Unfortunately, he fell from his horse in a race and was subsequently unable to engage in outdoor sports or do heavy manual labor.[46] Despite the apparent similarity of the actor Bater's mishap with that of the filmic character, a crucial difference is worth noting. In the film, Bater's legs were broken not in a horse race that brought him fame and glory but in an accident related to his use of dynamite to blast out a well.

This seemingly minor change is particularly meaningful, because it conditions our understanding of the nature of the risk society and its potential threat to the human body. Not a random mishap associated with a male-dominated sport, the film character's accident indicates the new pattern of risks in an industrial society that results from the scientization of everyday life. The film repeats this disastrous pattern, suggesting the risk of male castration by modern technology deployed to fight the local community's water crisis. Following in Bater's footsteps, Senge is determined to dig a well to get drinking water for people and cattle living in the area. He sells all his possessions to get a gigantic well-digging truck and hires several workers to help. However, the process stalls when they hit a thick layer of rock. Like Bater, Senge also resorts to the explosive power of dynamite to proceed.

The explosion sequence juxtaposes Tuya's laboring figure with Senge's monotonous detonations, one after another. After many failed attempts to penetrate the indestructible layer, Tuya is told that Senge was killed by a blast. She loses her usual composure, runs to the well, and hysterically screams out his name. In this chaotic scene, Wang's trademark jostling camera movements amplify the feeling of suspense and apprehension. Though it turns out that Senge is only unconscious, the false alarm suggests the possibility that he will duplicate Bater's failure to deal with modern technology. By the end the film, audiences still don't know if Senge's nearly suicidal attempt succeeds in bringing water to the community. The ambiguous ending implies that high-risk well digging and rock demolition must continue if this small Mongolian village is to hold fast to its traditional way of life in the face of escalating industrialization and desertification.

In addition to the physical castration caused by recurring incapacitating calamities, the male characters also experience emotional castration resulting from their failed marriages and collapsed families. Senge's wife abandons him for a wealthy man. To defend his honor and that of his family, the cuckolded Senge gives up herding and attempts to get rich by using modern machinery, a big truck, which, unfortunately, fails to bring him wealth and love. His obsession with modern technology and the urban lifestyle, together with his delicate physique, pale complexion, high-pitched voice, and whimsical actions, makes him look more like a Mongolian counterpart of those marginalized drifters in the urban cinema of Sixth Generation filmmakers than a stereotypically hypermasculine ethnic minority man.

Baolier (played by Baolier, who adopted the Han name Peng Hong-xiang), another Mongolian man who has lost his wife to the lure of urban modernity, is going through a similar process of emotional castration. When he was young, he went to the same middle school as Tuya. He fell in love with her but was beaten up by Bater, who was a champion horse racer at the time. After graduation, Baolier plunges into the sea of business as an oil merchant but is brought to the brink of bankruptcy when his oil wells produce nothing. Because of this, his wife divorces him. When he is about to commit suicide in despair, a sudden gusher saves his life with its abundant production of high-quality oil.

Now an oil tycoon, Baolier has enormous wealth, modern transportation (cars in place of horses or camels), scientific knowledge (suggested by his thick eyeglasses and prosperous oil business), and an urban lifestyle (his dream is to have Tuya become a full-time house-wife maintaining a blissful domestic interior in his luxury villa). Hearing about her divorce, Baolier returns to his hometown to seek Tuya's hand, to cure his homesickness and emotional trauma. However, his decision to send Bater to a modern-style nursing home puts the latter in a lonely and desperate situation. After Baolier and Tuya leave the nursing home, Bater wants to kill himself. When Senge learns of his suicide attempt, he sends Bater to the hospital and calls Tuya for help. Pretending that he is having a problem with reception on his cell phone, Baolier hangs up on Senge and conceals the whole thing from Tuya. Undeterred by his failure to get the message across via modern technology, the next day, Senge rides up on a horse, stops Baolier's car, and tells Tuya everything.

Baolier's selfish behavior violates Mongolian moral principles, which consequently drives Tuya away from him. Baolier is last seen as a lonely figure, separate from an intimate group of people composed of Tuya and Bater and their children, all sitting close together in the back of Senge's truck. Taking Tuya's and her family's point of view, the camera gradually moves away from the isolated and trivialized figure of Baolier, lingering alone, at a loss for words or direction, in the middle of the endless highway leading to the city.

Situated in such a temporal structure marked by the unavoidable recurrence of disaster, loss, and disorientation, the male characters' castration, physical or emotional, should not be regarded as a random accident that can be prevented with prudence. Rather, the modern risk culture is an inevitable outcome of a fundamental overhaul of economic, social, and ecological structures, or, more specifically in this Mongolian community, overindustrialization, uneven regional development, and degradation of natural conditions. Its locally grounded problems have a wider relevance, as the water crisis has already become a global problem that reaches beyond the Third World.[47] In other words, global connectedness manifests not only in the constant flows of transnational capital and cultural exchange but also in the form of deteriorating natural conditions and environmental problems all over the world.

THE LOCAL, THE NATURAL, AND THE MATERNAL

The high risk of male castration, physical and affective, in the modern age is softened by the cinematic representation of women as maternal figures firmly anchored in local culture and the primitive landscape. This connection between motherhood and ethnicity is made explicit by the director Wang Quan'an's selection of the shooting site. The film is based on the real-life story of a Han family living in Chengdu, Sichuan.[48] The director explained the change of location at the Berlin Film Festival:

> My mother was born in Inner Mongolia, not far from the film's location. This is why I've always liked Mongolians, their way of life and their music. When I learned about the extent to which massive industrial expansion is turning the steppe into a desert, and how local administrators are forcing the shepherds to leave their homelands, I decided to make a film that would record their lifestyle before it all disappears forever.[49]

Engaging with the tension-ridden relationship of the traditional and the modern, the filmic representation obviously favors the former, again, personified by the rural woman (e.g., Caifeng in ch. 1). Tuya, the title character, embodies a therapeutic recuperation of the disappearing motherland and its community ethics. Her maternal image is often viewed as the embodiment of the mythological figure of Mother Earth set against modern patriarchal societies.[50]

Throughout the film, viewers are privy to Tuya's frequent acts of saving the men around her. At the very beginning of the film, she saves Senge, who gets crazy drunk and falls off his motorcycle after his wife runs away with a wealthy man (see fig. 6). Tuya carries him home and rubs his chest with alcohol, treating him like a lost child.

Figure 6. Tuya saves Senge, who has drunkenly fallen off his motorcycle in response to his wife's running away with a wealthy man. (Source: *Tuya's Marriage*)

Her husband sits next to them, patting their young daughter to sleep. The following day, Senge brings three lambs to thank Tuya. However, Tuya refuses his offer of lambs and mockingly suggests that Senge sell them to get some extra money for a truck so that his wife will stay loyal to him. Though physically absent throughout the film, Senge's wife is set up as Tuya's negative foil, someone who zealously embraces the market logic of capital accumulation and commodity consumption. In contrast to this modern Mongolian woman indulging her desire for wealth and extramarital sexuality, Tuya is represented as the gendered icon of the natural (her name means "moonlight" in Mongolian) and ethical universe that resists the contamination of a post-natural and post-ethical modern society.

This self-sacrificing maternal affection reaches its apex when Tuya rides a giant camel out one evening to look for her boy Zhaya, who has gotten lost in a severe snowstorm. The moving camera follows Tuya's roaming figure as it merges with the gloomy natural background in long-shot cinematography. This scene of a lonely female figure superimposed against a natural disaster evokes cultural memories of the socialist "red classic" directed by Qian Yunda and Tang Cheng, *Heroic Little Sisters of the Grassland* (Caoyuan yingxiong xiao jiemei; 1965), which was reworked in 1975 as a ballet film, *Son and Daughter of the Grassland* (Caoyuan ernü; dir. Fu Jie). Based on a real-life story, the animated film features Longmei and Yurong, two young Mongolian girls who brave a ferocious snowstorm to protect public property—a flock of sheep that belongs to their commune. As a result, both girls are crippled due to frostbite. Rather than traumatizing them, their loss of mobility becomes the irrevocable bodily evidence of their wholehearted devotion to the revolutionary cause of constructing a socialist nation.

In this same spirit of self-sacrifice, the Mongolian woman Tuya performs the role of a protective mother in place of a revolutionary heroine. When she finally locates Zhaya, Tuya holds him tightly to her bosom, comforting him calmly: "Don't be scared. If wolf comes, Mom will eat it!" To push this emotionally charged moment a step closer to a cathartic climax, a female voice singing traditional Mongolian songs supplements the visuals of Tuya and her son returning home together, enhancing the ethereal aura of the maternal space. The acoustic and visual aestheticization of such an outlet of sublime maternal feelings neatly ties together the primitive natural environment (harsh for film characters but breathtakingly beautiful for spectators) and the ethical code of the nomadic community.

This return to the maternal and the natural is further underscored by the cinematic representation of other strong women characters in the film. For example, Bater's older sister raises six children single-handedly in the absence of a husband/father in the nuclear family. Despite her own heavy burden and dire financial situation, she insists on taking care of Bater after his divorce. In addition, a group of elderly Mongolian women who happen to pass by when Senge is wedged under his overturned truck immediately join Tuya's effort to save the unfortunate man. Patrolling the domestic or communal boundary rather than the national space, these Mongolian women change their gender role from politicized national subject to maternal figure. This trend in changing women's role corresponds to the post-socialist ideological shift that stresses individual fulfillment and domestic sentiments.

This portrayal of feminized local ethics even attaches a human face to the male-dominated modern bureaucracy. When Tuya and Bater go to the local government agency to get their divorce papers, viewers get a glimpse of the lower-level state judicial apparatus. Off center in the frame, the figure of a government official, a middle-aged man, is squeezed into the corner of a crowded room where many people are taking care of their individual business. Complementing this de-authorizing visual composition, the cadre's voice is also submerged in a cacophony of competing sounds and conversations. Bater remains silent through the whole process, while Tuya and his sister compete for his custody after the divorce. As a small space of everyday life, the court room weakens judicial authority and patriarchal power.

Impressed by Tuya's determination to remarry anyone who agrees to support Bater, the cadre helps spread the moving story about this unusual divorce case in the local community, which in turn attracts many suitors for Tuya. In this case, the divorce court becomes a link in the community ethics and moral sentiments rather than a symbol of the abstract notion of rule by law (discussed in ch. 2). The cinematic representation of a relatively easy and efficient procedure of the no-fault consensual divorce seems to indicate that state intervention is no longer as much of an obstacle as the risks of modernization in an individual's pursuit of happiness and security.

However, the sacred aura that surrounds the maternal and the local soon dissipates. Rather than reproducing the dichotomy of the traditional as an effective antidote to the post-natural and post-ethical modern world, the filmmaker relentlessly demonstrates just how fragile and problematic such an idealistic connection between the maternal and the ethical is. Playing a traditional Mongolian man's role, the masculinized female character Tuya also faces the risk of losing her ability to move freely. In this sense, the risk of male castration is transferred to the ailing woman who is equally enmeshed in the uneven development and unequal power relationships of modern society. In such a risk society, a profound sense of anxiety about the future, instead of romantic sentiments and domestic bliss, binds the man and the woman together.

By the same token, local community ethics are also more problematized than eulogized as a powerful countermeasure to risk culture. The way back to an idealized mythical past is carefully blocked. In what appears to be a conventional happy ending that affirms family values, Tuya finally agrees to marry Senge, who divorces his adulterous wife and swears to support Bater and the two young children. However, the film does not end on a "happily ever after" note after all. Instead, we see parallel editing of two fight scenes that connect the disorderly domestic and communal spaces, as well as the current moral dilemma and the unpredictable future. Inside the tent, Tuya and Senge, dressed in exquisite Mongolian wedding attire, are performing the ritual of respectfully serving wine to honored guests and family members. Sitting uneasily in the midst of the guests is Bater, looking dejected and singing a traditional Mongolian wedding song with his eyes closed. When Senge asks him to drink less for reasons of health, Bater yells at him, "Leave me alone!" The bickering between Senge and Bater leads to a brutal fight over reasserting patriarchal authority in this unconventional polyandrous marriage. If we view Bater's failed suicide as an attempt to escape from the moral dilemma, then this fight is his first violent confrontation with it.

At the same time, outside the tent, Tuya's son, Zhaya, gets into a fight with another teenage boy who has made fun of him, saying, "Now you have two fathers." Failing to stop either fight, Tuya curses furiously: "All men are bastards." Then she hurriedly walks away and hides herself in an empty tent, tears streaming down her face. Up to this point, the emotional tone of the filmic narrative has remained fairly reserved. We never see Tuya shed tears or Bater smile. Not until this concluding moment does Tuya have some alone time for a good cry, which is soon interrupted by Senge's anxious voice calling her name from offscreen. Looking in the direction of Senge's voice, Tuya covers her mouth with a trembling hand. A close-up shot of her sad face and teary eyes fades into darkness. Meanwhile, the melancholy music of the Mongolian horsehead fiddle (*morin khuur* in Mongolian) swells, ending the film on a sorrowful note (see fig. 7).

This bitter conclusion reproduces exactly the opening sequence of the film. The cyclical time frame questions the linear progressive temporality promised by a socialist construction or capitalist modernization. The excitement about and hope for a better tomorrow governed by the determinism of nature-conquering modern technology in 1980s films, such as *Wild Mountains*, *Old Well*, and many others discussed in chapter 1, are replaced by a grimmer vision of unresolvable conflicts between modern scientific positivism and a traditional way of life as shown in *Tuya's Marriage*.

Meanwhile, the melancholy ending also rewrites the cinematic tradition of celebrating the search for a home(land) in a modern society. The Fourth Generation filmmaker Xie Fei's film *A Mongolian Tale* (Ai zai caoyuan; 1995), adapted from Zhang Chengzhi's award-winning novella "The Black Steed" (Hei junma), is a representative work in this tradition, which visualizes the Mongolian grassland as "a mythical, unspoiled paradise of purity and harmony."[51] In such a paradise long lost in the postindustrial modern society, "even the patriarchal degradation of women [rape in this film] is made a virtue:

Figure 7. Tuya cries alone in a tent. (Source: *Tuya's Marriage*)

that the woman proves to be fertile is cause for celebration."[52] Deviating from this "minority cinema" tradition, the ambivalent closure of Wang Quan'an's filmic narrative questions the residual sexism persisting in local community ethics that further attests to a future of risk and uncertainty.

Wang Quan'an is not alone among the Sixth Generation filmmakers to zoom in on the moral dilemma of the maternal versus the scientific in a post-natural and post-ethical risk society. Wang Xiaoshuai's 2008 film *In Love We Trust* (Zuoyou) is also concerned with the increasing risks of disease and (state-regulated) infertility that force a middle-aged divorced woman to seek a second chance to carry out her reproductive duties. One year after Wang Quan'an received an award at Berlin, *In Love We Trust* won Wang Xiaoshuai a second Silver Bear (for best screenplay) at the fifty-eighth Berlin International Festival.

In Love We Trust, like *Tuya's Marriage*, is based on a true story that took place in Sichuan. The filmmaker changes its setting to Beijing, where a young girl's diagnosis of leukemia deals a fatal blow to her mother, Mei Zhu (played by Liu Weiwei), and stepfather, Xie Huaicai (played by Cheng Taisheng). In desperation, Mei Zhu swallows her pride and begs her ex-husband, Xiao Lu (played by Zhang Jiayi), who has also remarried, to help her conceive a sibling so that the stem cells from the newborn's umbilical cord can be used to save their sick child. This seemingly unthinkable plan compels all four adults, including Mei's current husband, and her ex-husband's second wife, Dong Fan (played by Yu Nan, who also plays Tuya in *Tuya's Marriage*), to cross a conventionally inviolable borderline. When the modern medical technology of in vitro fertilization does not work as hoped, the mother makes up her mind to revert to "natural" reproductive means--to conceive through sexual intercourse with her ex-husband.

The ethical dilemma and emotional strain are further intensified by China's national policy of family planning. If Mei conceives a baby with Xiao, then Xie's legal quota of biological children will be used up. This state-regulated fertility (or sterility) is made visible through cold-toned visual aesthetics—a gloomy picture of empty homes in a sterile modern city. Against the sterility of the modern city (the grayish color tone of the cityscape, steel and glass buildings, vacant and unfurnished apartments, fast-moving vehicles), shot with a detached but keen camera's eye, maternal instincts seem to offer the only hope for repopulating the empty domestic space. Navigating the uncharted realm beyond the accepted normality of a moral ethos and domestic sentiments, the divorced woman seeks a second chance for her child at any cost, including a second divorce. However, instead of endorsing self-sacrificing motherhood with a happy ending, the undetermined moment in a morally ambiguous ending suggests a pessimistic view of the reinvention of home/life whether through biogenetic engineering or maternal love and "natural" fertility.

CONCLUSION

The Chinese cinema of divorce is haunted by a strong sense of anxiety about estranged familial relationships and generational conflict in the midst of the "massive migration and dislocation" of post-revolutionary Chinese society.[53] Engaging with divorced women's border-crossing migration, social (im)mobility, and urban modernity, the cinema of divorce is populated by the figures of divorced women looming precariously on the edges of urban splendor.

In a hierarchical brave new world of internationalized Chinese urban centers, these middle-aged women do not enjoy the privilege of seemingly unlimited opportunities. Rather, they can perform only a parody of the cosmopolitan dream of unlimited social mobility by trading their bodies through marriage and divorce across regional borders or the rural/urban divide. Trapped in the whirlpool of diz-zying social change, however, women are not simply victims of dis-jointed gender relationships and collapsed family structure, as the conventional wisdom assumes. They often take the initiative to press for divorce in the hopes of getting a second chance to support their families and plan for the indeterminate future in the face of ferocious risk and uncertainty.

Neither film encourages us to idealize such a feminized risk-man-agement endeavor. Instead, divorce films in the new millennium bear witness to the broken marriages, failed mothers, and empty homes that can be found in every corner of today's global risk society. In this light, it is not hard to understand why a number of divorce films dis-cussed in this chapter share a similar open ending that shows a mid-dle-aged divorced woman looking blankly into an uncertain future. This suspenseful ending enhances the sense of failure and helplessness felt by the female risk subjects. Such a picture of insecurity, stagna-tion, immobility, and a hollowed-out domestic interior, along with the degradation of the health of the human body and the environ-ment, calls into question not only the meaning of the modern conjugal family but also the teleological linearity of progressive historic time.

CHAPTER SIX

A New Divorce Culture

Rupture and Reconstruction

Cultural stereotypes often assume that Chinese people have enjoyed a stable family culture with low divorce rate, given the long Confucian tradition of prioritizing the maintenance of proper domestic order, familial relationships, and ethics. This theory has been proved completely wrong by the statistical figures of China's skyrocketing divorce rate in recent years. Since China's program of economic reform, launched in 1978, the divorce rate has soared for various reasons: relaxed state control of citizens' private lives; increasing social mobility and massive dislocation; improvement of women's educational level and financial situation; and people's changing concepts of romance, marriage, and family. As Chinese society is navigating a paradigmatic shift, the escalating divorce rate illustrates the impact of such epochal changes on the most personal thread of the social fabric. Meanwhile, visual media have gained increasing popularity in rechanneling the popular desire for and imagination of new lifestyles and domestic space.

New legal codes and cultural discourses concerning divorce continue to develop, and an in-depth analysis of these most recent changes is beyond the scope of this book. The following snapshots provide a window to the ongoing family revolution in a society in transition.

The most recent judicial interpretation of marriage law makes divorce a battlefield of public opinion and cultural representation. On August 12, 2011, the Supreme People's Court (SPC) issued the third interpretation of the marriage law, putting exclusive emphasis on the economic regulation of marital relationships. Property division, particularly home ownership, is the focal point of the concomitant debate. The most hotly argued parts are Article 7, which states that the property given as a gift to one spouse by his or her parents may not be considered family property or conjugal property jointly owned by both spouses, and Article 10, which states that real estate purchased before marriage is exempt from property division upon divorce.

It is a time-honored tradition for the wife to contribute a dowry, while the husband, or his parents, contributes private housing to the joint property. After the new interpretation, many women worried that they would lose their right to the housing unit after divorce. Days after the reinterpretation was issued, "women . . . scrambled to add their names to their husbands' housing contracts." A woman wrote on her microblog (Weibo, a Chinese version of Twitter): "I want to make sure I don't end up in the street [after divorce]."[1] Meanwhile, men applauded this new judgment because it legalized their "rights" to punish those "gold diggers."

Clearly, in a market economy, the legitimacy of private property ownership outweighs the familialist consideration of protecting the rights of the disadvantaged party (normally, women, children, and seniors).[2] Now that property ownership has become a dominant concern of marital life, the younger generation has begun to negotiate new strategies to deal with the growing tension between romance and economics. The changing meanings and practices of love, marriage, and divorce can be summed up in several popular neologisms: "naked marriage" (luohun), "snail marriage" (wohun), and "AA system marriage" (AA zhi hunyin).

Luohun literally means "naked wedding" or "getting married naked." It refers to a couple who marries without spending a large amount of money on private property such as engagement rings, automobiles, and, most important, a housing unit. It is said that those who choose to get married naked need only ¥9 (approximately $1.41), the cost of a marriage certificate.[3]

A 2011 television melodrama, The Age of the Naked Wedding (Luohun shidai), registers this new social phenomenon through the story of a young couple of the post-1980s (80 hou) generation: those born after the promulgation of the notorious one-child policy. Liu Yiyang (played by Wen Zhang), the male lead, is from a working-class family, and Tong Jiaqian (played by Yao Di), the female lead, is from a middle-class family. They get married without purchasing a private home, despite Tong's parents' objection. However, this naked marriage forged out of mutual affection ends up in divorce, because the young couple's shortage of financial resources leads to everyday ordeals that hit them hard. This TV series has struck a nerve, particularly among the generation who grew up during China's reform era and have experienced insecurity and anxiety in the face of the soaring housing prices and divorce rate.

A related neologism, "snail marriage," refers to divorced couples who continue to live under the same roof because they cannot afford a second housing unit. The term is probably derived from the title of *Snail House* (Woju), a 2009 prime-time megahit centered on the emerging urban middle-class and their "Chinese dream" of owning private housing in big cities. This TV drama also popularized the term "house slaves" (*fangnu*), which refers to aspiring urban professionals who are caught in financial crises caused by the radical marketization of private housing.

Members of their parents' generation practiced snail marriage, as depicted in Zhang Yuan's 1996 film *Sons* and Ann Hui's 2006 film *The Postmodern Life of My Aunt* (discussed in ch. 5). A 2010 film, *Ma Wen's Battle* (Ma Wen de zhanzheng), shows the increasing pressure of skyrocketing housing costs on the younger generation. Adapted from Ye Zhaoyan's novella of the same title, *Ma Wen's Battle* is directed by the Seventh Generation filmmaker Chang Zheng. Ma Wen (played by Cheng Taisheng), the eponymous protagonist, is a laid-off worker. For financial reasons, he has to live with his ex-wife, Yang Xin (played by Jiang Hongbo), and her current husband. This unconventional domestic arrangement results in a series of comical twists and farcical confrontations. Throughout the film, the constant tight framing of a claustrophobic interior space captures the emotional alienation of a generation struggling to find domestic bliss and emotional fulfillment in the midst of a dizzying social transformation.

AA System Marriage is the title of a popular novel first circulated online and then adapted into a TV serial in 2012. The Chinese term, which literally means "All Average system," refers to "splitting the bill equally" or "going Dutch." In an AA system marriage, the husband and wife split all their daily expenses and pay equal shares for everything.

The TV series *AA System Marriage* shows a new way of organizing and managing a family economy. In this show, the young couples of the post-1980 generation sign and implement a contract in which they agree to equally divide the household expenses. The core idea, that even in a marriage everyone is a free individual whose autonomy is guaranteed by his or her private property rights, reveals the direct impact the 2011 judicial interpretation of the marriage law had on Chinese people's understanding of conjugality and individuality.

The sweeping popularity of a new gadget called a "divorce calculator" (*lihun jisuan qi*) testifies to the increasing importance of financial concerns and rational calculations in intimate relationships in the domestic site. Invented by the Consumer Financial Education Body, a British government agency, this calculator can be used online and, more important, anonymously. One may calculate the financial costs of a divorce (alimony, child support, property settlement, litigation fees, and so on) by entering the financial information (stipends, pensions, savings account interests, mortgage, insurance premiums, and so on) of both spouses.[4]

Seemingly an antidote to this prevailing trend of individualizing and economizing one's marital life, a counterbalancing cultural imagination tends to return the calculating *homo economicus* in a "negotiated family" to a close-knit network of mutual support, moral bonds, and domestic affection.[5] Even more intriguingly, the meaning of domesticity goes beyond the definition of modern nuclear family that has been held as *the* new ideal of home since the May Fourth generation. Rather, it reverts back to the anachronistic model of the traditional extended family and communal bonding. Some well-received TV dramas, including *Let's Dance* (Buru tiaowu; 2010), *Old Maid Gets Married* (Danü dangjia; 2010), and *Li Chuntian's Springtime* (Li Chuntian de chuntian; 2011), portray how multiple generations of an extended family, particularly grandparents, and different social groups in a neighborhood play the essential role of providing a peaceful haven for divorcees who return to their natal homes or local communities in search of financial security and emotional comfort.

Sometimes life imitates art. In 2011, a fifty-seven-year-old woman in Taiyuan, Shanxi, divorced her adulterous husband. She held a grand divorce ceremony, obviously a real-life reenactment of the comical scene in Feng Xiaogang's film *If You Are the One II* (Feicheng wurao 2; 2010). After the sensational ritual, the divorcee's children and brothers accompanied her on a triumphant walk from her conjugal home to her natal home.[6]

Therefore, I coin the term "kinship individualism" to describe this unexpected turn to a revitalization of kinship network and community ethics in cultural representations and everyday practices.

Seemingly an oxymoron, it highlights the improbably close connections between social formations that are conventionally deemed contradictory, that is, kinship and individuality. Rather than constraining individual freedom, the kinship network offers financial, moral, and emotional support for the expression and performance of a person's individuality, particularly his or her freedom to choose to end an unhappy marriage. Of course, the growing dependence of individuals on their kinship network risks the "re-feudalization" (*zai fengjian hua*) of marriage and divorce practices.[7] In other words, while offering more financial resources and moral support, the older generation in a tight kinship-based community will also exert more decisive influence on the younger's generation's life choices, including those involving marriage and divorce. Parents' opinions have played an increasingly dominant role in the divorce decisions of post-1980s generation youths.[8] This is caused by the stronger parent-child bonding resulting from the one-child policy and the younger generation's increasing financial dependence on the older generation for private housing purchases, wedding costs, and childcare duties in an age of global recession.

Shedding new light on the dialectics of the collective and the individual, and the traditional and the revolutionary, these new social phenomena continue the story of the new divorce culture told in the previous chapters of this book. This new divorce culture, along with unprecedented social mobility and massive dislocation, a global middle-class culture, the privatization of property ownership, and the dismantling of the socialist state welfare system, contributes to the ongoing family revolution in post-revolutionary China.

In a post-revolutionary age, family revolution is made possible not through Maoist class struggle or socialist revolution, including the marriage reform campaign and women's liberation. Rather, it is more a result of economic marketization and the fundamental restructuring of social relationships and institutional environments. Family revolution refers to an overhaul of the family structure, marital practices, and gender relationships—namely, the drastic transformation of home from an extension of socialist work units during the Mao era to a privatized physical space and economic partnership defined and regulated by the new legal and cultural codes, going along with the paradigmatic shift of post-revolutionary China's evolution from high socialism to high capitalism.

This paradigmatic shift, particularly the relaxation of state control in the domestic realm, promises more individual agency and a greater degree of freedom as well as more social tolerance for divorce. However, it would be naive to see the situation as a simple black-and-white case of the oppressive state versus the free individual. Rather, an array of complex historic conditions affect the ongoing family revolution, which is also a subjectivizing project, disseminating new notions of domestic culture and reproducing new gender and class positions. Therefore, overemphasizing the private and autonomous nature of the domestic interior and its naturalized association with women's affective and reproductive labor obscures the fact that family is a historically situated and ideologically mediated social institution with multiple links to other sociopolitical institutions.

The formation of a new domestic culture and affective economy—defined in terms of a spatial segregation of public and private, individual autonomy in life choices and commodity consumption, naturalized reproductive sexuality and gendered division of labor—has led to the exclusion of the question of women from public discussions and intellectuals' concerns. In the face of "the crisis of home," women are often said to be responsible for failed marriages due to their lack of the proper gendered qualities. While domesticated femininity becomes a sign of exchange value in male-centered family ethics, the labor, stress, and structural inequality and exploitation behind it are often brushed aside as a matter of personal privacy. On the one hand, the rising trend of "affective individualism" in post-revolutionary China tends to emphasize an increasing awareness of self-interest, individualized identity, and "a growing recognition of the individual's right to pursue his or her own goals."[9] On the other hand, as a result of the dismantling of the social welfare system, the maintenance and reproduction of a stable domestic order depends on vast investments of time, energy, money, and labor from conjugal partners, particularly women, often at the expense of their own educational, professional, and emotional fulfillment.

The lack of a critical examination of this fundamental contradiction—unequal distribution of socioeconomic resources, hierarchical division of labor, and women's conflicting public and private roles in marital life—leads to the privatization of gender-related problems. It is not surprising that the story of marital strife is retold in mainstream cultural production as a personal (particularly a woman's) problem while its sociopolitical underpinnings are often dismissed.

Instead, the allegory of free market competition of gendered bodies and sexualized femininities is brought in to redesign the domestic order. Hence, the central question of this book is, exactly how free is free marriage/divorce when a life situation is contingent on a person's position in a "free" market economy, an economy that is already embedded in the unequal division of labor along regional, gender, class, age, and ethnic lines?

This new divorce culture does not simply mean an ideological rupture with the past, just as divorce does not necessarily mean a complete severance of all past emotional and ethical ties. Repressed historical memories, anachronistic ethical codes, and structures of feeling frequently come back to haunt the domestic interior. These specters of history are often embodied by middle-aged divorcees who have experienced China's radical transition from high socialism to high capitalism. Their contending voices and nostalgic gazes open up a critical public space for cultural reflections and political engagement in multiple ways, indicating a new course of "de-unifying and de-simplifying our image of the past."[10] Meanwhile, some de-revolutionizing trends such as the return of conservative family ethics sanctioned by the official "harmonious society" rhetoric can also be found in this extensive family transformation and popular cultural imagination. All these earlier modes of life call into question the dominant discourse of developmentalism, manifested in various forms of progressive scientific and legalistic modernity, economic advancement, evolutionary masculinity, and middle-class wifely quality in the genres of divorce narrative discussed throughout this book.

Exposing the fissures, conflicts, wounds, and traumas that destabilize the boundaries of a privatized domestic interior, divorce in post-revolutionary China is a highly contested locus at which different narratives and rhetoric come into play, negotiating and competing with each other to constantly rewrite our knowledge of gender, class, and family. As a result, family revolution is an ongoing project, characterized by the dialectic of rupture and reconstruction and the interface of sentimentality, morality, and legality, generating a more complex and fluid relationship between individual, family, society, and market-state in post-revolutionary China.

Not until the 1990s did mainstream Chinese visual culture, particularly TV dramas, become less concerned with social change and public events and begin to focus more on private matters and domestic affairs.[1] This recent trend is the result of a global emphasis on visuality and the relaxation of governmental control of cultural production. Literary works that connect marital strife to grand intellectual discourses have gradually lost their mass appeal.

Given the huge amount of domestic melodramas produced in the past two decades, this list cannot claim to be exhaustive. One dominant trend worth noting is that the settings of the majority of these popular series are urban and sometimes foreign environments.

Release Date	Title	Director	Setting
1990	*Yearning* (Kewang)	Lu Xiaowei	Urban
1992	*Indisputable Love* (Aini mei shangliang)	Zhang Yu	Urban
1992	*Beauties against Wind and Rain* (Fengyu liren)	Zhang Jingbin	Urban
1992	*Craving for Love* (Guoba yin)	Zhao Baogang	Urban
1993	*Beijing Natives in New York* (Beijing ren zai Niuyue)	Zheng Xiaolong and Feng Xiaogang	Foreign
1995	*Foreign Babes in Beijing* (Yangniu zai Beijing)	Li Jianxin	Urban
1995	*Sun and Rain* (Dongbian richu xibian yu)	Zhao Baogang	Urban

Release Date	Title	Director	Setting
1995	*Autumn Stories in Beijing* (Beijing shenqiu de gushi)	Teng Wenji	Urban
1999	*Divorce* (Lihun)	Ma Junxiang	Urban (Republican Beijing)
1999	*Year after Year* (Yinian you yinian)	An Zhanjun and Zheng Xiaolong	Urban
1999	*Holding Hands* (Qianshou)	Yang Yang	Urban
2000	*Dangerous Passion* (Weixian zhenqing)	Liu Erwei	Urban
2000	*Divorce Reports* (Lihun qishi lu)	Jiang Junge	Urban
2000	*Deadly Encounter* (Zhiming xiehou)	Ding Hei	Urban
2001	*Love Rules* (Rang ai zuozhu)	Zhang Jiandong	Urban
2001	*How Far Is Forever* (Yongyuan you duoyuan)	Chen Weiming	Urban
2002	*Empty Mirror* (Kong jingzi)	Yang Yazhou	Urban
2002	*Married for Ten Years* (Jiehun shinian)	Gao Xixi	Urban
2003	*Romantic Stories* (Langman de shi)	Yang Yazhou	Urban
2003	*So Long, Vancouver* (Biele, Wengehua)	Zhao Baogang	Foreign
2003	*Don't Touch My Drawer* (Biedong wo de chouti)	Li Tong	Urban
2004	*Tree of Familial Feelings* (Qinqing shu)	Xia Gang	Urban
2004	*Chinese-Style Divorce* (Zhongguoshi liyun)	Shen Yan	Urban
2004	*Women behind Women* (Nüren beihou de nüren)	Jiang Junge	Urban
2004	*Yesterday Once More* (Haitang yiju)	Huang Jianzhong	Urban
2004	*Empty Home* (Kong fangzi)	Chen Guoxing	Urban

Release Date	Title	Director	Setting
2004	*The Enemy of Marriage* (Hunyin de diren)	Qin Pingyuan	Urban
2004	*Loved Me, Release Me* (Ai guo wo, fang le wo)	Sun Hao	Urban
2005	*The Present Tense of Divorce* (Lihun jinxing shi)	Xu Zongzheng	Urban
2005	*Divorce Lawsuits* (Lihun guansi)	Zhang Yuanlong and Chu Xiaomei	Urban
2005	*Divorced Women* (Lihun nüren)	Zeng Lizhen	Urban
2005	*Happy as a Flower* (Xingfu xiang hua'r yiyang)	Gao Xixi	Army
2005	*Halfway Couples* (Banlu fuqi)	Liu Huining	Urban
2005	*Love and the City* (Haoxiang haoxiang tan lian'ai)	Liu Xingang	Urban
2005	*Ma Dashuai II*	Zhao Benshan	Urban
2006	*Chinese Mother* (Zhongguo muqin)	Jing Quan	Small town
2006	*Let's Get Remarried* (Women fuhun ba)	Peng Fu	Urban
2006	*Mid-life Plans* (Zhongnian jihua)	Chen Wujian	Urban
2006	*Cannot Live without You* (Buneng shiqu ni)	Zhang Fanfan	Urban
2007	*Dear Brothers* (Qinxiong redi)	Huang Lijia	Urban
2007	*Between Wife and Mother* (Shuangmian jiao)	Teng Huatao	Urban
2007	*Dream Links* (Youjian yilian youmeng)	Zeng Lizhen and Mai Dajie	Urban
2007	*Golden Anniversary* (Jinhun)	Zheng Xiaolong	Urban
2007	*Struggle* (Fendou)	Zhao Baogang and Wang Ying	Urban
2008	*Uxorilocal Son-in-Law* (Shangmen nüxu)	Zhang Xiaochun	Rural
2008	*Ma Wen's Battle* (Ma Wen de zhanzheng)	Yu Chun	Urban

Release Date	Title	Director	Setting
2008	*Blind Romance* (Sanqi zhuangshang ershiyi)	Ma Xiaogang	Urban
2009	*Who Calls the Shots of My Youth?* (Wode qingchun shei zuozhu)	Zhao Baogang and Wang Ying	Urban
2009	*Nanny Mom* (Baomu mama)	Liu Xin	Urban
2009	*Daughter-in-Law's Happy Age* (Xifu de meihao shidai)	Liu Jiang	Urban
2009	*Our 1980s II—Plunging into the Sea* (Women de bashi niandai II—Xiahai)	Wang Yichi	Urban
2009	*Big Life* (Da shenghuo)	Huang Lijia	Urban
2009	*At Middle Age* (Rendao zhongnian)	Dou Qi	Urban
2010	*Old Maids Should Get Married* (Danü dangjia)	Sun Hao	Urban
2010	*Let's Dance* (Buru tiaowu)	Luo Chang'an	Urban
2010	*Marriage Battle* (Hunyin baowei zhan)	Zhao Baogang	Urban
2010	*My Ex-wife's Train Station* (Qianqi de chezhe)	Dou Qi	Urban
2010	*Cell Phone* (Shouji)	Shen Yan and Wang Lei	Urban and rural
2010	*Naked Wedding* (Luohun)	Wang Xiaokang	Urban
2010	*Remarry* (Fuhun)	Dong Zhiqiang	Urban
2010	*Country Love Stories* (Xiangcun aiqing gushi)	Zhao Benshan and Xu Zhengchao	Rural

This list cannot claim to be exhaustive, since almost every recent film about urban China touches on the issues of divorce, infidelity, and marital strife. Similar to television representations, the majority of these divorce films are set in an urban milieu.

Release Date	Title	Director	Setting
2000	*Breaking the Silence* (Piaoliang mama)	Sun Zhou	Urban
2000	*Happy Times* (Xingfu shiguang)	Zhang Yimou	Urban
2000	*A Sigh* (Yisheng tanxi)	Feng Xiaogang	Urban
2001	*Beijing Bicycle* (Shiqi sui de danche)	Wang Xiaoshuai	Urban
2001	*Lan Yu*	Stanley Kwan (aka Guan Jinpeng)	Urban
2001	*Fish and Elephant* (Jinnian xiatian)	Li Yu	Urban
2001	*I Love Beijing* (Xiari nuan yangyang)	Ning Ying	Urban
2002	*Shanghai Women* (Jiazhuang mei ganjue)	Peng Xiaolian	Urban
2003	*Ma Shiqing Gets a Divorce* (Ma Shiqing lihun)	Pan Jingchen	Urban
2003	*I Love You* (Wo ai ni)	Zhang Yuan	Urban

Release Date	Title	Director	Setting
2003	*Cell Phone* (Shouji)	Feng Xiaogang	Urban
2004	*The Parking Attendant in July* (Kanche ren de qiyue)	An Zhanjun	Urban
2004	*Jasmine Women* (Moli huakai)	Hou Yong	Urban
2005	*Eat Hot Tofu Slowly* (Xinji chi bu liao re doufu)	Feng Gong	Urban
2005	*Dam Street* (Hongyan)	Li Yu	Small town
2005	*Sunflower* (Xiangrikui)	Zhang Yang	Urban
2006	*Still Life* (Sanxia haoren)	Jia Zhangke	Small town
2006	*Never Ever Say "I Love You"* (Dasi bushuo wo ai ni)	Fang Gangliang	Urban
2006	*Tuya's Marriage* (Tuya de hunshi)	Wang Quan'an	Rural/ ethnic
2006	*The Postmodern Life of My Aunt* (Yima de hou xiandai shenghuo)	Ann Hui (aka Xu Anhua)	Urban
2007	*Home Run* (Huijia de lu)	Fang Gangliang	Urban
2007	*Call for Love* (Aiqing hujiao zhuanyi)	Zhang Jianya	Urban
2007	*Lost in Beijing* (Pingguo)	Li Yu	Urban
2007	*The Other Half* (Ling yiban)	Ying Liang	Small town
2008	*24 City* (Ershi si cheng ji)	Jia Zhangke	Urban
2008	*In Love We Trust* (Zuoyou)	Wang Xiaoshuai	Urban
2009	*My Ex-Wife* (Qianqi)	Qiao Liang	Urban
2010	*Ma Wen's Battle* (Ma Wen de zhanzheng)	Chang Zheng	Urban
2010	*Apart Together* (Tuanyuan)	Wang Quan'an	Urban
2010	*If You Are the One II* (Feicheng wurao 2)	Feng Xiaogang	Urban
2010	*The Piano in a Factory* (Gang de qin)	Zhang Meng	Urban
2010	*Love Repair Station* (Aiqing weixiu zhan)	Wang Ning	Urban
2010	*Driverless* (Wuren jiashi)	Zhang Yang	Urban

All translations are the author's, unless otherwise indicated.

INTRODUCTION

1. Wang and Di, "1.61 Million Couples Break Up in 2004," 2.
2. Wang and Chen, "Divorce Rate Rises for Seven Straight Years in China," http://english.people.com.cn/90882/8134709.html (accessed September 2, 2013).
3. Ministry of Civil Affairs, *Minzheng bu fabu 2010 nian shehui fuwu fazhan tongji baogao*, http://www.mca.gov.cn/article/zwgk/mzyw/201106/20110600161364.shtml (accessed October 2, 2011).
4. Chen Huafei. "Pandian Zhongguo lihunlü zuigao de shida chengshi," http://health.people.com.cn/GB/14740/106977/10120416.html (accessed September 2, 2013).
5. Maureen Fan, "Chinese Slough Off Old Barriers," A01. For a comprehensive statistical report on the married and divorced populations from 1980 to 2007 in Shanghai, see Shanghai tongji ju, *Shanghai tongji nianjian 2008*, 43.
6. Faison, "In China, Rapid Social Changes Bring a Surge in the Divorce Rate," http://www.nytimes.com/1995/08/22/world/in-china-rapid-social-changes-bring-a-surge-in-the-divorce-rate.html?pagewanted=all&src=pm (accessed August 17, 2003).
7. Xia Yinlan, "Zhongguo shi lihun zui ziyou de guojia," http://news.sina.com.cn/c/sd/2009-07-07/140718171866_4.shtml (accessed May 27, 2010).
8. Sun, "Zhongguo shi lihun zui ziyou"; Lü, "'Lihun nan' neng jiang lihun lü ma?" A05.
9. Morley, *Home Territories*, 29.
10. The use of the term "middle class" in contemporary Chinese society has been greatly contested. Even the translation of the term has not yet been fixed. Instead of *zhongchan jieji*, a politicized social segment that seems to suggest an explicit connection with the Maoist ideology of class struggle, "middle class" has often been translated as *zhongchan jieceng* or *zhongjian jieceng*, referring to the social group of well-educated affluent

urbanites sharing a certain capacity and taste for commodity consumption. A number of prominent sociologists such as Zhou Xiaohong and Lu Xueyi have investigated the demographic constitution of the Chinese middle class. Some intend to define the great contribution of a stable and affluent middle class to the building of a "harmonious society." See Zhou Xiaohong, *Zhongguo zhongchan jieceng diaocha*; Lu Xueyi, *Dangdai zhongguo shehui jieceng yanjiu baogao*; Zhu Yaoqun, *Zhongchan jieceng yu hexie shehui*. Rather than establishing the clear-cut boundaries of the Chinese middle class through the use of standardized survey questionnaires or statistical numbers, in this book I am more inclined to examine the imagination, identification, and circulation of a middle-class domestic culture in cultural representations. As Charles Seller has aptly put it, "The so-called middle class was constituted not by modes and relations of production but by ideology" (*The Market Revolution*, 237).

11. Xu Anqi, "Lihun yu nüxing diwei ji quanyi zhi tantao," 199.

12. Wong, "Family Reform through Divorce Law in the PRC"; and Diamant, *Revolutionizing the Family*, 317.

13. The seven conditions include a wife's barrenness, wanton conduct, neglect of her husband's parents, loquacity, theft, jealousy, and chronic illness. However, a wife could not be expelled under three conditions (*san buqu*): if she observed three years of mourning for her parents-in-law, if she had no natal family to return to, and if she had gone through adversity with her husband (from rags to riches). The wife could request a divorce if her husband deserted her for more than three years or if she was abused by her husband. See Wong, "Family Reform through Divorce Law in the PRC," 269; Philip Huang, "Women's Choices under the Law," 12; and Bernhardt, "Women and the Law," 189.

14. Haiyan Lee, *Revolution of the Heart*, 95–96.

15. She, "Toward Ideology."

16. Zhang Xipo, *Zhongguo hunyin lifa shi*, 74.

17. Ibid., 77.

18. Lao She, *Lihun*. The passage is quoted from *The Quest for Love of Lao Lee*, trans. Helena Kuo, 52. Mr. Li is transliterated as Lao Lee in this edition.

19. Foucault, *The History of Sexuality*, vol. 1, 4–5.

20. Larson, *From A Q to Lei Feng*, 1.

21. Haiping Yan, *Chinese Women Writers and the Feminist Imagination*, 17.

22. Ibid., 16.

23. Leo Lee, *The Romantic Generation of Modern Chinese Writers*.

24. Haiping Yan, *Chinese Women Writers and the Feminist Imagination*, 15. Recently, a biography of Zhu An—Lu Xun's first wife from an arranged marriage, who was illiterate, short, and had bound feet—was published. See Qiao, *Wo ye shi Lu Xun de yiwu*.

25. When Eileen Chang was a young child, her mother, a pioneering figure of the modern new woman, divorced her father. It is hard to gauge to what extent the fictional divorce case is based on her mother's experience.

But it is quite safe to conclude that Chang is sensitive to the particular social issue of divorce and what it meant for Chinese women at that transitional moment. In 1947, Chang divorced her first husband, Hu Lancheng, due to his infidelity.

26. Haiyan Lee, *Revolution of the Heart*, 134.

27. "Stale Mates" was written in English and published in *The Reporter*, September 12, 1956. Chang published the Chinese-language version in *Wenxue zazhi*, January 20, 1957.

28. Nicole Huang, *Women, War, Domesticity*, 38.

29. Tonglin Lu, *Misogyny, Cultural Nihilism, and Oppositional Politics*, 12.

30. For more details about the Shaanxi-Gansu-Ningxia Border Region marriage law and rural women's agency in this political campaign, see Cong, "Zuo Run su Wang Yinsuo."

31. See Wong, "Family Reform through Divorce Law in the PRC"; and Bernhardt, "Women and the Law."

32. Philip Huang, "Women's Choices under the Law," 33; Wong, "Family Reform through Divorce Law in the PRC," 273; and Diamant, *Revolutionizing the Family*.

33. Xia Yinlan, "Zhongguo shi lihun zui ziyou de guojia," http://news.sina.com.cn/c/sd/2009-07-07/140718171866_4.shtml (accessed May 27, 2010).

34. Yeh, "The Paradox of Autonomy," 42

35. Fu, "The New Marriage Law of People's China," 122.

36. Meijer, "Marriage Law and Policy in the People's Republic of China," 437.

37. Alford and Shen, "Have You Eaten? Have You Divorced?" 238.

38. Philip Huang, "Women's Choices under the Law," 33.

39. *Beijing Review*, September 12, 1983. Quoted in Davis and Harrell, introduction to *Chinese Families in the Post-Mao Era*, 5.

40. Wong, "Family Reform through Divorce Law in the PRC," 275.

41. See Diamant, *Revolutionizing the Family*, particularly the introduction.

42. See Andors, *Unfinished Liberation of Chinese Women*; Stacey, *Patriarchy and Socialist Revolution in China*; and Wolf, *Revolution Postponed*.

43. Zhao Shuli composed the story to popularize the idea of "family reform" endorsed by the New Marriage Law. "Dengji" was first published in *Shuoshuo changchang*, a monthly devoted to folk arts and performance. Zhao subsequently made some revisions, and the story was republished as a small pamphlet by Gongren chubanshe in Beijing.

44. Another well-known work promoting the new marriage law is *Liu Qiao'er* (1956), which was based on a matrimonial dispute mediated by Ma Xiwu (1898–1962) in 1943 in the Shaanxi-Gansu-Ningxia Border Region (Shaan-Gan-Ning Bianqu) and later adapted as various local operas. In this 1956 film, the new state ideology not only endorses women's right to marital freedom but also incorporates the political discourse of class struggle into the formation of new forms and meanings of marriage and family. For a

more detailed analysis of the transformation of the legal case into a series of popular cultural products, see Wu Xueshan, "Suzao hunyin."

45. McDougall and Louie, *The Literature of China in the Twentieth Century*, 222.

46. Foucault, "The Repressive Hypothesis," 313.

47. Fang Ji's story was first published in *Renmin wenxue* (1950: 3). For more details concerning the controversy over the story, see Hang, "*People's Literature* and the Construction of a New Chinese Literary Tradition," 102.

48. Ban Wang, *The Sublime Figure of History*, 134.

49. Diamant, *Revolutionizing the Family*, 290.

50. Thanks to an anonymous reviewer for bringing this film to my attention.

51. Jianmei Liu, *Revolution Plus Love*, 185.

52. For a more comprehensive discussion of the changing idea of work, see Entwisle and Henderson, *Re-drawing Boundaries: Work, Households, and Gender in China*, particularly part 1, "Perspectives on Work."

53. Tsou Tang, *The Cultural Revolution and Post-Mao Reforms*, 145.

54. Zhonghua renmin gongheguo zuigao renmin fayuan, *Sifa jieshi quanji*, 1086. Quoted in Philip Huang, "Divorce Law Practices and the Origins, Myths, and Realities of Judicial 'Mediation' in China," 156.

55. Zhonghua renmin gongheguo zuigao renmin fayuan, *Sifa jieshi quanji*, 1086. Quoted in Philip Huang, "Divorce Law Practices and the Origins, Myths, and Realities of Judicial 'Mediation' in China," 156.

56. Benjamin, *The Arcades Project*, 20.

57. Armstrong, *Desire and Domestic Fiction*; and Brown, *Domestic Individualism*.

58. Cott, *The Bonds of Womanhood*, xviii.

59. Quoted in Xiaobing Tang, *Chinese Modern*, 302.

60. Ibid., 304.

61. Ibid., 306.

62. Ibid., 308.

63. Rofel, *Desiring China*, 3.

64. Read, "Property Rights and Homeowner Activism in New Neighborhoods," 41.

65. See Li Zhang, *In Search of Paradise*, particularly ch. 4.

66. Zhang and Ong, introduction to *Privatizing China*, 2.

67. Yunxiang Yan, *The Individualization of Chinese Society*, 288.

68. Ibid., 289.

69. Hu Fayun, *Di sidai nüxing*, 55.

70. Ibid., 54.

71. Lauretis, "Aesthetic and Feminist Theory," 167.

72. For an in-depth study of China's turn to consumerism as the essential means of boosting the domestic economy, see Yunxiang Yan, "The Politics of Consumerism" in *The Individualization of Chinese Society*. Also see Myers, "China's Consumer Revolution."

73. Zhen Zhang, "Mediating Time," 94.

74. Thanks to Lin Danya for bringing this point to my attention.

75. Nicole Huang. *Women, War, Domesticity*, 42.

76. Ding Ling's most controversial essay, "Sanba jie yougan" (My thoughts on March 8), published March 9, 1942, highlights this problem and exposes the cultural and political stigma attached to divorced women in Yan'an, the revolutionary base of the Chinese Communist Party (1936-1948).

77. Jieyu Liu, *Gender and Work in Urban China*, 143–44.

78. Negra, *What a Girl Wants?* 4.

79. Lock, *Encounters with Aging*, 366.

80. Negra, *What a Girl Wants?* 4.

81. Negra, *What a Girl Wants?*

82. Xueping Zhong, "Hou funü jiefang yu ziwo xiangxiang." In her book *Mainstream Culture Refocused*, Zhong defines the "post-women's-liberation age" as "the post-Mao era (1976 to the present) with a focus on changes in women's and gender issues" (125).

83. Hai Ren, "The Neoliberal State and Risk Society," 105.

CHAPTER ONE

1. Xudong Zhang, *Chinese Modernism in the Era of Reforms*, 13.

2. For a dynamic scholarly conversation centering on 1980s intellectuals' great debate concerning Enlightenment and scientific knowledge, see Barlow, "Zhishifenzi [Chinese Intellectuals] and Power"; Xiaomei Chen, *Occidentalism*; Jing Wang, *High Culture Fever*; Wang Hui, "Contemporary Chinese Thought and the Question of Modernity"; and He Guimei, *"Xin qimeng" zhishi dang'an*.

3. For a comprehensive analysis of "scientific policymaking" in the 1980s, see Greenhalgh, *Just One Child*.

4. Jing Wang, *High Culture Fever*, 89.

5. Louie, "Love Stories," 68.

6. Andreas, *Rise of the Red Engineers*, 258.

7. Greenhalgh's book *Just One Child*, particularly its introduction, offers an in-depth discussion of the radical transition from the Maoist party policy formulated mainly on ideological grounds to Dengist "scientific policymaking."

8. Alvin Toffler was so influential in China that articles about his works even appeared on Chinese government websites such as the official website of the Chinese embassy in the United States and the premier CCP news portal *Renmin ribao*, www.people.com.cn. See Damm and Thomas, "Introduction: Chinese Cyberspaces," 7.

9. Simon, "China's Scientists and Technologists in the Post-reform Era," 136.

10. Jin Qi, "New Technology," 4.

11. The Four Modernizations are the modernization of China's agriculture, industry, science and technology, and national defense. The CCP first put forward this policy in 1964. In 1975, Premier Zhou Enlai called for the Four Modernizations, with an emphasis on economic development. For more details, see Hsu, *China without Mao*.

12. Barlow, *"Zhishifenzi* [Chinese Intellectuals] and Power," 222.

13. Ji Shi, "Meiyou zhishifenzi jiu meiyou xiandaihua," 14.

14. Simon, "China's Scientists and Technologists in the Post-reform Era," 141.

15. Andreas, *Rise of the Red Engineers*, 7.

16. For a more detailed account of the historic changes in China's educational policies, see Andreas, *Rise of the Red Engineers*, "Part 4: The New Era (1976–Present)."

17. Bourdieu, "The Economics of Linguistic Exchanges," 652.

18. Li Zehou, *Li Zehou zhexue meixue wenxuan*, 178.

19. Lin Xingzhai. "Wenming de jidi—Shi yu shuxue de tongyi,'" *Wenxue pinglun* (1985:4). Quoted in He Guimei, *"Xin qimeng" zhishi dang'an*, 227.

20. Lin Xingzhai, "Wenming de jidi." Quoted in He Guimei, *"Xin qimeng" zhishi dang'an*, 227.

21. Li Zehou, *Zhongguo xiandai sixiang shi lun*, 116.

22. Ye Junjian, "Xu," 5.

23. He Guimei, *"Xin qimeng" zhishi dang'an*, 226.

24. Wang and Sun, *Xu Chi yanjiu zhuanji*, 8.

25. For a more detailed description of the production and reception of the play, see Xiaomei Chen, *Occidentalism*, 62–63.

26. Li Ming, "Popularizing Science in China," 21; and *Beijing Review*, "Popular Science Writing," 30.

27. Wagner, "Lobby Literature," 60.

28. Gao and Wu, "Bushi huanxiang de huanxiang gushi," 62-63.

29. Jin and Liu, "Xin *Qingnian* minzhu guannian de yanbian," 30.

30. Wang Hui, *Xiandai Zhongguo sixiang de xingqi*, 1123.

31. Williams, *The Country and the City*, 32.

32. This practice of recommending peasants as well as workers and soldiers for college was established during the Cultural Revolution to replace the meritocratic college-entrance examination system. It aimed to narrow the gap between the city and the countryside by recruiting a higher percentage of college students from proletarian families. Ideally, upon graduation, these students would return to their home regions in the spirit of Mao Zedong's July 21 Directive. For more details about this recommendation system, see Andreas, *Rise of the Red Engineers*, particularly ch. 8.

33. Anagnost, *National Past-times*, 4.

34. Shi's wife, in her thirties, would have grown up around the time when state-sponsored basic education in the form of "illiteracy-elimination class" (*sao mang ban*) was expanding in the countryside. According to the 1982 population census, "only 23 percent of men and women aged 15 or over were illiterate, a vast improvement when contrasted with pre-1949 illiteracy rates of between 70 and 80 percent" (Bramall, *The Industrialization of Rural China*, 152). Therefore, readers might wonder whether the authors created Caifeng's illiteracy to fit the imagined backwardness of the rural environment and to emphasize her contrast with the image of an urban-based Miss Science. My thanks to Matt A. Hale for this insight.

35. Bourdieu, "The Economics of Linguistic Exchanges," 651.

36. Williams, *The Country and the City*, 32.

37. Chen and Ma, "Dujuan tigui," 155.

38. Mohanty, "Cartographies of Struggle," 13.

39. Farrer, *Opening Up*, 306.

40. Nanyue Dadui Tuanzhibu, "'Qingchun jiang' pingxuan huodong xiaoji," 50.

41. For examples of such criticisms, see Zhao Guangde, "Ganqing shewang yu daode yueshu"; and Zhong Chengxiang, "Shenghuo, aiqing, daode."

42. Wu Xin, "Zhenshi de miaoxie, dadan de tansuo," 53.

43. Dong Jian, "Tan 'Dujuan tigui' de xinyi," 58–60.

44. The foreign scientists' names are given as "L. Wegener" and "M. Ening" in the original Chinese-language text.

45. Chen and Ma, "Feixiang yuanfang," 207.

46. Lyotard, *The Postmodern Condition*, 35.

47. Williams, *The Country and the City*, 210.

48. Ibid.

49. Greenhalgh, *Just One Child*, 24.

50. For a comprehensive study of this formula, see Jianmei Liu, *Revolution Plus Love*.

51. Farrer, *Opening Up*, 127.

52. "Guowuyuan guanyu renzhen guanche zhixing Xin Hunyinfa de tongzhi" [State council notice concerning earnestly implementing and executing the New Marriage Law], December 10, 1980. Quoted in Li and Friedman, "Wedding of Marriage, Nation, and State in Modern China," 11.

53. Greenhalgh, *Just One Child*, 20.

CHAPTER TWO

1. Shek, "Midlife Crisis in Chinese Men and Women," 109; and Jaques, "Death and the Mid-life Crisis."

2. Hairong Yan, *New Masters, New Servants*, 58.

3. Ocko, "Women, Property, and Law in the People's Republic of China," 315.

4. Wang Ruoshui, "Guanyu 'yihua' de gainian." " Quoted in Xueping Zhong, *Masculinity Besieged*, 90

5. Guo Xiaodong, "Muxing tuteng," 91.

6. Liu Binyan, "Man Is the Aim, Man Is the Center," 121.

7. Jianmei Liu, *Revolution Plus Love*, 24.

8. Wu Ruozeng, "Nanzihan," 130. In her book *Masculinity Besieged*, Xueping Zhong reads the heated debate of *yinsheng yangshuai* in the 1980s as the male intellectuals' effort to change their marginal position in the wake of the Cultural Revolution.

9. Leo Lee, "Afterword," 364.

10. David Wang, *Fin-de-Siècle Splendor*, 6.

11. Zhang Chunsheng, "*Liyi* zai Wu Ruozeng de chuangzuo zhong," 79.

12. Giddens, *Modernity and Self-Identity*, 76.

13. Wu Ruozeng, *Liyi*, 158. Nan Yang can be seen as the self-projection of the author, Wu Ruozeng, within the textual framework. Nan Yang establishes himself in the literary circle with his work *Strange Tales of the Cai Village* (Cai Zhuang yiwen), which apparently alludes to Wu's *The Cai Village Series*.

14. Ibid., 165.

15. Ibid., 160.

16. For a reference to Chen Shimei, see ch. 2.

17. Wu Ruozeng, *Liyi*, 163.

18. Ibid., 162.

19. Dikötter, *Sex, Culture, and Modernity in China*, 186.

20. Larson, *From A Q to Lei Feng*, 3.

21. Wu Ruozeng, *Liyi*, 182–83.

22. Ibid., 162.

23. In her book *National Past-Times*, Anagnost has argued that "'[s]peaking bitterness' provided a narrative structure in which oppressed members of the 'old society' took center stage to vent their rage in a compelling performance that made the working of history palpably 'real'" (17). Rofel provides an overview of the narrative and talks about its use among post-Mao intellectual narratives during the Dengist reform era in her *Desiring China* (48–54). For the use of the mechanism of speaking bitterness in peasantry mobilization during the Mao era, also see Guo and Sun, "Suku."

24. Wu Ruozeng, *Liyi*, 258.

25. Wu Ruozeng, "Dangdai wenxue fenlei ABC," 195.

26. Lean, *Public Passions*, 110–11.

27. Philip Huang, "Divorce Law Practices and the Origins, Myths, and Realities of Judicial 'Mediation' in China," 170.

28. Ibid.

29. Hsiau, "The Moral Dilemma of China's Modernization," 204.

30. Wu Ruozeng, *Liyi*, 186.

31. Diamant, *Revolutionizing the Family*, 331.

32. Merry, *Getting Justice and Getting Even*, 64. A similar point is also discussed in Baumgarten's *The Moral Order of a Suburb*.

33. Wu Ruozeng, *Liyi*, 197.

34. Lean, *Public Passions*, 15.

35. Wu Ruozeng, *Liyi*, 201.

36. Ibid., 203.

37. The fictional character's observation goes along with the gender-divided statistics of real-life divorce lawsuits. Johnson's *Women, the Family, and Peasant Revolution in China* and Palmer's "The Re-emergence of Family Law in Post-Mao China" offer empirical evidence for gender disparity in divorce lawsuits in the 1950s and the 1980s respectively. Thanks to Ke Li for bringing these scholarly works to my attention.

38. Wu Ruozeng, *Liyi*, 214.

39. In *Public Passions*, Lean criticizes the dichotomy of modern (Western) rule by law versus traditional (Chinese) rule by man by providing an insightful analysis of the complex entanglements and constant negotiations between

communal sentimentality and modern legality in Republican China. She points out particularly the revolutionary potential of feminized "public passions," which questions the limitations of Habermasian ideas of the public sphere and civil society that tend to emphasize the participatory politics of rational (male) bourgeois individuals.

40. Wu Ruozeng, *Liyi*, 228.

41. Ibid., 229. Isadora Duncan has been another influential cultural figure in modern Chinese history, although not as extensively studied as Ibsen's Nora. Her artistic career and unconventional lifestyle indicate an alternative model of femininity outside of heterosexual domesticity, which has inspired different generations of Chinese young women ranging from Xie Bingying, the first woman soldier-writer in Chinese history, to the student-turned-revolutionary Lin Daojing in Yang Mo's semiautobiographical *Qingchun zhi ge*, to Jin Dao, a sexual libertine in this 1980s divorce narrative. For multiple references to Isadora Duncan and Irma Duncan, her student and adopted daughter, see Xie, *A Woman Soldier's Own Story*, 71; Tian, "Shuofeng," 83–86; and Yang Mo, *Qingchun zhi ge*, 78. Thanks to Liang Luo for directing my attention to the first two pieces.

42. Ibid., 232.

43. Ibid., 249.

44. The ten chaotic years of the Cultural Revolution are hardly conceived as an integral part of modern Chinese history but more of a rupture, a loss of youth, meaning, and progressive temporality. Chen Rong's "Jianqu shi sui" published in 1986, best illustrates Chinese intellectuals' discontent with the Cultural Revolution.

45. Doane, *Femmes Fatales*, 2–3.

46. Wu, *Liyi*, 261.

47. Ibid.

48. Ibid., 205.

49. See Vittinghoff, "Jiang Qing and Nora." Anagnost argues that "[t]his 'feminization of evil' has now become a pervasive image of the Cultural Revolution period. The irony of this image lies in the fact that the Cultural Revolution, despite its horrors, was the most successful period in the erasure of gender inequality in its assaults on Confucian ideology." Anagnost, "Transformations of Gender in Modern China," 323. In "State-Society Relations and Women's Political Participation," Qi Wang also points out that "[t]he proportion of basic-level woman cadres has declined sharply since the early 1980s" (19).

50. Wu Ruozeng, "Funü jiefang zhi qianti dang wei nanren zhi jiefang," 178.

51. Butler, *Gender Trouble*, 135.

52. Su Tong, "Zixu," 1.

53. Fang Ping, "Pingyong disu de cipin xiaoshuo," 45.

54. "Lihun zhinan" was first published in *Shouhuo* (1991:5) and then reprinted in *Hunyin jijing*. An English-language version, translated by Josh Stenberg, is in *Tattoo*.

55. Su Tong, "Zixu," 2.

56. Su Tong, "A Divorce Handbook," 73.

57. Ibid., 1.

58. Ibid., 35. My emphasis.

59. Yue Meng, "Su Tong de 'jiashi' yu 'lishi' xiezuo," 93.

60. Yue Meng's article also provides an insightful analysis of Su Tong's use of "gaze" as a narrative device for establishing a connection between fictional family genealogy and historical writings.

61. Su Tong, "A Divorce Handbook," 15.

62. For more details on the intellectuals' discussion, see a series of articles on the "loss of the humanist spirit" published in *Dushu* (1994). Also see Wang Xiaoming, *Renwen jingshen xinsi lu*; and McGrath, *Postsocialist Modernity*, particularly ch. 2.

63. Su Tong, "A Divorce Handbook," 24.

64. Ibid., 61. I have made minor modifications in Stenberg's translation of this passage.

65. Xiaobing Tang, *Chinese Modern*, 236.

66. "Yihun nanren" was first published in *Zuojia* (1990:4) and then reprinted in *Hunyin jijing*.

67. Su Tong, "Yihun nanren," 166.

68. Guo Wu, "Subversion of the Feminist Myth in Chinese Film and Its Dilemma," 330.

69. Judovitz, *Subjectivity and Representation in Descartes*, 13. Judovitz posits the origins of modernity in the Cartesian sense of self as an "individualized essence."

70. Wu Ruozeng, "Zai nanyi xiaohua de lishi yu xianshi mianqian zhi dubai," 25.

71. Glosser, "'The Truths I Have Learned'," 139.

CHAPTER THREE

1. "Fangzhou" was first published in *Shouhuo* (1982: 2). A translation by Stephen Hallett was included in *Love Must Not Be Forgotten*, a collection of English-language translations of Zhang's representative works.

2. Barlow, *The Question of Women in Chinese Feminism*, 299–300.

3. "Ai, shi buneng wangji de" was first published in *Beijing Wenyi* (1979:11). An English-language translation by Gladys Yang was included in *Love Must Not Be Forgotten*.

4. Chi, "Taiyang chushi," 171.

5. Emphasizing the significance of an intersubjective space between women, Patricia Sieber compiles an anthology of women writers' works on "female-sex relations." In her introduction to the anthology *Red Is Not the Only Color*, Sieber sketches out a brief genealogy of Chinese women's practices, fictional and historical, of "same-sex intimacy" from ancient China to the contemporary period. In *The Emerging Lesbian: Female Same-Sex Desire in Modern China*, Tze-lan D. Sang examines "the shifting terms of the representations of female-female relations through time and their varied constructive and/or regulatory effects" (15). In addition to homoerotic

tales of women's bonding in fictional works, other forms of sisterhood are also represented in post-reform Chinese literature. Xueping Zhong explores the representations of close yet ambivalent relationships between women in contemporary Chinese fiction. See Xueping Zhong, "Sisterhood?" In this article, Zhong reads female-female relationships in both stories as a collective attempt to resist gender norms; however, the "patriarchal and ahistorical" notion of the self-identity of a "free individual" seriously undermines the cultural significance of sororal union (171).

6. Zhang Jie, "Love Must Not Be Forgotten," 2.

7. Yu-shih Chen, "Harmony and Equality," 170.

8. This debate occupies a central position in many 1980s literary works. For instance, in Dai Houying's novel *Ren ah ren* (1980), the heroic protagonist He Jingfu, a middle-aged male intellectual who was labeled a Rightist in 1957, also participated in this debate and published a controversial book *Makesi zhuyi yu rendao zhuyi* (*Marxism and humanism*).

9. Larson, "Women, Writers, Social Reform," 180.

10. Zhang Jie, "The Ark," 166.

11. Bailey, "Traveling Together," 98.

12. Zhang Jie, "The Ark," 140.

13. Ibid., 137.

14. Ibid., 126, 122.

15. Hall and Jacques, *The Politics of Thatcherism*, 10–11.

16. Lauretis, "Aesthetic and Feminist Theory," 165. Original emphasis.

17. Farquhar, *Appetites*, 189.

18. Zhang Jie, "Love Must Not Be Forgotten," 7.

19. Ibid.

20. Jingyuan Zhang, "Breaking Open," 164.

21. Zhang Jie, "The Ark," 166.

22. Ibid., 122.

23. To name a few examples of such criticisms, see Xu Dancheng, "'Xiaojie nizao' zhong de xingbie yishi"; Shang, "Cong *Wuzi* dao 'Fangzhou'"; and Zhou Airong, "Jiexi Chi Li xiaoshuo 'Xiaojie nizao' de dianshiju gaibian."

24. For the origin of the term "new urbanite fiction," see Xiaobing Tang, "Decorating Culture," 536; and Gong, "Constructing a Neorealist Reality," which situates neorealist writings in the larger tradition of literary realism in China and beyond.

25. For a more detailed account of Chi Li's career trajectory in postsocialist China, see McGrath, *Postsocialist Modernity*, ch. 3.

26. Chi, "Xiaojie nizao," 157.

27. I am indebted to Jingyuan Zhang for this insight.

28. McGrath, *Postsocialist Modernity*, 67.

29. Jin Yihong, "Rethinking the 'Iron Girls'," 621.

30. Ibid.

31. Naihua Zhang, "In a World Together Yet Apart," 19. This memoir provides a personal account that bears witness to shifting feminine ideals from the Mao era to the post-Mao era.

32. Fengzhi Dong, "On the Obstacles to Women's Participation in Politics on the Part of Women Themselves," 45

33. Chi, "Jinxiu shatan," 307.

34. Suying Yang, "Gender Construction in the Novels of Zhang Kang-kang and Liang Xiaosheng," 121.

35. Chi, "Xiaojie nizao," 102.

36. Schiebinger, introduction to *Feminism & the Body*, 14

37. Dikötter's *Sex, Culture, and Modernity in China* (esp. 40–48) also registers 1930s intellectuals' promotion of modern sexual hygiene and their attacks on traditional (read: rural) beliefs and practices in the realm of reproductive health.

38. The term is borrowed from Rogaski's book *Hygienic Modernity*, which examines how the concept of hygiene (*weisheng*) has become an essential measurement of Chinese modern consciousness since the nineteenth century. In this chapter, I particularly emphasize the gendered aspect of this idea of "hygienic modernity" in contemporary China.

39. For a meticulous description of the pregnancy check-up, see Chi, "Tai-yang chushi," 122–25.

40. Barlow, "Wanting Some," 313.

41. Ibid., 330. My emphasis.

42. Chi, "Xiaojie nizao," 152.

43. Doane, *Femmes Fatales, Film Theory, Psychoanalysis*, 25.

44. Chi, "Xiaojie nizao," 96.

45. Ibid., 90. A nearly identical passage is on p. 112.

46. The original Chinese phrase for "send him back to his 1970s home-town" is *rang ta huidao qishi niandai de laojia qu*. Ai proposed this plan as retaliation against Wang. Ibid., 152.

47. Jones, *Developmental Fairy Tales*, 10.

48. For more comprehensive studies of courtesan culture from late imperial China to early Republican China, see Widmer and Sun Chang, *Writing Women in Late Imperial China*, particularly the first three chapters by Paul S. Ropp, Wai-yee Li, and Dorothy Ko; Hershatter, *Dangerous Pleasures*; and McMahon, *Polygamy and Sublime Passion*, in which McMahon translates *qing* as "sublime passion," which "embodies a form of feminine subjectivity that shuns the world of promiscuous male sexual drive" (7).

49. Chow, "Virtuous Transactions," 94.

50. Butler, *Gender Trouble*, 139. Original emphasis.

51. Chi, "Xiaojie nizao," 154.

52. Thanks to Jingyuan Zhang for bringing this point to my attention. An important *runwu* allusion can be found in Du Fu's famous poem "Chunye xiyu," composed around 761CE while the poet was living in Chengdu. The second couplet goes like this: "Wind-borne, it steals softly into the night, / nourishing, enriching, delicate, and soundless" (Suifeng qian ruye, / runwu xi wusheng). The English translation is from Burton Watson's *The Selected Poems of Du Fu*, 85.

53. Chi, "Xiaojie nizao," 125.

54. Ibid., 317.

55. Chi, *Suoyi*, 254.

56. Robinson, "Of Women and Washing Machines," 51. Also see Dikötter's *Imperfect Conceptions* for an insightful analysis of the stipulation of women's responsibilities, state-promoted eugenic discourse, and practices.

57. Haiyan Lee, *Revolution of the Heart*, 207.

58. Butler, *Gender Trouble*, 92.

59. Chi, "Xiaojie nizao," 155.

60. Chi, "Zhenshi de rizi," 19.

61. Chi, "Liaotian," 124.

62. Gong, "Constructing a Neorealist Reality," 71.

63. Ibid., 84.

64. Zheng Wang, *Women in the Chinese Enlightenment*, 173. Also see Ko, *Teachers of the Inner Chambers*; and Lieberman, *The Mother and Narrative Politics in Modern China*.

65. Zurndorfer, "Gender, Higher Education, and the 'New Woman'," 452.

66. Barlow, "Gender and Identity in Ding Ling's *Mother*," 124.

67. Yeh, "The Paradox of Autonomy," 49, 50.

CHAPTER FOUR

1. Wang Hailing's best-selling novels *Qianshou* (1999), *Zhongguo shi lihun* (2004), and *Xin jiehun shidai* (2006), all of which have been adapted into well-received television series, are often put together and labeled the "marriage trilogy."

2. Xueping Zhong, *Mainstream Culture Refocused*, 132.

3. The question of whether China is fully neoliberalized still arouses many scholarly debates and discussions. See Harrison, "Serving the Market or Serving the Party"; Harvey, *A Brief History of Neoliberalism*; Wang and Huters, *China's New Order*; and Rofel, *Desiring China*. I concur with Harvey's argument about contemporary China's "neoliberalism with Chinese characteristics." That means that although China remains a socialist country in name with its one-party bureaucratic system largely intact, it has been radically neoliberalizing in terms of its accelerating marketization and privatization of state-owned enterprises and other public properties as well as the dismantling of the welfare system. Furthermore, I would add that the rhetoric of state-sanctioned and market-informed neoliberal competition and self-governance has gained popular currency in contemporary Chinese society as the regime of the party-state has become more sophisticated and "modernized." In this sense, neoliberalism is not only an economic model but also a subjectivizing project.

4. Meng Xiaoyun, "Wang Hailing: 'Hunyin diyi xieshou'," 7.

5. Tang Jian, "*Zhongguoshi lihun* re le hunyinju," November 10, 2004, 11.

6. Qiu Lihua, "*Zhongguoshi lihun* shoushilü Shanghai 'gaoshao' butui guanzhong dangcheng jiaokeshu," B7.

7. One male viewer of the serial half-jokingly told me that Lin's image in this scene reminded him of the "abandoned woman" ghost in Japanese horror films such as *The Ring*.

8. Diamant, *Revolutionizing the Family*.

9. In several places of the novel and the serial drama *Chinese-Style Divorce*, the female protagonist's "low quality" is criticized. In a popular talk show targeted at female audiences, Wang Hailing states that a married woman should invest in self-development in order to prevent marital crises. See Tengxun yule, "Yang Lan fawen *Zhongguoshi lihun*, Jiang Wenli zuoke *Tianxia Nüren*," http://ent.qq.com/a/20050524/000152.htm (accessed January 3, 2009).

10. Tang and Hu, "Ziwo sangshi he jingshen weihun," 37–38.

11. Liu Siqian, "Hunyin wuyu," 177.

12. Williams, *The Country and the City*, 32.

13. In *The Divorce Revolution*, particularly ch. 5, Weitzman provides an incisive examination of the issue of gender inequality in accumulating and, upon divorce, dividing intangible assets in the 1980s United States.

14. Anagnost, "The Corporeal Politics of Quality (*Suzhi*)," 190.

15. Ibid., 196.

16. Xueping Zhong, *Mainstream Culture Refocused*, 139.

17. Zheng Wang, *Women in the Chinese Enlightenment*, 20.

18. Yeh, "The Paradox of Autonomy," 44. Hoffman also mentions this new social phenomenon in *Patriotic Professionalism in Urban China*, 125.

19. Weitzman, *The Divorce Revolution*, 111.

20. Ibid., 111, 374.

21. Jie Lu, "Cultural Invention and Cultural Intervention," 126, 129.

22. Chi, *To and Fro*, 28–29.

23. Ibid., 40–43.

24. DeWoskin, *Foreign Babes in Beijing*, 213, 223.

25. Ibid., 29.

26. Young and DeWoskin, "Foreign Babe in Beijing," 12.

27. Sheldon Lu, *China, Transnational Visuality, Global Postmodernity*, 221.

28. DeWoskin, *Foreign Babes in Beijing*, 23, 136.

29. Young and DeWoskin, "Foreign Babe in Beijing," 16.

30. DeWoskin, *Foreign Babes in Beijing*, 220.

31. For an in-depth discussion of the idea of "self-ownership," see Knight, *The Heart of Time*.

32. Tang Xinyong, "Wei chenggong zhangfu dazao wanmei nüren," 70–71.

33. Barlow, "Theorizing Woman," 267.

34. Sheldon Lu, *China, Transnational Visuality, Global Postmodernity*, 213, 233.

35. In addition to this new vision of romantic individualism embedded in television melodramas, published "factual oral accounts" (*koushu shilu*) of personal feelings and failed intimacy in conjugal relationships have drawn people's attention and contributed to the changing perception

of privacy. Popular examples include An Dun's best-selling series *Juedui yinsi* (1998), Liu Jian's *Zhongguo shi lihun baogao* (2005), and Wang Ru's *Women weishenme lihun* (2006). These accounts appeal to readers' voyeuristic desires. On a practical level, they also serve as a combination of admonitory lesson and self-help handbook on issues related to marital life.

36. Dai Jinhua's "Redemption and Consumption" offers an in-depth analysis of this trend of consuming revolutionary memories.

37. In this article, Wang Hailing also states that a married woman's gendered quality is the most important factor in promoting children's education. See Sha, "Zhongguoshi lihun lu zai hefang," 30–36.

38. Rofel, "'Yearnings'," 711.

39. Baudrillard, *Simulacra and Simulation*, 14, 50.

40. Giddens, *Transformation of Intimacy*, 188.

41. Harvey, *A Brief History of Neoliberalism*, 125.

42. For a more comprehensive discussion of the "socialist mainstream melody" culture, see Rui Zhang, *The Cinema of Feng Xiaogang*; and Xueping Zhong, *Mainstream Culture Refocused*.

43. Ji Bingxuan, "Changxiang zhu xuanlü, duochu jingpin ju," 3.

44. Hu Jintao, the former president of China, is credited with the concept of a "harmonious society," which is considered a major contribution to Chinese political thought. The Chinese government first proposed it in 2002, during the sixteenth National Congress of the Chinese Communist Party, in the face of increasing social disparities and conflicts. Marking the historical discontinuity with the Maoist ideology of class struggle, Hu's campaign aims to serve the ultimate harmony of a middle-class-oriented "affluent society" (*xiaokang shehui*). In his series of talks about his vision of a "harmonious society," Hu cites lengthy paragraphs from Confucian canons and emphasizes the key role that ethical education, including the rehabilitation of domestic virtues, should play in realizing social harmony. In general, "[t]he cardinal features of what the party envisions as 'a harmonious society' include democracy and the rule of law, equality and justice, trust and love, stability and order, and finally a harmonious coexistence between humans and nature" (Li Zhang, *In Search of Paradise*, 213). As a result, "harmonious society" has become the central theme of many state-sponsored and state-sanctioned cultural products and activities such as the annual CCTV Spring Festival Gala, television melodramas celebrating "Asian values," and Yu Dan's best-selling spin-offs of traditional classics. For more details about this campaign, see ibid., 212–14.

45. Dangdang.com, Editor's recommendation for *Jinhun* DVD, http://product.dangdang.com/product.aspx?product_id=20215676&ref=search-1-pub (accessed November 19, 2011).

46. Shen, *Beijiangou de nüxing*, 209.

47. *Zhongguo daxuesheng jiuye*, "2004 Zhongguo zhiye bailing shenghuo zhiliang diaocha," 41–42.

48. Ren Qiuling, "Jiayou xianqi de nanren bi danshenhan zhuanqian duo."

49. In addition to giving a series of lectures about "cultivating a harmonious soul" (*goujian hexie xinling*), Yu Dan has published a book and DVD titled *Yu Dan's Thoughts on Harmony* (Yu Dan hexie xinde). In an interview, Yu suggests that Chinese women should consult traditional classics such as the *Analects* (Lunyu) for guidance on building a harmonious interior world for self-cultivation and domestic bliss. See *Zhongguo funü*, "Yu Dan fangtan," 6.

50. Yu Jun, "Shuangxing hexie," 238–39.

51. Kong, "Family Matters," 83.

52. This being said, what should not be ignored is the fact that even during the Mao era, the heavily gendered division of labor still persisted in the domestic sphere and the burden of domestic labor fell largely on women. The Maoist tenet that one's value is fulfilled through one's social labor enhanced the devaluation of unpaid domestic and reproductive labor.

53. For references to practices of modern concubinage, see Shih, "Gender and a New Geopolitics of Desire"; and DeWoskin, "Wife Sentence." The term *ernai* literally means "second wives" in Chinese. The term "*ernai* adoption contract" refers to the agreement signed by a wealthy married man and a young single woman who consents to be his mistress. Normally it details the obligations of each party, such as housing arrangements, living expenses, and a certain amount of compensation that the man should provide for the woman, who, in return, would cohabit with him in a second home established outside the institution of marriage.

54. An exception is the recent megahit *Snail House* (Woju; 2009). This extremely popular TV serial not only touches on the issue of a high-ranking CCP cadre's practices of corruption and concubine adoption but also exposes the enormous financial pressure faced by urban middle-class professionals in dealing with skyrocketing housing prices in big cities like Shanghai.

55. Foucault, "Governmentality," 92.

56. Li Zhang, *In Search of Paradise*, 19. My emphasis.

57. For instance, see Li Xiaojiang, "From 'Modernization' to 'Globalization'," 1274–78. In addition, the self-development rhetoric is central to the women-oriented CCTV program *Half of the Sky* (Banbian tian).

58. Xueping Zhong, "Hou funü jiefang yu ziwo xiangxiang," 13–20.

59. Tonglin Lu, *Misogyny, Cultural Nihilism, and Oppositional Politics*, 14.

CHAPTER FIVE

1. For more details on the evolution of the PRC marriage law, see chapter 1.

2. Jason McGrath's study examines two distinct narrative trends of what he calls "the cinema of infidelity" produced between the 1980s and 2000: the rural cinema of infidelity often features a strong-willed woman character's extramarital affair as a fable of rural modernization, and the urban cinema of infidelity tends to characterize an adulterous male "successful personage" (*chenggong renshi*), who has become a stock figure embodying the

disorientation many men experience when faced with the new possibilities, desires, and anxieties of post-revolutionary China. McGrath, *Postsocialist Modernity*, 95–96.

3. Xueping Zhong, "Mr. Zhao On and Off the Screen," and Cui, "Ning Ying's Beijing Trilogy," analyze the depiction of male desire and its discontents in *Mr. Zhao* and *I Love Beijing* respectively.

4. For someone familiar with Chinese cinema, this character will immediately bring to mind Tian Zhuangzhuang's banned film *Blue Kite* (1993), in which the female protagonist (played by Lü Liping) experiences multiple traumatic disruptions in her marriages due to the tumultuous political campaigns of socialist China.

5. Jerry White and Shuqin Cui note this conspicuous lack in their close analysis of Ning Ying's earlier cinematic works. See White, "The Films of Ning Ying"; and Cui, "Ning Ying's Beijing Trilogy."

6. The cast selection is also noteworthy. The amateur actresses Hong Huang and Liu Suola are cultural luminaries. Together with the filmmaker herself, they participated actively in the 1980s "culture fever" and played a critical role in pushing a wave of nostalgia for that decade. For a more comprehensive analysis of this film, see Hui Faye Xiao, "Interiorized Feminism and Gendered Nostalgia."

7. Browne, 'Society and Subjectivity," 43.

8. For more details about "quality education," see ch. 5.

9. Wallerstein and Blakeslee, *Second Chances*, 278.

10. Beck, *Risk Society*, 21. Original emphasis.

11. Giddens, "Risk and Responsibility," 3.

12. Ibid., 2.

13. Beck, *Risk Society*, 46. Original emphasis.

14. Giddens, "Risk and Responsibility," 3. Original emphases.

15. See Giddens, *Modernity and Self-Identity*, particularly the introduction, for a full discussion of such a transformation in an age of high modernity.

16. Hai Ren, "The Neoliberal State and Risk Society," 105.

17. Ibid.

18. Giddens, *Modernity and Self-Identity*, 28.

19. Podvin, "Tale of the Dark Side/Director Ann Hui Explores the Seamy Side of Postmodern Shanghai," http://blog.hkcinemagic.com/thomas-podvin/index.php/2007/10/17/292-the-postmodern-life-of-my-aunt-ann-hui (accessed June 10, 2010).

20. Marchetti, "Gender Politics and Neoliberalism in China," 123–40.

21. Ann Hui was born in Anshan to a Chinese father and a Japanese mother. The second character, *an*, of her Chinese name, Xu Anhua, indicates her birthplace, Anshan City in Liaoning, and the third character, *hua*, means "China."

22. For an intertextual reference, Wang Bing's lengthy documentary *West of the Tracks* (Tie xi qu; 2003) best captures the historical memories and everyday experiences of factory workers in the industrial complex of

Manchuria who are trapped in the paradigmatic shift in contemporary Chinese society. Also see Ching Kwan Lee, *Against the Law,* particularly chs. 3 and 4.

23. Ye Xin, a popular sent-down youth writer, wrote about this massive reverse flow of human resources from the country to the city. In 1992, he published another best-selling novel, *Niezhai,* which was adapted into a television serial. It narrates various stories of Shanghai sent-down youths abandoning their ethnic minority wives and children in the rural Xishuangbanna area of Yunnan in the late 1970s. Even though many sent-down youths had their sexual awakening and encounters with local ethnic minorities in Xishuangbanna, which is depicted as a pastoral place, they choose to return to Shanghai, where many end up doing poorly paid backbreaking work in cramped factories. Shanghai, with its aura of scientific modernity and economic development, lures people by appearing to be the only legitimate site in which a modern lifestyle is possible. Therefore, the abandonment of marriage and children in the rural areas is justified as a commonsense choice made by those sent-down youths who married during their years of rustication and then decide to go back to the city no matter the cost. See Deng Xian, "Zhongguo zhiqing meng," 105–8. Xu Mingyu's story "Diaodong" (1979) and Zhu Lin's novel *Shenghuo de lu* (1979) also tell stories of female sent-down youths who sacrifice their loved ones to find their way back to the city. Lai-fong Leung's study "In Search of Love and Self" compared the two works, noting that the female was punished with sexual exploitation followed by a tragic death at the end of the novel while the male returned successfully to the city.

24. Clarke, introduction to *The Cinematic City,* 4.

25. Simmel, *The Philosophy of Money,* 227.

26. He Dan, "Marriage Database to Go Online," http://english.peopledaily.com.cn/90001/90776/90882/7246513.html (accessed September 1, 2013).

27. Ye's confident statement resonates with the famous line of Elsa Bannister (played by Rita Hayworth) "You need more than luck in Shanghai" in the 1947 crime thriller *The Lady from Shanghai.* Since its emergence as a semicolonial cosmopolitan city, Shanghai has enjoyed notoriety as the "paradise of adventurers," so much so that the city name has become a verb meaning "to put aboard a ship by force often with the help of liquor or a drug," "to put by force or threat of force into or as if into a place of detention," and "to put by trickery into an undesirable position" (merriam-webster.com). Such an impressionist vision of the metropolis not only is exploited and reproduced in early Chinese cinema but also connects directly to Orientalist representations in classic Hollywood cinema. For example, the 1932 Hollywood adventure-romance *Shanghai Express* features a witty, sexy, and mysterious woman [Shanghai Lily, played by Marlene Dietrich] who travels from Peking to Shanghai. Likewise, in *The Lady from Shanghai,* the dangerous sexual appeal of the femme fatale Elsa Bannister is reinforced by her enigmatic past adventures in Shanghai. The above-quoted line "You need more than luck in Shanghai" evokes the legendary urban decadence of the "Paris

of the Orient," which is also closely associated with modern technology in the Chinese "literature of modernity," such as Mu Shiying's story "Shanghai de hubuwu" (1932), Mao Dun's novel *Ziye* (1933), and Zhang Henshui's novel *Ping Hu tongche* (1935), which share a setting and femme fatale figure similar to those in the film *Shanghai Express*.

28. Clarke, introduction to *The Cinematic City*, 3–4.

29. Kaplan, "Is the Gaze Male?" 119–38.

30. Haiyan Lee, "*Woman, Demon, Human*," 244.

31. Yue Meng, *Shanghai and the Edges of Empires*, 206.

32. Giddens, *Modernity and Self-Identity*, 119.

33. Stringer, "Boat People," 45.

34. Negra, *What a Girl Wants?* 16–18.

35. Beck, *Risk Society*, 21. Original emphasis.

36. Ibid.

37. Zhen Zhang, "Bearing Witness," 1.

38. Zhen Zhang, "Urban Dreamscape, Phantom Sisters, and the Identity of an Emergent Art Cinema," 345.

39. Yingjin Zhang, "From 'Minority Film' to 'Minority Discourse'," 89.

40. For a critique of the practice of exoticizing ethnic minorities, see Yingjin Zhang, "From 'Minority Film' to 'Minority Discourse'," and Gladney, "Representing Nationality in China."

41. *Urtiin duu* is a time-honored form of Mongolian folk singing that originated around two thousand years ago in the Mongolian grasslands. For more information about this musical genre, see the Silk Road Project, http://www.silkroadproject.org/MusicArtists/Instruments/Urtiinduulongsong/tabid/331/Default.aspx (accessed September 15, 2011).

42. Ban Wang, *Illuminations from the Past*, 237.

43. Zan, "Realism Is a Big Hit," 44.

44. Benjamin, *Illuminations*, 257–58.

45. Mei Zhang, "Rural Privatisation and Women's Labour," 187.

46. See Yu Nan's blog, http://blog.sina.com.cn/s/blog_4c2862ef010007as.html (accessed August 16, 2011).

47. Mies and Shiva, *Ecofeminism*, 81.

48. Li Yu, a woman filmmaker born in 1973, made a documentary on this polyandryist family, which aired on the popular program *Life Space* (Shenghuo kongjian) on CCTV. Inspired by Li's documentary, Wang Quan'an decided to make a feature film based on the real-life story, but set in the Inner Mongolian steppe at the foot of Mount Helan. *Chengdu ribao*, "Yuanzi Chengdu zhenshi gushi, *Tuya de hunshi* duo Jinxiong," http://www.scta.gov.cn/web/main.jsp?go=newsDetail&pid=8&cid=15&id=16091 (accessed September 17, 2011).

49. Berlinale.de, "Short Synopsis of *Tuya's Marriage*," http://www.berlinale.de/en/archiv/jahresarchive/2007/02_programm_2007/02_Filmdatenblatt_2007_20070854.php (accessed August 30, 2011).

50. For this type of interpretation of the film, see Ya-chen Chen, "Mother Earth *Tuya's Marriage*."

51. Ban Wang, *Illuminations from the Past*, 121.

52. Ibid., 122.

53. Zhen Zhang, "Urban Dreamscape, Phantom Sisters, and the Identity of an Emergent Art Cinema," 368.

CHAPTER SIX

1. Reuters, "China Reinterprets Untying the Knot," http://www.reuters.com/article/2011/08/30/us-china-divorce-idUSTRE77T0K020110830 (accessed May 30, 2012).

2. For a more thorough discussion of this judicial interpretation and its social impact, see Huang Zongzhi, "Zhongguo de xiandai jiating."

3. Hu Yijun, "Getting 'Naked'," 19.

4. *Daily Mail* reporter, "Divorce Calculator Puts Price on Your Marriage"; Yu Ying, "Yingguo · lihun chengben · Shangwang gusuan," 4; and Fan Fu, "Shidai reci," B08.

5. Beck, *Risk Society*, 89.

6. Chen Lifang, "Fuqi lihun yishi fang *Feicheng wurao* 2 yin weiguan," *Shanxi Wanbao wang*, June 20, 2011, http://news.qq.com/a/20110620 /000379.htm (accessed June 20, 2012).

7. Qiang, "Sifa nengdong xia de zhongguo jiating," 28.

8. *Jiazhi zhongguo*, "'Zhonguo shi lihun' shidai," *China Value*, http://focus.chinavalue.net/General/2011-12-9/372270.html (accessed July 7, 2012).

9. "Affective individualism" is Lawrence Stone's term, used to describe the prioritizing of individual rights over the "good of the family" during the period of the Industrial Revolution in England. See Stone, *The Family, Sex and Marriage in England, 1500–1800*. Cited in Weitzman, *The Divorce Revolution*, 375.

10. Calinescu, *Five Faces of Modernity*, 283.

APPENDIX I

1. Kong, "Family Matters," 75.

Abel, Elizabeth. "(E)Merging Identities: The Dynamics of Female Friendship in Contemporary Fiction by Women." *Signs* 6.3 (1981): 413–35.

Alford, William P., and Shen Yuanyuan. "Have You Eaten, Have You Divorced? Debating the Meaning of Freedom in Marriage in China." In *Realms of Freedom in Modern China*, edited by William C. Kirby, 234–63. Stanford: Stanford University Press, 2004.

An Dun. *Juedui yinsi* [Absolute privacy]. Beijing: Xin shijie chubanshe, 1998.

Anagnost, Ann. "The Corporeal Politics of Quality (*suzhi*)." *Public Culture* 16.2 (Spring 2004): 189–208.

———. *National Past-times: Narrative, Representation, and Power in Modern China*. Durham, NC: Duke University Press, 1997.

———. "Transformations of Gender in Modern China." In *Gender and Anthropology: Critical Reviews for Research and Teaching*, edited by Sandra Morgan, 313–42. Washington, DC: American Anthropological Association, 1989.

Andors, Phyllis. *Unfinished Liberation of Chinese Women*. Bloomington: Indiana University Press, 1983.

Andreas, Joel. *Rise of the Red Engineers: The Cultural Revolution and the Origins of China's New Class*. Stanford: Stanford University Press, 2009.

Armstrong, Nancy. *Desire and Domestic Fiction: A Political History of the Novel*. New York: Oxford University Press, 1987.

Bailey, Alison. "Traveling Together: Narrative Technique in Zhang Jie's 'The Ark'." In *Modern Chinese Women Writers: Critical Appraisals*, edited by Michael S. Duke, 96–111. Armonk, NY. and London: M. E. Sharpe, 1989.

Barlow, Tani E. "Gender and Identity in Ding Ling's *Mother*." *Modern Chinese Literature* 2.2 (Fall 1986): 123–42.

———. *The Question of Women in Chinese Feminism*. Durham, NC: Duke University Press, 2004.

————. "Theorizing Woman: *Funü, Guojia, Jiating* (Chinese Woman, Chinese State, Chinese Family)." In *Body, Subject and Power in China*, edited by Angela Zito and Tani Barlow, 253–89. Chicago: The University of Chicago Press, 1994.

————. "Wanting Some: Commodity Desire and the Eugenic Modern Girl." In *Women in China: The Republican Period in Historical Perspective*, edited by Mechthild Leutner and Nicola Spakowski, 312–50. Münster, Germany: LIT, 2005.

————. "*Zhishifenzi* [Chinese Intellectuals] and Power." *Dialectical Anthropology* 16.3–4 (1991): 209–32.

Baudrillard, Jean. *For a Critique of the Political Economy of the Sign.* Translated by Charles Levin. Saint Louis, MO: Telos Press, 1981.

————. *Simulacra and Simulation.* Translated by Sheila Faria Glaser. Ann Arbor: The University of Michigan Press, 1994.

Baumgarten, M. P. *The Moral Order of a Suburb.* Oxford: Oxford University Press, 1988.

Beck, Ulrich. *Risk Society: Toward a New Modernity.* Translated by Mark Ritter. London: Sage Publications, 1992.

Beijing Review. "China Needs World-Class Universities." *Beijing Review,* no. 50 (December 15, 1986): 26–27.

————. "Chinese Literary Criticism Flourishes." *Beijing Review,* no. 48 (December 1, 1986): 31–32.

————. "Freedom of Divorce Affirmed." *Beijing Review,* no. 43 (October 27, 1980): 8.

————. "Liberal Arts Reform in Colleges." *Beijing Review,* no. 10 (March 8, 1982): 26.

————. "No Prize for China: Nobel's Loss?" *Beijing Review,* no. 47 (November 24, 1986): 21–22.

————. "Nobel Prize: Critical Appraisal." *Beijing Review,* no. 47 (November 24, 1986): 22–23.

————. "Popular Science Writing." *Beijing Review,* no. 40 (October 3, 1983): 30.

————. "Selecting Cadres from among College Students." *Beijing Review,* no. 32 (August 11, 1980): 7.

————. "Shanghai Scientists Seek International Works." *Beijing Review,* no. 34 (August 22, 1983): 28.

————. "Women Writers." *Beijing Review,* no. 36 (September 8, 1980): 29.

Benjamin, Walter. *The Arcades Project.* Translated by Howard Eiland and Kevin McLaughlin. Cambridge, MA: The Belknap Press of Harvard University Press, 1999.

————. *Illuminations: Essays and Reflections.* Edited by Hannah Arendt. Translated by Harry Zohn. New York: Schocken, 1969.

Berlinale.de. "Short Synopsis of *Tuya's Marriage.*" http://www.berlinale. de/en/archiv/jahresarchive/2007/02_programm_2007/02_Filmdaten-blatt_2007_20070854.php (accessed August 30, 2011).

Bernhardt, Kathryn. "Women and the Law: Divorce in the Republican Period." In *Civil Law in Qing and Republican China*, edited by Kathryn Bernhardt and Philip C.C. Huang, 187–214. Stanford: Stanford University Press, 1994.

Bernstein, Thomas P. *Up to the Mountains and Down to the Villages: The Transfer of Youth from Urban to Rural China.* New Haven: Yale University Press, 1977.

Bourdieu, Pierre. "The Economics of Linguistic Exchanges." Translated by Richard Nice. *Social Science Information* 16. 6 (1977): 645–68.

Bramall, Chris. *The Industrialization of Rural China.* New York: Oxford University Press, 2007.

Bronfen, Elizabeth. "Castration Complex." In *Feminism and Psychoanalysis*, edited by Elizabeth Wright, 41–45. Oxford: Blackwell, 1992.

Brown, Gillian. *Domestic Individualism: Imagining Self in Nineteenth-Century America.* Berkeley: University of California Press, 1990.

Browne, Nick. "Society and Subjectivity: On the Political Economy of Chinese Melodrama." In *New Chinese Cinemas: Forms, Identities, Politics*, edited by Nick Browne, Paul G. Pickowicz, Vivian Sobchack, and Esther Yau, 40–56. Cambridge: Cambridge University Press, 1994.

Bu Wen. "Lihun" [Divorce]. *Renmin wenxue* [People's literature] (1957:2): 50–55.

Butler, Judith. *Bodies That Matter.* New York: Routledge, 1990.

————. *Gender Trouble: Feminism and the Subversion of Identity.* New York: Routledge, 1990.

Calinescu, Matei. *Five Faces of Modernity.* Durham: Duke University Press, 1987.

Cao Keying. *Xiao nüxu* [Little husband]. Beijing: Baowentang shudian, 1954.

Certeau, Michel de. *The Practice of Everyday Life.* Translated by Steven Rendall. Berkeley: University of California Press, 1988.

Chen Duxiu. "Dongxi minzu genben sixiang zhi chayi" [Differences of basic thought between Eastern and Western people]. *Xin qingnian* [New youth] 1. 4 (1915): 283–86.

Chen Huafei, ed. "Pandian Zhongguo lihunlü zuigao de shida chengshi" [Top ten Chinese cities with the highest divorce rate]. *Renmin wang* [People's daily online], September 26, 2009. http://health.people.com.cn/GB/14740/106977/10120416.html (accessed September 2, 2013).

Chen Kexiong and Ma Ming. "Dujuan tigui" [Return, cries the cuckoo]. In *"Dujuan tigui": Daxuesheng duanpian xiaoshuo ji* ["Return, cries the cuckoo": An anthology of short stories by college students], 143–70. Shanghai: Fudan daxue chubanshe, 1989.

———. "Feixiang yuanfang—Xu "Dujuan tigui" [Flying afar—a sequel to "Return, cries the cuckoo"]. In *"Dujuan tigui": Daxuesheng duanpian xiaoshuo ji* ["Return, cries the cuckoo": An anthology of short stories by college students], 171–207. Shanghai: Fudan daxue chubanshe, 1989.

Chen Lifang. "Fuqi lihun yishi fang *Feicheng wurao 2* qin weiguan" [A couple's divorce ritual imitates the ceremony in the film *If You Are the One II* and attracts spectators] *Shanxi Wanbao wang*, June 20, 2011. http://news.qq.com/a/20110620/000379.htm (accessed June 20, 2012).

Chen Rong (Shen Rong). "Jianqu shi sui" [Ten years deducted]. *Renmin wenxue* [People's literature] (1986:2): 7–18.

———. "Lande lihun" [Too lazy to divorce]. *Jiefangjun wenyi* [People's Liberation Army literature and art] (1988:6): 4–35.

———. "Rendao zhongnian" [At middle age]. *Chinese Literature* (October 1980): 3–63.

———. "Yongyuan shi chuntian" [Springtime forever]. *Shouhuo* [Harvest] (1979:3): 117–73.

Chen, Xiaomei. *Occidentalism: A Theory of Counter-discourse in Post-Reform China*. New York: Oxford University Press, 1995.

Chen, Ya-chen. "Mother Earth *Tuya's Marriage*." *Asian Cinema* 19. 2 (Fall–Winter 2008): 195–214.

Chen, Yu-shih. "Harmony and Equality: Reflections on 'Mimosa' and 'Ark'." *Modern Chinese Literature* 4, nos. 1–2 (Spring and Fall 1988): 163–70.

Chengdu ribao [Chengdu daily]. "Yuanzi Chengdu zhenshi gushi, *Tuya de hunshi* duo Jinxiong" [Based on a true story in Chengdu, *Tuya's Marriage* won the Golden Bear Award]. *Chengdu ribao* [Chengdu daily], Feburary 19, 2007. http://www.scta.gov.cn/web/main.jsp?go=newsDetail&pid=8&cid=15&id=16091 (accessed September 17, 2011).

Chi Li. "Bugan yu ni tongku—Zhi Zhang Jie" [Dare not to cry together with you—to Zhang Jie]. In *Chi Li Wenji* [Anthology of Chi Li's works], vol. 4, 108–12. Nanjing: Jiangsu wenyi chuban she, 1995.

———. "Butan aiqing" [Apart from love]. In *Chi Li Wenji* [Anthology of Chi Li's works], vol. 2, 55–109. Nanjing: Jiangsu wenyi chuban she, 1995.

———. "Jinxiu shatan" [Brocade beach]. In *Chi Li Wenji* [Anthology of Chi Li's works], vol. 2, 289–333. Nanjing: Jiangsu wenyi chuban she, 1995.

———. "Kanzhe wo de yanjing" [Look at my eyes]. In *Chi Li Wenji*

[Anthology of Chi Li's works], vol. 3, 383–96. Nanjing: Jiangsu wenyi chuban she, 1995.

———. *Lailai wangwang* [To and fro]. Beijing: Zuojia chubanshe, 1998.

———. "Liaotian" [Chitchat]. In *Chi Li Wenji* [Anthology of Chi Li's works], vol. 4, 117–25. Nanjing: Jiangsu wenyi chuban she, 1995.

———. "Shenghuo xiu" [The life show]. In *Shenghuo Xiu* [The life show], 1-112. Kunming: Yunnan renmin chubanshe, 2002.

———. *Suoyi* [Therefore]. Beijing: Renmin wenxue chubanshe, 2007.

———. "Taiyang chushi" [Sunrise]. In *Chi Li Wenji* [Anthology of Chi Li's works], vol. 2, 110–82. Nanjing: Jiangsu wenyi chuban she, 1995.

———. Excerpts from *To and Fro*. Translated by Wang Mingjie. *Chinese Literature* (1999:4): 13–63.

———. "Xiaojie nizao" [Good morning, miss]. In *Yun po chu* (Cloud breaking), 87–157. Beijing: Huaxia chubanshe, 1998.

———. "Zhenshi de rizi" [Real life]. In *Chi Li Wenji* [Anthology of Chi Li's works], vol. 4, 13–20. Nanjing: Jiangsu wenyi chubanshe, 1995.

Chi Li and Xiao Yun. *Kouhong* [Lipstick]. Nanjing: Jiangsu wenyi chubanshe, 2000.

Chodorow, Nancy. *The Reproduction of Mothering: Psychoanalysis and the Sociology of Gender.* Berkeley: University of California Press, 1978.

Chow, Rey. "Virtuous Transactions: A Reading of Three Short Stories by Ling Shuhua." In *Gender Politics in Modern China: Writing and Feminism*, edited by Tani E. Barlow, 90–105. Durham, NC: Duke University Press, 1993.

Clarke, David, ed. *The Cinematic City.* London and New York: Routledge, 1997.

Comaroff, Jean, and John L. Comaroff, eds. *Millennial Capitalism and the Culture of Neoliberalism.* Durham, NC: Duke University Press, 2001.

Cong, Xiaoping. "Zuo Run su Wang Yinsuo: 20 shiji 40 niandai Shaanganning Bianqu de funü, hunyin yu guojia jiangou" [Zuo Ren versus Wang Yinsuo: Women, marriage and state-making in the Shaan-Gan-Ning Border Region of the 1940s]. *Kaifang shidai* [Open times] (October 2009): 62–79.

Conroy, Richard. "Patterns of Divorce in China." *Australian Journal of Chinese Affairs* 17 (January 1987): 53–75.

Cott, Nancy F. *The Bonds of Womanhood.* New Haven: Yale University Press, 1977.

Cowan, Ruth Schwartz. *More Work for Mother: The Ironies of Household Technology from the Open Hearth to the Microwave.* New York: Basic Books, 1983.

Croll, Elisabeth J. *The Politics of Marriage in Contemporary China*. New York: Cambridge University Press, 1981.

Cudd, Ann E., and Robin O. Andreasen, eds. *Feminist Theory: A Philosophical Anthology*. Oxford, UK, and Malden, MA: Blackwell, 2004.

Cui, Shuqin. "Ning Ying's Beijing Trilogy: Cinematic Configurations of Age, Class, and Sexuality." In *The Urban Generation: Chinese Cinema and Society at the Turn of the Twenty-first Century*, edited by Zhen Zhang, 241–63. Durham, NC, and London: Duke University Press, 2007.

Dai Houying. *Ren ah ren* [Ah, humanity!]. Guangzhou: Huacheng chubanshe, 1980.

Dai Jinhua, "Redemption and Consumption: Depicting Culture in the 1990s." In *Cinema and Desire: Feminist Marxism and Cultural Politics in the Work of Dai Jinhua*, edited by Jing Wang and Tani E. Barlow, 172-188. London and New York: Verso, 2002.

Dai, Qing. *Jia de yingxiang: Zhongguo dianshiju jiating lunli xushi yanjiu* [The image of home: A study of narratives of family ethics in Chinese TV dramas]. Beijing: Zhongguo chuanmei daxue chubanshe, 2008.

Daily Mail reporter. "Divorce Calculator Puts Price on Your Marriage: Government Body's Online Gadget That Undermines Commitment." *Daily Mail*, December 31, 2010. http://www.dailymail.co.uk/news/article-1342809/Government-launches-online-divorce-calculator-tell-separating-partners-get.html (accessed June 20, 2012).

Damm, Jens, and Simona Thomas, eds. *Chinese Cyberspaces: Technological Changes and Political Effects*. London and New York: Routledge, 2006.

Davis, Deborah, and Stevan Harrell, eds. *Chinese Families in the Post-Mao Era*. Berkeley: University of California Press, 1993.

Deng Xian. "Zhongguo zhiqing meng" [Dreams of Chinese sent-down youths]. *Dangdai* [Contemporary] (1992:5): 4–117.

Deng Youmei. "Zai xuanya shang" [On the cliff]. In *Deng Youmei duanpian xiaoshuo xuan* [Selected stories of Deng Youmei], 197–236. Beijing: Beijing chubanshe, 1981.

DeWoskin, Rachel. *Foreign Babes in Beijing: Behind the Scenes of a New China*. New York: W. W. Norton & Company, 2005.

———. "Wife Sentence." *Sunday Times Magazine*. October 22, 2006. http://www.timesonline.co.uk/article/0,,2099-2409883,00.html (accessed June 4, 2009).

Diamant, Neil J. "Pursuing Rights and Getting Justice on China's Ethnic Frontier, 1949–1966." *Law & Society Review* 35 (2001): 799–840.

———. "Re-examining the Impact of the 1950 Marriage Law: State Improvisation, Local Initiative and Rural Family Change." *China Quarterly* 161 (2000): 171–98.

———. *Revolutionizing the Family: Politics, Love, and Divorce in Urban and Rural China, 1949–1968*. Berkeley: University of California Press, 2000.

Dikötter, Frank. *Imperfect Conceptions: Medical Knowledge, Birth Defects, and Eugenics in China*. New York: Columbia University Press, 1998.

———. *Sex, Culture, and Modernity in China*. Honolulu: University of Hawai'i Press, 1995.

Ding Ling. *Muqin* [Mother]. Hong Kong: Huijin shudian, 1965.

———. "Sanba jie yougan" [My thoughts on March 8]. *Jiefang ribao*, March 9, 1942.

———. "Shafei nüshi de riji" [Diary of Miss Sophie]. In *Ding Ling zuopin xinshang* [Appreciating Ding Ling's works], edited by Guo Cheng and Chen Zongmin, 16–57. Guilin: Guangxi renmin chubanshe, 1986.

Ding Yun. "Qimeng zhutixing yu sanshinian sixiangshi—yi Li Zehou wei zhongxin" [Enlightenment subjectivity and the intellectual history of the past three decades—with a focus on Li Zehou]. *Dushu* [Reading] (2008:11): 17–27.

Dissanayake, Wimal, ed. *Melodrama and Asian Cinema*. Cambridge: Cambridge University Press, 1993.

Doane, Mary Ann. *Femmes Fatales: Feminism, Film Theory and Psychoanalysis*. New York: Routledge, 1991.

Donald, Stephanie. "Chinese Women and Chinese Film: Problems with History and Feminism." In *Women and Market Societies: Crisis and Opportunity*, edited by Barbara Einhorn and Eileen Janes Yeo, 84–95. Aldershot: E. Elgar, 1995.

Dong, Fengzhi. "On the Obstacles to Women's Participation in Politics on the Part of Women Themselves." In *Chinese Law and Government: Women and Politics in China* (2) 26.6 (November–December 1993): 39–49.

Dong Jian. "Tan "Dujuan tigui" de xinyi" [On the innovation of "Return, cries the cuckoo"]. In *Gui cheng* [Ghost city], 58–60. Shanghai: Shidai wenyi, 2000. Originally published in *Xinhua ribao* [Xinhua daily], October 13, 1980.

Dong, Madeleine Yue and Joshua Goldstein, eds. *Everyday Modernity in China*. Seattle: University of Washington Press, 2006.

Duggan, Lisa. *The Twilight of Equality?: Neoliberalism, Cultural Politics, and the Attack on Democracy*. Boston: Beacon Press, 2003.

Duke, Michael S. "Chinese Literature in the Post-reform Era: The Return of 'Critical Realism'." *Bulletin of Concerned Asian Scholars* 16.3 (1984): 2–5.

Engels, Friedrich. *The Origins of the Family, Private Property, and the State*. New York: Pathfinder, 1972.

Entwisle, Barbara, and Gail E. Henderson, eds. *Re-drawing Boundaries: Work, Households, and Gender in China.* Berkeley: University of California Press, 2000.

Evans, Harriet. *Women and Sexuality in China: Female Sexuality and Gender since 1949.* New York: Continuum, 1997.

Faison, Seth. "In China, Rapid Social Changes Bring a Surge in the Divorce Rate." *New York Times,* August 22, 1995. http://www.nytimes.com/1995/08/22/world/in-china-rapid-social-changes-bring-a-surge-in-the-divorce-rate.html?pagewanted=all&src=pm (accessed August 17, 2003).

Falü chubanshe (Law Press), ed. *Lihun wenti lunwen xuanji* [Selected essays on divorce]. Beijing: Falü chubanshe, 1958.

Fan Fu. "Shidai reci: Lihun jisuan qi" [Buzzword of our age: Divorce calculator]. *Xin jingbao* [Beijing news], June 25, 2011, B08.

Fan, Maureen. "Chinese Slough Off Old Barriers to Divorce." *Washington Post,* April 7, 2007, A01.

Fang Ji. "Rang shenghuo biande geng meihao ba" [Let's make life even better]. *Renmin wenxue* [People's literature] (1950: 3): 55–60.

Fang Ping. "Pingyong disu de cipin xiaoshuo—Ping 'Lihun zhinan" [Vulgar low-quality fiction—a review of "A divorce handbook"]. *Zuopin yu zhengming* [Works and debates] (1992:3): 45, 24.

Farquhar, Judith. *Appetites: Food and Sex in Post-Socialist China.* Durham, NC: Duke University Press, 2002.

Feng Cun. "Yige lihun anjian" [A divorce case]. *Benliu* [Torrents] (Febuary 1957): 1–10.

Foucault, Michel. "Governmentality." In *The Foucault Effect: Studies in Governmentality,* edited by Graham Burchell, Colin Gordon, and Peter Miller, 87–104.Chicago: The University of Chicago Press, 1991.

———. *The History of Sexuality: An Introduction,* vol. 1. Translated by Robert Hurley. New York: Vintage Books, 1990.

———. "Technologies of the Self." In *Technologies of the Self: A Seminar with Michel Foucault,* edited by Luther H. Martin, Huck Gutman, and Patrick Hutton, 16–49. Amherst: University of Massachusetts Press, 1988.

Freud, Sigmund. "A Case of Hysteria." In *Freud Reader,* edited by Peter Gay. New York: Norton, 1989.

———. "Femininity." In *The Standard Edition of the Complete Psychological Works of Sigmund Freud,* vol. 22 (1932–36), edited by James Strachey, 112–35. London: The Hogarth Press and the Institute of Psycho-analysis, 1964.

Fu, S. L. "The New Marriage Law of People's China." In *Contemporary*

China, edited by E. Stuart Kirby, vol. 1, 115–38. Hong Kong: Hong Kong University Press, 1955.

Gao Zhizhong and Wu Shiliu. "Bushi huanxiang de huanxiang gushi: Weilai de jiating shenghuo" [A fantasy story that's not a fantasy: Family life of the future]. *Shaonian kexue* [Youth science] (1981:12): 61–67.

Gates, Hill. "The Commoditization of Chinese Women." *Signs* 14.4 (Summer 1989): 799–832.

Geng Huanmei. *Ruhe rang nanren ai ni yisheng* [How to make a man to love you for a lifetime]. Beijing: Zhongguo qingnian chubanshe, 2009.

Giddens, Anthony. *Transformation of Intimacy: Sexuality, Love & Eroticism in Modern Societies*. Stanford: Stanford University Press, 1992.

———. *Modernity and Self-Identity: Self and Society in the Late Modern Age*. Stanford: Stanford University Press, 1991.

———. "Risk and Responsibility." *Modern Law Review* 62.1 (January 1999): 1–10.

Gilmartin, Christina Kelley. *Engendering the Chinese Revolution: Radical Women, Communist Politics, and Mass Movements in the 1920s*. Berkeley: University of California Press, 1995.

Gilmartin, Christina Kelley Gail Hershatter, Lisa Rofel, and Tyrene White, eds. *Engendering China*. Cambridge, MA: Harvard University Press, 1994.

Gladney, Dru. "Representing Nationality in China: Refiguring Majority/Minority Identities." *Journal of Asian Studies* 53.1 (1994): 92–123.

Glosser, Susan, ed. and trans. *Li Fengjin: How the New Marriage Law Helped Chinese Women Stand Up*. Portland, OR: Pal Mogus Books, 2005.

Goldman, Merle, Timothy Cheek, and Carol Lee Hamrin, eds. *China's Intellectuals and the State*. Cambridge, MA: Harvard University Press, 1987.

Grieder, Jerome B. *Intellectuals and the State in Modern China*. New York: The Free Press, 1981.

Gong, Haomin. "Constructing a Neorealist Reality: Petty Urbanites, Mundaneness, and Chi Li's Fiction." *Modern Chinese Literature and Culture* 22.1 (2010): 59–95.

———. *Uneven Modernity: Literature, Film, and Intellectual Discourse in Postsocialist China*. Honolulu: University of Hawai'i Press, 2012.

Greenhalgh, Susan. *Just One Child: Science and Policy in Deng's China*. Berkeley: University of California Press, 2008.

Grossberg, Lawrence. *We Gotta Get Out of This Place: Popular Conservatism and Postmodern Culture*. New York: Routledge, 1992.

Guo Xiaodong. "Nüren zai qinxie de shijie li" [Women in a tilted world]. *Piping jia* [Critics] (1988:6): 15–19.

———. "Muxing tuteng: Zhiqing wenxue de yizhong jingshen biange" [The totem of maternity: A change of heart in sent-down youth literature]. *Shanghai wenxue* [Shanghai literature] (1988:1): 90–96.

Guo Yuhua and Sun Liping. "Suku: Yizhong nongmin guojia guannian xingcheng de zhongjie jizhi" [Speaking bitterness: A mediating mechanism for the shaping of peasants' idea of the state]. *Zhongguo xueshu* [Chinese scholarship] 12 (2002:4): 130–57.

Hall, Stuart, and Martin Jacques, eds. *The Politics of Thatcherism*. London: Lawrence and Wishart, 1983.

Han Aili. "Tianyuan" [Pastorale]. *Shouhuo* [Harvest] (1981:4): 59–68.

Hang, Krista Van Fleit. "*People's Literature* and the Construction of a New Chinese Literary Tradition." *Journal of Modern Literature in Chinese* 9.2 (2009): 88–107.

Harrison, Graham. "Serving the Market or Serving the Party: Neo-liberalism in China." In *The Neo-liberal Revolution: Forging the Market State*, edited by Richard Robison, 114–31. Basingstoke and New York: Palgrave Macmillan, 2006.

Harvey, David. *A Brief History of Neoliberalism*. New York: Oxford University Press, 2005.

Haug, W. F. *Critique of Commodity Aesthetics, Appearance, Sexuality and Advertising in Capitalist Society*. Minneapolis: University of Minnesota Press,1986.

He Dan, "Marriage Database to Go Online." *Renmin wang* [*People's daily* online], December 30, 2010. http://english.peopledaily.com. cn/90001/90776/90882/7246513.html (accessed September 1, 2013).

He Guimei. *"Xin qimeng" zhishi dang'an: 80 niandai zhongguo wenhua yanjiu* ["New Enlightenment" knowledge archives: A study of 1980s Chinese culture]. Beijing: Beijing University Press, 2010.

Hebei Ji Xian Nanyue Dadui Tuanzhibu [Nanyue Brigade Branch of the Communist Youth Colleague of Ji County, Hebei]. "'Qingchun jiang' pingxuan huodong xiaoji" [A record of the "Youth Award" selection meeting]. *Qingchun* [Youth] (1981:4): 50–51.

Hegel, Robert E., and Richard C. Hessney, eds. *Expressions of Self in Chinese Literature*. New York: Columbia University Press, 1985.

Hershatter, Gail. *Dangerous Pleasures: Prostitution and Modernity in 20th-Century Shanghai*. Berkeley: University of California Press, 1997.

Hou, Denghua, and Zhang Jiasheng. *Lihun jiufen* [Divorce disputes]. Beijing: Zhongguo fazhi chubanshe, 2007.

Hsiau, A-chin. "The Moral Dilemma of China's Modernization: Rethinking

Zhang Yimou's *Qiu Ju da guansi.*" *Modern Chinese Literature* 10.1 (1998): 191–206.

Hsu, Immanuel C. Y. Hsu. *China without Mao: The Search for a New Order.* New York: Oxford University Press, 1990.

Hu Fayun. *Di sidai nüxing* [The fourth-generation women]. Wuhan: Changjiang wenyi chubanshe, 2000.

Hu Yijun "Getting 'Naked'." *China Daily* (December 2, 2011): 19.

Huang, Nicole. *Women, War, Domesticity: Shanghai Literature and Popular Culture of the 1940s.* Leiden and Boston: Brill, 2005.

Huang, Philip (Huang Zongzhi). "Divorce Law Practices and the Origins, Myths, and Realities of Judicial 'Mediation' in China." *Modern China* 31 (2005): 151–203.

———. "Women's Choices under the Law: Marriage, Divorce, and Illicit Sex in the Qing and the Republic." *Modern China* 27 (2001): 3–58.

———. "Zhongguo de xiandai jiating: Laizi jingji shi he falü shi de shijiao" [The modern Chinese family: In light of economic and legal history]. *Kaifang shidai* [Open times] (2011:5): 82–105.

Huang, Ping. "Talking about Gender, Globalization, and Labor in a Chinese Context." *Signs* 26.4 (Summer 2001): 1278–81.

Jaques, Elliott. "Death and the Mid-life Crisis." *International Journal of Psychoanalysis* 46 (1965): 502–14.

Jefferson, Margo. "The Return of the Shrew, and Other TV Woes." *New York Times*, September 6, 2005, E5.

Ji Bingxuan. "Changxiang zhu xuanlu, duochu jingpin ju" [Promote the mainstream melody, produce more quality dramas]. Speech given at the 2000 Television Drama Subject Advisory Meeting. *Zhongguo dianshi* [Chinese television] (2000:7): 3.

Ji Shi. "Meiyou zhishifenzi jiu meiyou xiandaihua" [Without intellectuals there will be no modernization]. In *Zhishifenzi wenti wenxuan* [Collection of essays on the problem of intellectuals], edited by Zhonggong Zhongyang Zuzhi bu Yanjiu shi [Chinese Communist Party Central Committee Organization Unit Research Office], 14–24. Beijing: Renmin chubanshe, 1983.

Jia Pingwa. "Jiwowa de renjia" [Households in the Chicken Nest Lowland]. In *Jiwowa de renjia* [Households in the Chicken Nest Lowland], 112–25. Beijing: Renmin wenxue chubanshe, 2006.

Jiazhi zhongguo. "'Zhonguo shi lihun' shidai" [The age of "Chinese-style divorce"]. *Jiazhi zhongguo* [China value]. http://focus.chinavalue.net/General/2011-12-9/372270.html (last accessed July 7, 2012).

Jin Guantao and Liu Qingfeng. "*Xin Qingnian* minzhu guannian de yanbian" [Evolution of the idea of democracy in *New Youth*]. *Ershiyi shiji* [Twenty-first century] 56 (1999:12): 29–41.

———. *Xingsheng yu weiji: Lun Zhongguo shehui chao wending jiegou* [Prosperity and crisis: on the ultra-stable structure of Chinese society]. Changsha: Hunan renmin chubanshe, 1984.

Jin Qi. "New Technology: Opportunity and Challenge." *Beijing Review*, no. 50 (December 12, 1983): 4.

Jin Yihong. "Rethinking the 'Iron Girls': Gender and Labour during the Chinese Cultural Revolution." Translated by Kimberley Ens Manning and Lianyun Chu. *Gender and History* 18.3 (November 2006): 613–34.

Johnson, Kay Ann. *Women, the Family, and Peasant Revolution in China.* Chicago: The University of Chicago Press, 1983.

Jones, Andrew F. *Developmental Fairy Tales: Evolutionary Thinking and Modern Chinese Culture.* Cambridge, MA, and London: Harvard University Press, 2011.

Judovitz, Dalia. *Subjectivity and Representation in Descartes: The Origins of Modernity.* Cambridge and New York: Cambridge University Press, 1988.

Kaplan, Amy. "Manifest Domesticity." *American Literature* 70.3 (September 1998): 581–606.

Kaplan, E. Ann. "Is the Gaze Male?" In *Feminism and Film*, edited by E. Ann Kaplan, 119–38. Oxford and New York: Oxford University Press, 2000.

Ke Ren. *Qizi bingfa* [Wife's art of war]. Beijing: Zhongguo yanshi, 2007.

Klein, Christina. *Cold War Orientalism: Asia in the Middlebrow Imagination, 1945–1961.* Berkeley: University of California Press, 2003.

Knight, Sabina. *The Heart of Time: Moral Agency in Twentieth-Century Chinese Fiction.* Cambridge, MA, and London: Harvard University Asia Center, 2006.

Ko, Dorothy. *Teachers of the Inner Chambers: Women and Culture in Seventeenth-Century China.* Stanford: Stanford University Press, 1994.

Kong, Shuyu. "Family Matters: Reconstructing the Family on the Chinese Television Screen." In *TV Drama in China*, edited by Ying Zhu, Michael Keane, and Ruoyun Bai, 75–88. Hong Kong: Hong Kong University Press, 2008.

Lao She. *Lihun* [Divorce]. Beijing: Renmin wenxue chubanshe, 1981.

———. *The Quest for Love of Lao Lee.* Translated by Helena Kuo. New York: Reynal & Hitchcock, 1948.

Larson, Wendy. *From Ah Q to Lei Feng: Freud and Revolutionary Spirit in 20th Century China.* Stanford: Stanford University Press, 2009.

———. "Women, Writers, Social Reform: Three Issues in Shen Rong's Fiction." In *Modern Chinese Women Writers: Critical Appraisals*, edited by Michael S. Duke, 174–95. Armonk, NY, and London: M. E. Sharpe, 1989.

Lasch, Christopher. *Haven in a Heartless World*. New York: Basic Books, 1977.

Lauretis, Teresa de. "Aesthetic and Feminist Theory: Rethinking Women's Cinema." *New German Critique* 34 (Winter 1985): 154–75.

———. *Technologies of Gender: Essays on Theory, Film, and Fiction*. Bloomington: Indiana University Press, 1987.

Lean, Eugenia. *Public Passions: The Trial of Shi Jianqiao and the Rise of Popular Sympathy in Republican China*. Berkeley: University of California Press, 2007.

Lee, Ching Kwan. *Against the Law: Labor Protests in China's Rustbelt and Sunbelt*. Berkeley: University of California Press, 2007.

Lee, Haiyan. "*Woman, Demon, Human*: The Spectral Journey Home." In *Chinese Films in Focus II*, edited by Chris Berry, 243–49. London: BFI and Palgrave Macmillan, 2008.

———. *Revolution of the Heart: A Genealogy of Love in China, 1900–1950*. Stanford: Stanford University Press, 2006.

Lee, Leo Ou-fan. "Afterword: Reflections on Change and Continuity in Modern Chinese Fiction." In *From May Fourth to June Fourth: Fiction and Film in Twentieth-Century China*, edited by Ellen Widmer and David Der-wei Wang, 361–84. Cambridge, MA: Harvard University Press, 1993.

———. *The Romantic Generation of Modern Chinese Writers*. Cambridge, MA: Harvard University Press, 1973.

Leung, Lai-fong. "In Search of Love and Self: The Image of Young Female Intellectuals in Post-Reform Women's Fiction." In *Modern Chinese Women Writers: Critical Appraisals*, edited by Michael S. Duke, 135–51. Armonk, NY, and London: M. E. Sharpe, 1989.

———. *Morning Sun: Interviews with Chinese Writers of the Lost Generation*. Armonk, NY: M. E. Sharpe, 1994.

Li, Ke, and Sara L. Friedman. "The Wedding of Marriage, Nation, and State in Modern China: Legal Consequences for Divorce, Property, and Women's Rights." In *Domestic Tensions, National Anxieties: Global Perspectives on Modern Marriage Crises*, edited by Kristin Celello and Hanan Kholoussy. New York: Oxford University Press, forthcoming.

Li Ming. "Popularizing Science in China." *Beijing Review*, no. 9 (March 1, 1982): 20–26.

Li Xiaojiang. "Economic Reform and the Awakening of Chinese Women's Collective Consciousness." In *Engendering China: Women, Culture and the State*, edited by Christina K. Gilmartin, Gail Hershatter, Lisa Rofel, and Tyrene White, 360–82. Cambridge, MA: Harvard University Press, 1994.

————. "From 'Modernization' to 'Globalization': Where Are Chinese Women?" Translated by Tani E. Barlow. *Signs* 26. 4 (2001): 1274–78.

————. *Xiawa de tansuo: Funü yanjiu lungao* [Eve's exploration: Papers in women's studies]. Zhengzhou: He'nan renmin chubanshe, 1988.

Li Zehou. *Li Zehou zhexue meixue wenxuan* [Selected essays of Li Zehou on philosophy and aesthetics]. Changsha: Hunan renmin chubanshe, 1985.

————. *Zhongguo xiandai sixiang shi lun* [A history of modern Chinese thought]. Tianjin: Shehui kexueyuan, 2003.

Liang Xiaosheng. *Nüren Xinqing* [Women's feelings]. Beijing: Zhongguo qingnian chubanshe, 1999.

Ling, L. H. M. "The Limit of Democratization for Women in East Asia." In *Democracy and the Status of Women in East Asia*, edited by Tose J. Lee and Cal Clark, 169–82. Boulder, CO: Lynne Rienner Publishers, 2000.

Liu Binyan. "Man Is the Aim, Man Is the Center." Translated by John Beyer. In *Chinese Literature for the 1980s: The Fourth Congress of Writers and Artists*, edited by Howard Goldblatt, 121–31. Armonk, NY: M. E. Sharpe, 1982.

Liu, Jian. *Zhongguoshi lihun baogao* [Chinese-style divorce reports]. Beijing: Zhongguo guangbo dianshi chubanshe, 2004.

Liu, Jianmei. *Revolution Plus Love: Literary History, Women's Bodies, and Thematic Repetition in Twentieth-Century Chinese Fiction*. Honolulu: University of Hawai'i Press, 2003.

Liu, Jieyu. *Gender and Work in Urban China: Women Workers of the Unlucky Generation*. London and New York: Routledge, 2007.

Liu Liu. "Yun" [Fortune]. In *Fu shi hui* [Portraits of the floating world], 143–51. Beijing: Zhongguo funü chubanshe, 2009.

Liu, Lydia. "Invention and Intervention: The Making of a Female Tradition in Modern Chinese Literature." In *Chinese Femininities, Chinese Masculinities: A Reader*, edited by Susan Brownell and Jeffrey N. Wasserstrom, 149–74. Berkeley: University of California Press, 2002.

Liu Siqian. "Hunyin wuyu" [The tale of marriage]. *Zhongguo nüxingzhuyi* [Chinese feminism] 4 (Summer 2005): 177.

Liu Zaifu. "The Subjectivity of Literature Revisited." Translated by Mary Scoggin. In *Politics, Ideology, and Literary Discourse in Modern China: Theoretical Interventions and Cultural Critique*, edited by Liu Kang and Xiaobing Tang, 56–69. Durham, NC: Duke University Press, 1993.

Lock, Magaret M. *Encounters with Aging: Mythologies of Menopause in Japan and North America*. Berkeley: University of California Press, 1993.

Louie, Kam. "Love Stories: The Meaning of Love and Marriage in China." In *After Mao: Chinese Literature and Society 1978–1981*, edited by

Jeffrey C. Kinkley, 63–87. Cambridge, MA, and London: Harvard University Press, 1985.

———. *Theorising Chinese Masculinity: Society and Gender in China*. Cambridge: Cambridge University Press, 2002.

Lu, Jie. "Cultural Invention and Cultural Intervention: Reading Chinese Urban Fiction of the Nineties." *Modern Chinese Literature and Culture* 13. 1 (Spring 2001): 107–39.

Lu, Sheldon Hsiao-peng. *China, Transnational Visuality, Global Postmodernity*. Stanford: Stanford University Press, 2001.

Lu, Tonglin, ed. *Gender and Sexuality in Twentieth-Century Chinese Literature and Society*. Albany: State University of New York Press, 1993.

———. *Misogyny, Cultural Nihilism, and Oppositional Politics*. Stanford: Stanford University Press, 1995.

Lu Xueyi. *Dangdai zhongguo shehui jieceng yanjiu baogao* [A research report on contemporary Chinese social strata]. Beijing: Shehui kexue wenxian chubanshe, 2002.

Lu Xun. "Kuangren Riji" [Diary of a madman]. In *Lu Xun quanji* [The complete works of Lu Xun], vol. 1, 422–33. Beijing: Renmin wenxue chubanshe, 1981.

———. "Lihun" [Divorce]. In *Lu Xun quanji* [The complete works of Lu Xun], vol. 2, 144–55. Beijing: Renmin wenxue chubanshe, 1982.

———. "Nala zouhou zenyang" [What happens after Nora leaves home]. In *Lu Xun quanji* [The complete works of Lu Xun], vol. 1, 158–65. Beijing: Renmin wenxue chubanshe, 1981.

Lu Yin. "Lishi de riji" [Lishi's diary]. In *Lu Yin xuanji* [Selected works of Lu Yin], edited by Xiao Feng and Sun Ke, 47–58. Tianjin: Baihua wenyi chubanshe, 1983.

Lü Pin. "'Lihun nan' neng jiang lihun lü ma?" [Can "difficult divorce procedures" lower the divorce rate?]. *Xin jingbao* [Beijing news], March 11, 2010, A05.

Lyotard, Jean-François. *The Postmodern Condition: A Report on Knowledge*. Translated by Geoff Bennington and Brian Massumi. Minneapolis: University of Minnesota Press, 1984.

Mao Dun. *Ziye* [Midnight]. Shanghai: Kaiming shudian, 1933.

Mao Zedong. "To Fully Bring Out Women's Initiative in the Revolutionary Construction." *Hongqi* [Red flag] (1971:10): 60–64.

Marchetti, Gina. "Gender Politics and Neoliberalism in China: Ann Hui's *The Postmodern Life of My Aunt*." *Visual Anthropology* 22. 2 (2009): 123–40.

McDougall, Bonnie, and Kam Louie. *The Literature of China in the Twentieth Century*. New York: Columbia University Press, 1997.

McGrath, Jason. *Postsocialist Modernity: Chinese Cinema, Literature, and Criticism in the Market Age*. Stanford: Stanford University Press, 2008.

McMahon, Keith. *Misers, Shrews, and Polygamists: Sexuality and Male-Female Relations in Eighteenth-Century Chinese Fiction*. Durham, NC: Duke University Press, 1995.

——. *Polygamy and Sublime Passion: Sexuality in China on the Verge of Modernity*. Honolulu: University of Hawai'i Press, 2010.

Meade, Teresa A., and Merry E. Wiesner-Hanks, eds. *A Companion to Gender History*. Oxford: Blackwell Publishing, 2006.

Meijer, Marinus J. "Marriage Law and Policy in the People's Republic of China." In *Chinese Family Law and Social Change in Historical and Comparative Perspective*, edited by David C. Buxbaum, 436–83. Seattle: University of Washington Press, 1978.

Meisner, Maurice. *Deng Xiaoping's Era*. New York: Hill & Wang, 1996.

Meng Xiaoyun. "Wang Hailing: 'Hunyin diyi xieshou'" [Wang Hailing: "The best writer on marriage"]. *Renmin ribao* [People's daily], overseas edition, March 1, 2007.

Meng, Yue. *Shanghai and the Edges of Empires*. Minneapolis: University of Minnesota Press, 2006.

——. "Su Tong de 'jiashi' yu 'lishi' xiezuo" [On Su Tong's writings of "family genealogy" and "history"]. *Jintian* [Today] (1990:2): 84–93.

Merry, Sally Engle. *Getting Justice and Getting Even: Legal Consciousness among Working-Class Americans*. Chicago: The University of Chicago Press, 1990.

Mies, Maria, and Vandana Shiva. *Ecofeminism*. New Delhi: Gayatri Offset Press, 1993.

Millman, Marcia, and Kanter Moss, eds. *Another Voice: Feminist Perspectives on Social Life and Social Science*. New York: Anchor Books, 1975.

Ministry of Civil Affairs. "Minzheng bu fabu 2010 nian shehui fuwu fazhan tongji baogao" [2010 statistics of social services]. Ministry of Civil Affairs, June 16, 2011.

http://www.mca.gov.cn/article/zwgk/mzyw/201106/20110600161364.shtml (accessed October 2, 2011).

Mohanty, Chandra. "Under Western Eyes: Feminist Scholarship and Colonial Discourses." *Feminist Review* 30 (1988): 61–88.

Mohanty, Chandra, Ann Russo, and Lourdes Torres, eds. *Third World Women and the Politics of Feminism*. Bloomington: Indiana University Press, 1991.

Morley, David. *Home Territories: Media, Mobility, and Identity*. London and New York: Routledge, 2000.

Mu Ling. "Literary Criticism in the 1980s." *Modern China* 4 (October 1995): 420–27.

Mu Shiying. "Shanghai de hubuwu" [Shanghai foxtrot]. In *Mu Shiying daibiaozuo* [Representative works of Mu Shiying], edited by Li Jin, 153–64. Beijing: Huaxia chubanshe, 1998.

Myers, Ramon. "China's Consumer Revolution: The 1990s and Beyond." *Journal of Contemporary China* 7. 18 (1998): 351–68.

Nan, Fan. "Wenxue: chengshi yu xiangcun" [Literature: Urban and rural]. *Shanghai wenlun* [Shanghai literary theories] (1990:4): 29–33.

Negra, Diane. *What a Girl Wants?: Fantasizing the Reclamation of Self in Postfeminism*. London: Routledge, 2008.

Ni Zhengmao. "Establishing Intellectuals' Constitutional Status." *Beijing Review*, no. 50 (December 15, 1986): 18.

Ocko, Jonathan K. "Women, Property, and Law in the People's Republic of China." In *Marriage and Inequality in Chinese Society*, edited by Rubie S. Watson and Patricia Buckley Ebrey, 313–46. Berkeley: University of California Press, 1991.

Ong, Aihwa. *Flexible Citizenship: The Cultural Logics of Transnationality*. Durham, NC: Duke University Press, 1999.

Ono, Kazuko. *Chinese Women in a Century of Revolution, 1850–1950*. Edited by Joshua A. Fogel, translated by Kathryn Bernhardt et al. Stanford: Stanford University Press, 1989.

Palmer, Michael. "The Re-Emergence of Family Law in Post-Reform China: Marriage, Divorce and Reproduction." *China Quarterly* 141 (1995): 110–34.

———. "Transforming Family Law in Post-Deng China: Marriage, Divorce and Reproduction." *China Quarterly* 191 (2007): 675–95.

Podvin, Thomas. "Tale of the dark side/director Ann Hui explores the seamy side of Postmodern Shanghai." *Hong Kong Cinemagic*. http://blog.hkcinemagic.com/thomas-podvin/index.php/2007/10/17/292-the-postmodern-life-of-my-aunt-ann-hui (accessed June 10, 2010).

Poovey, Mary. *Uneven Developments: The Ideological Work of Gender in Mid-Victorian England*. Chicago: The University of Chicago Press, 1988.

Pransky, George S. *Lihun wujiyushi: Ruhe tiaozheng yu wanjiu hunyin* [Divorce is not the answer: A change of heart will save your marriage]. Translated by Wang shizhen. Beijing: Zhongyang bianyi chubanshe, 1998.

Qiang Shigong. "Sifa nengdong xia de zhongguo jiating: Cong zuigao fayuan guanyu 'Hunyin fa' de sifa jiashi tanqi" [Chinese families under judicial activism: Thoughts on the Supreme Court's judicial interpretation of the marriage law]. *Wenhua zongheng* [Beijing cultural review] (Febuary 2011): 24–30.

Qiao Lihua. *Wo ye shi Lu Xun de yiwu—Zhu An zhuan* [I am also Lu Xun's legacy: A biography of Zhu An] . Shanghai: Shanghai shehui kexue chubanshe, 2009.

Qiu Lihua. "*Zhongguoshi lihun* shoushilü Shanghai 'gaoshao' butui guanzhong dangcheng jiaokeshu" [The viewer ratings of *Chinese-Style Divorce* remain high in Shanghai, audiences take it as a textbook]. *Xinwen chenbao* [Shanghai morning post], November 24, 2004, B7.

Read, Benjamin L. "Property Rights and Homeowner Activism in New Neighborhoods." In *Privatizing China: Socialism from Afar*, edited by Li Zhang and Aihwa Ong, 41–56. Ithaca, NY, and London: Cornell University Press, 2008.

Ren, Hai. "The Neoliberal State and Risk Society: The Chinese State and the Middle Class." *Telos* 151 (Summer 2010): 105–28.

Ren Qiuling. "Jiayou xianqi de nanren bi danshenhan zhuanqian duo" [Men with good wives at home can make more money than bachelors]. *Shenghuo bao*, July 8, 2005.

Renmin ribao [People's daily]. "Minzhu yu fazhi" [Democracy and rule by law]. *Renmin ribao* [People's daily], July 13, 1978.

Reuters. "China Reinterprets Untying the Knot." Reporting by the Beijing newsroom, edited by Chris Buckley and Elaine Lies, August 30, 2011. http://www.reuters.com/article/2011/08/30/us-china-divorce-idUS-TRE77T0K020110830 (accessed May 30, 2012).

Richards, I. A. *Science and Poetry*. New York: Norton, 1926.

Roberts, Rosemary A. "Images of Women in the Fiction of Zhang Jie and Zhang Xinxin." *China Quarterly* 120 (December 1989): 800–813.

Robinson, Jean C. "Of Women and Washing Machines: Employment, Housework, and the Reproduction of Motherhood in Socialist China." *China Quarterly* 101 (March 1985): 32–57.

Rofel, Lisa B. *Desiring China: Experiments in Neoliberalism, Sexuality, and Public Culture*. Durham, NC: Duke University Press, 2007.

———. "'Yearnings': Televisual Love and Melodramatic Politics in Contemporary China." *American Ethnologist* 21.4 (November 1994): 700–722.

Rogaski, Ruth. *Hygienic Modernity: Meanings of Health and Disease in Treaty-Port China*. Berkeley: University of California Press, 2004.

Sang, Tze-Lan D. *The Emerging Lesbian: Female Same-Sex Desire in Modern China*. Chicago: The University of Chicago Press, 2003.

Schiebinger, Londa. Introduction to *Feminism & the Body*, edited by Londa Schiebinger, 1–21. Oxford: Oxford University Press, 2000.

Schmalzer, Sigrid. "On the Appropriate Use of Rose-Colored Glasses: Reflections on Science in Socialist China." In *Mr. Science and Chairman Mao's Cultural Revolution: Science and Technoglosy in Modern China*, edited by Chuanjuan Nancy Wei and Darryl E. Brock, 347–61. Lanham, MD: Lexington Books, 2013.

Scott, Joan W. "Gender: A Useful Category of Historical Analysis." *American Historical Review* 91.5 (2001): 1053–75.

Seller, Charles. *The Market Revolution: Jacksonian America, 1815–1846.* New York: Oxford University Press, 1991.

Sha Lin. "Zhongguoshi lihun lu zai hefang—Wang Hailing de hunyin gushi" [Where is the way out of the Chinese-style divorce—a story of Wang Hailing's marriage]. *Zhuanji wenxue* [Biographic literature] (2005:1): 30–36.

Shang Wenxiang. "Cong *Wuzi* dao 'Fangzhou': Jiedu 'Xiaojie nizao'" [From *Wordless* to "The Ark": Interpreting "Good Morning, Miss"]. *Anhui wenxue* [Anhui literature] (2007:9): 22.

Shanghai tongji ju, ed. *Shanghai tongji nianjian 2008* [Shanghai statistical yearbook 2008]. Beijing: Zhongguo tongji chubanshe, 2008.

She, Colleen S. "Toward Ideology: Views of the May Fourth Intelligentsia on Love, Marriage, and Divorce." *Issues and Studies* 27.2 (1991): 104–32.

Shek, Daniel T. L. "Midlife Crisis in Chinese Men and Women." *Journal of Psychology* 130.1 (1996): 109–19.

Shen Yifei. *Beijiangou de nüxing* [The constructed woman]. Shanghai: Renmin chubanshe, 2005.

Shih, Shu-Mei. "Gender and a New Geopolitics of Desire: The Seduction of Mainland Women in Taiwan and Hong Kong Media." *Signs* 23.2 (Winter 1998): 287–319.

Sieber, Patricia, ed. *Red Is Not the Only Color: Contemporary Chinese Fiction on Love and Sex between Women, Collected Stories.* Lanham, MD: Rowman & Littlefield, 2001.

Simmel, Georg. *The Philosophy of Money.* London: Rutledge, 1978.

Simon, Denis Fred. "China's Scientists and Techonologists in the Post-reform Era: A Retrospective and Prospective Glimpse." In *China's Intellectuls and the State: In Search of a New Relationship*, edited by Merle Goldman with Timothy Cheek and Carol Lee Hamrin, 129–156. Cambridge, MA, and London: The Council on East Asian Studies, Harvard University, 1987.

Siu, Helen F. *Furrows, Peasants, Intellectuals, and the State: Stories and Histories from Modern China.* Stanford: Stanford University Press, 1990.

Smedley, Agnes. *Portraits of Chinese Women in Revolution.* Old Westbury, NY: Feminist Press, 1976.

Stacey, Judith. *Patriarchy and Socialist Revolution in China.* Berkeley: University of California Press, 1983.

Stanley, Liz, and Sue Wise, eds. *Breaking Out: Feminist Consciousness and Feminist Research.* London: Routledge, 1983.

Stone, Lawrence. *The Family, Sex and Marriage in England, 1500–1800*. New York: Harper and Row, 1977.

Stringer, Julian. "Boat People: Second Thoughts on Text and Context." In *Chinese Films in Focus II*, edited by Chris Berry, 40–47. London and New York: BFI and Palgrave Macmillan, 2008.

Su Liwen. "'Aiqing re' manbu Zhongguo wentan" [A "craze for love" sweeps the Chinese literary circle]. *Qishi niandai* [The 1970s] (1982:2): 76–79.

Su Qing. *Jiehun shinian* [Married for ten years]. Beijing: Zhongguo funü chubanshe, 2009/1943.

Su Tong. "A Divorce Handbook." In *Tattoo: Three Novellas*, translated by Josh Stenberg, 1–74. Portland, ME: MerwinAsia, 2010.

———. "Kuangben" [Running wild]. *Zhongshan* [Bell Mountain] (1991:1): 123–27.

———. "Lihun zhinan" [A divorce handbook]. In *Hunyin jijing* [Snapshots of married life], 197–246. Nanjing: Jiangsu wenyi chubanshe, 1993.

———. "1934 nian de taowang" [1934 escapes]. *Shouhuo* [Harvest] (1987: 5): 55–74.

———. "Tao" [Escapes]. *Qingnian wenxue* [Youth literature] (1989:3): 44–47.

———. "Yihun nanren" [A married man]. In *Hunyin jijing* [Snapshots of married life], 165–96. Nanjing: Jiangsu wenyi chubanshe, 1993.

———. "Zixu" [Preface]. In *Hunyin jijing* [Snapshots of married life], 1–2. Nanjing: Jiangsu wenyi chubanshe, 1993.

Sun Lung-kee. *Zhongguo wenhua de shenceng jiegou* [The deep structure of Chinese culture]. Hong Kong: Yishan chubanshe, 1983.

Sun Qian. *Qiyi de lihun gushi* [A Strange Tale of Divorce]. Wuhan: Changjiang wenyi chubanshe, 1956.

Sun Ying. "Zhongguo shi lihun zui ziyou" [Chinese-style divorce is the freest]. *Beijing wanbao* [Beijing evening post], March 22, 2010.

Su Xiaokang. "Yin yang da liebian" [The great fission of yin and yang] in *Yin yang da liebian* [The great fission of yin and yang], 1–69. Nanjing: Jiangsu wenyi chubanshe, 1987.

Tan Renjiu. *Zhongguo de lihun yanjiu* [A study of divorce in China]. Shanghai: Zhonghua Jidujiao Nüqingnian hui quanguo xiehui, 1932.

Tang Jian. "*Zhongguoshi lihun* re le hunyinju" [*Chinese-Style Divorce* has caused a fever for marriage dramas]. *Shanghai xingqisan* [Shanghai Wednesday], November 10, 2004. 11.

Tang Ling and Hu Yusun. "Ziwo sangshi he jingshen weihun—*Zhongguoshi Lihun* de nüxing beiju tanyin" [Lost self and spiritual besiegement—an analysis of the woman's tragedy in *Chinese-Style Divorce*]. *Dangdai dianshi* [Contemporary television] 201 (2005:1): 37–38.

Tang, Tsou. *The Cultural Revolution and Post-Mao Reforms: A Historical Perspective*. Chicago: The Chicago University Press, 1986.

Tang, Xiaobing. "Decorating Culture: Notes on Interior Design, Interiority, and Interiorization." *Public Culture* 10.3 (1998): 530–548.

———. *Chinese Modern: The Heroic and the Quotidian*. Durham, NC: Duke University Press, 2000.

Tang Xinyong. "Wei chenggong zhangfu dazao wanmei nüren" [Producing perfect woman for her successful husband]. *Zhongwai funü wenzhai* [World women's digest] (2005:1): 70–71.

Tengxun yule [Tencent entertainment]. "Yang Lan fawen *Zhongguoshi lihun*, Jiang Wenli zuoke *Tianxia Nüren*" [Yang Lan inquires about *Chinese-Style Divorce*, Jiang Wenli is invited to the talk show *Women under the Heaven*]. http://ent.qq.com/a/20050524/000152.htm (accessed January 3, 2009).

Tian Han. "Shuofeng" [Northern wind]. In *Tian Han quanji* [The complete works of Tian Han], vol. 13, 83–86. Shijiazhuang: Huashan wenyi chubanshe, 2000.

Visser, Robin. *Cities Surround the Countryside: Urban Aesthetics in Postsocialist China*. Durham, NC: Duke University Press, 2010.

Vittinghoff, Natascha. "Jiang Qing and Nora: Drama and Politics in the Republican Period." In *Women in China: The Republican Period in Historical Perspective*, edited by Mechthild Leutner and Nicola Spakowski, 208–41. Münster: LIT, 2005.

Wagner, Rudolph G. "Lobby Literature: The Archeology and Present Functions of Science Fiction in China." In *After Mao: Chinese Literature and Society 1978–1981*, edited by Jeffrey C. Kinkley, 17–62. Cambridge, MA, and London: Harvard University Press, 1985.

Wallerstein, Judith S., and Sandra Blakeslee. *Second Chances: Men, Women, and Children a Decade After Divorce*. Boston and New York: Houghton Mifflin, 2004/1989.

Wang, Ban. *Illuminations from the Past: Trauma, Memory, and History in Modern China*. Stanford: Stanford University Press, 2004.

———. *The Sublime Figure of History*. Stanford: Stanford University Press, 1997.

Wang Danru, ed. *Erqiao lihun* [Erqiao gets a divorce]. Xi'an: Chang'an shudian, 1953.

Wang, David Der-wei. *Fin-de-siècle Splendor: Repressed Modernities of Late Qing Fiction, 1849–1911*. Stanford: Stanford University Press, 1997.

Wang Fengbo and Sun Luqian, eds. *Xu Chi yanjiu zhuanji* [Studies on Xu Chi]. Hangzhou: Zhejiang wenyi chubanshe, 1989.

Wang Fuxiang. "'Nüxing wenxue' zhiyi" [Questioning "women's literature"]. *Dangdai wenyi sichao* [Trends in contemporary literature and art] (1984:2): 16–22.

Wang Hailing. *Qianshou* [Holding hands]. Beijing: Renmin wenxue chubanshe, 1999.

———. *Xin jiehun shidai* [New age of marriage]. Beijing: Zuojia chubanshe, 2006.

———. *Zhongguoshi lihun* [Chinese-style divorce]. Beijing: Beijing Press, 2004.

Wang Hui. "Contemporary Chinese Thought and the Question of Modernity." *Social Text* 55 (Summer 1998): 9–44.

———. *Xiandai Zhongguo sixiang de xingqi* [The emergence of modern Chinese thoughts]. Beijing: Sanlian shudian, 2004.

Wang Hui and Theodore Huters. *China's New Order: Society, Politics, and Economy in Transition.* Cambridge, MA: Harvard University Press, 2003.

Wang, Jing. *High Culture Fever.* Berkeley: University of California Press, 1996.

Wang Kai. "Qunni lihun ji" [The story of Qunni's divorce]. In *Qunni lihun ji* [The story of Qunni's divorce], 85–106. Shanghai: Huadong renmin chubanshe, 1951.

Wang Meng. "Duobi chonggao" [Stay away from the sublime]. *Dushu* [Reading] (1993:1): 10–16.

Wang, Qi. "State-Society Relations and Women's Political Participation." In *Women of China: Economic and Social Transformation*, edited by Jackie West, Zhao Minghua, Chang Xiangqun, and Cheng Yuan, 19–44. New York: St. Martin's Press, 1999.

Wang, Qingbin, and Qin Zhou. "China's Divorce and Remarriage Rates: Trends and Regional Disparities." *Journal of Divorce & Remarriage* 51.4 (2010): 257–67.

Wang Ru. *Women weishenme lihun* [Why do we divorce]. Beijing: Wenjin chubanshe, 2005.

Wang Xiaoming, ed. "Kuangye shang de feixu—wenxue he renwen jingshen de weiji" [Ruins on the open field—Literature and the crisis of the humanist spirit]. *Shanghai wenxue* [Shanghai literature] (1993:6): 63–71.

———. *Renwen jingshen xinsi lu* [Reflections on the humanist spirit]. Shanghai: Wenhui chubanshe, 1996.

Wang Xin, and Chen Lidan, eds. "Divorce Rate Rises for Seven Straight Years in China." *Renmin wang* [People's daily], February 19, 2013.

http://english.people.com.cn/90882/8134709.html (accessed September 2, 2013).

Wang Ying and Di Fang. "1.61 Million Couples Break Up in 2004." *China Daily* (March 2, 2005): 2.

Wang, Zheng. *Women in the Chinese Enlightenment: Oral and Textual Histories*. Berkeley: University of California Press, 1999.

Wang Zunsan. "Feng Junying lihun" [Feng Junying gets a divorce]. In *Feng Junying lihun* [Feng Junying gets a divorce], 1–9. Beijing: Baowentang shudian, 1952.

Watson, Burton. *The Selected Poems of Du Fu*. New York: Columbia University Press, 2002.

Watson, Rubie S., and Patricia Buckley Ebrey, eds. *Marriage and Inequality in Chinese Society*. Berkeley: University of California Press, 1991.

Weitzman, Lenore J. *The Divorce Revolution: The Unexpected Social and Economic Consequences for Women and Children in America*. New York and London: The Free Press, 1985.

Wen Yong and Quan Fu. *Nijing · lizhi · chengcai* [Adversities · resolution · success]. Chengdu: Sichuan renmin chubanshe, 1984.

White, Jerry. "The Films of Ning Ying: China Unfolding in Miniature." *Cineaction* 42.1 (1997): 2–9.

Widmer, Ellen, and Kang-I Sun Chang, eds. *Writing Women in Late Imperial China*. Stanford: Stanford University Press, 1997.

Williams, Raymond. *The Country and the City*. New York: Oxford University Press, 1973.

———. "Structures of Feeling." In *Marxism and Literature*, 128–35. Oxford: Oxford University Press, 1977.

Wolf, Margery. *Revolution Postponed: Women in Contemporary China*. Stanford: Stanford University Press, 1985.

Wong, Linda. "Family Reform through Divorce Law in the PRC." *UCLA Pacific Basin Law Journal* 1.2 (Fall 1982): 265–84.

Wu Deqing. *Dangdai zhongguo lihun xianzhuang ji fazhan qushi* [The patterns and trends of divorce in contemporary China]. Beijing: Wenwu chubanshe, 1999.

Wu, Guo. "Subversion of the Feminist Myth in Chinese Film and Its Dilemma." *Asian Cinema* 16.1 (2005): 325–33.

Wu Ruozeng. *Dangdai wenxue fenlei ABC* [Contemporary literature categorization ABC]. In *Wu Ruozeng zawen suibi zixuanji* [A self-selection of Wu Ruozeng's essays], 193–99. Beijing: Qunyan chubanshe, 1994.

———. "Funü jiefang zhi qianti dang wei nanren zhi jiefang" [The precondition of women's liberation must be men's liberation]. In *Wu Ruozeng zawen suibi zixuanji* [A self-selection of Wu Ruozeng's essays], 175–78. Beijing: Qunyan chubanshe, 1994.

———. *Liyi: Yige dangdai zhongguo nanren de neixin dubai* [Divorce: An interior monologue of a contemporary Chinese man]. *Shiyue* [October] 48 (1986:6): 158–268.

———. "Nanzihan—nanren de lixiang" (Real man—man's ideal). In *Wu Ruozeng zawen suibi zixuanji* [A self-selection of Wu Ruozeng's essays], 127–33. Beijing: Qunyan chubanshe, 1994.

———. "Zai nanyi xiaohua de lishi yu xianshi mianqian zhi dubai" [A monologue in the face of indigestible history and reality]. In *Wu Ruozeng zawen suibi zixuanji* [A self-selection of Wu Ruozeng's essays], 25–29. Beijing: Qunyan chubanshe, 1994.

Wu Xin. "Zhenshi de miaoxie, dadan de tansuo" [Realistic depiction, brave exploration]. In *Gui cheng* [Ghost city], 50–53. Shanghai: Shidai wenyi, 2000. Originally published in *Xinhua ribao* [Xinhua daily], September 3, 1980.

Wu Xueshan. "Suzao hunyin" [Forging marriage]. Translated by Hui Xiao. *Inter-Asia Cultural Studies* 7.3 (2006): 502–10.

Xia Yinlan. "Zhongguo shi lihun zui ziyou de guojia" [China is the freest country in terms of divorce]. *Xiaokang* [Well-being], July 7, 2009. http:// news.sina.com.cn/c/sd/2009–07–07/140718171866_4.shtml (accessed May 27, 2010).

Xia Zhongyi. "Cong Xianglin sao, Shafei nüshi dao 'Fangzhou'" [From Xianglin's wife and Miss Sophie to "The Ark"]. *Dangdai wenyi sichao* [Trends in contemporary literature and art] (1983:5): 58–63.

Xiao, Hui Faye. "Interiorized Feminism and Gendered Nostalgia of the 'Daughter-Generation' in Ning Ying's *Perpetual Motion*." *Journal of Chinese Cinemas* 5.3 (2011): 253–68.

Xiao Yemu. "Women fufu zhijian" [Between the two of us]. *Renmin wenxue* [People's literature] (1950: 1): 37–45.

Xie Bingying. *A Woman Soldier's Own Story: The Autobiography of Xie Bingying.* Translated by Lily Chia Brissman and Barry Brissman. New York: Columbia University Press, 2001.

Xinhuanet. "Dianji 2004 Zhongguo 'reci' zheshe Zhongguo zhengzhi, shehui bianqian" [Clicking 2004 Chinese "hot words" reflecting political and social transformations of China]. http://news.xinhuanet.com/ newscenter/2004–12/28/content_2388092.htm (accessed April 20, 2009).

Xu Anqi. "Lihun yu nüxing diwei ji quanyi zhi tantao" [A study of divorce and women's status and rights]. *Zhejiang xuekan* [Zhejiang academic journal] (2007:1): 198–206.

Xu Chi. "Dizhi zhi guang" [The light of geology]. *Renmin wenxue* [People's literature] (1977:10): 4–15.

———. "Gedebahe Caixiang" [Goldbach's Conjecture]. *Renmin wenxue* [People's literature] (1978:1): 53–68.

Xu Dancheng. "'Xiaojie nizao' zhong de xingbie yishi" [Gender consciousness in "Good Morning, Miss"]. *Wenyi lilun yu piping* [Literary theories and criticism] (2003: 6): 121–25.

Xu Dishan (Luo Huasheng). "Chuntao." In *Chuntao*, 1–36. Shanghai: Shenghuo shudian, 1935.

Xu, Gary, and Susan Feiner. "*Meinü Jingji*/China's Beauty Economy: Buying Looks, Shifting Value, and Changing Place." *Feminist Economics* 13.3–4 (2007): 307–23.

Xu Mingyu. "Diaodong" [Transfer]. In *Zhengming zuopin xuanbian* [A selection of controversial works], vol. 1, 325–97. Beijing: Beijing wenlian yanjiubu, neibu ziliao, 1981.

Yan, Haiping. *Chinese Women Writers and the Feminist Imagination, 1905–1948*. New York: Routledge, 2006.

Yan, Hairong. *New Masters, New Servants: Migration, Development, and Women Workers in China*. Durham, NC: Duke University Press, 2008.

Yan, Yunxiang. *The Individualization of Chinese Society*. Oxford and New York: Berg, 2009.

———. *Private Life under Socialism: Love, Intimacy, and Family Change in a Chinese Village, 1949–1999*. Stanford: Stanford University Press, 2003.

Yang Gang. "Fragment from a Lost Diary." In *Writing Women in Modern China: The Revolutionary Years, 1936–1976*, edited by Amy D. Dooling, 37–49. New York: Columbia University Press, 2005.

Yang, Gladys. "Zhang Jie, a Controversial, Mainstream Writer." In *The Time Is Not Yet Ripe—Contemporary China's Best Writers and Their Stories*, edited by Ying Bian, 253–59. Beijing: Foreign Languages Press, 1991.

Yang Mo. *Qingchun zhi ge* [Song of youth]. Hong Kong: Sanlian shudian, 1959.

Yang, Suying. "Gender Construction in the Novels of Zhang Kangkang and Liang Xiaosheng." In *Gender, Discourse and the Self in Literature: Issues in Mainland China, Taiwan and Hong Kong*, edited by Kwok-kan Tam and Terry Siu-han Yip, 109–24. Hong Kong: The Chinese University Press, 2010.

Ye Junjian. "Xu" [Preface]. In *Xiandai xiaoshuo jiqiao chutan* [A preliminary study of modernist fiction techniques], Gao Xingjian, 1–7. Guangzhou: Huacheng chubanshe, 1981.

Ye Yonglie. *Xiao lingtong manyou weilai* [The adventures of Little Talent in the future]. Beijing: Shaonian ertong chubanshe, 1978.

Ye Xin. *Niezhai* [The wages of sin]. Nanjing: Jiangsu wenyi chubanshe, 1992.

Ye Zhaoyan. "Ma Wen de zhanzheng" [Ma Wen's battle]. In *Ma Wen de zhanzheng* [Ma Wen's battle], 59–112. Beijing: Beijing shiyue wenyi chubanshe, 2009.

Yeh, Wen-hsin. "The Paradox of Autonomy: Nation, Revolution, and Women through the Chinese Looking Glass." In *Women in China: The Republican Period in Historical Perspective*, edited by Mechthild Leutner and Nicola Spakowski, 40–56. Münster: LIT, 2005.

Young, Bob, and Rachel DeWoskin. "Foreign Babe in Beijing." *Transpacific* 67 (1996): 12.

Yu Dafu. *Riji jiuzhong* [Nine diaries]. Shanghai: Beixin shuju, 1927.

Yu Hua. "Gudian aiqing" [Classical love]. In *Gudian Aiqing* [Classical love], 1–39. Beijing: Renmin wenxue chubanshe, 2006.

———. *Huozhe* [To live]. Wuhan: Changjiang wenyi chubanshe, 1993.

Yu Jun. "Shuangxing hexie, yingshiju dui aiqing lixiang de buxie zhuiqiu— yi Qiong Yao yanqingju weili" [Harmony of opposite sexes, the constant pursuit in the ideal love of the films and TV shows—a case study of Qiong Yao's romance melodramas]. *Zhongguo nüxingzhuyi* [Chinese feminism] 5 (Fall and Winter 2005): 238–39.

Yu Ying. "Yingguo· lihun chengben· shangwang gusuan" [Britain· divorce costs· online estimate]. *Wenhui bao* [Wenhui daily] January 23, 2011, 4.

Zan Jifang. "Realism Is a Big Hit." *Beijing Review*, no. 10 (March 8, 2007): 44–45.

Zeng, Yi, ed. *Zhongguo bashi niandai lihun yanjiu* [A study of divorce in 1980s China]. Beijing: Beijing daxue chubanshe, 1995.

Zeng, Yi, and Wu Deqing. "Regional Analysis of Divorce in China since 1980." *Demography* 37.2 (May 2000): 215–19.

Zhang Ailing (Eileen Chang). "Hong meigui yu bai meigui" [Red rose, white rose]. In *Zhang Ailing Wenji* [Selected works of Zhang Ailing], vol. 2, edited by Jin Hongda and Yu Qing, 125–63. Heifei: Anhui wenyi chubanshe, 1992.

———. "Qingcheng zhi lian" [Love in a fallen city]. In *Zhang Ailing Wenji* [Selected works of Zhang Ailing], vol. 2, edited by Jin Hongda and Yu Qing, 48–84. Heifei: Anhui wenyi chubanshe, 1992.

———."Wusi yishi" [Stale mates]. In *Zhang Ailing Wenji* [Selected works of Zhang Ailing], vol. 1, edited by Jin Hongda and Yu Qing, 270–79. Heifei: Anhui wenyi chubanshe, 1992.

Zhang Chengzhi. "Hei junma" [The black steed]. In *Zhang Chengzhi daibiaozuo* [Representative works of Zhang Chengzhi], edited by Zhang Caixin, 177–243. Zhengzhou: Huanghe wenyi chubanshe, 1988.

Zhang Chunsheng. "*Liyi* zai Wu Ruozeng de chuangzuo zhong" [*Divorce in Wu Ruozeng's oeuvre*]. *Tianjin shehui kexue* [Tianjin social sciences] (1988:1): 76–81, 37.

Zhang Henshui. *Ping Hu tongche* [Shanghai express]. Shanghai: Baixin shudian, 1941.

Zhang Jie. "Ai, shi buneng wangji de" [Love must not be forgotten]. *Beijing wenyi* [Beijing literature and art] (1979:11): 19–27.

———. "The Ark." Translated by Stephen Hallett. In *Love Must Not Be Forgotten*, 113–201. San Francisco and Beijing: China Books and Panda Books, 1986.

———. "Cong senlinli laide haizi" [The music of the forests]. *Beijing wenyi* [Beijing literature and art] (1978:7): 19–27.

———. "Fangzhou" [The ark]. *Shouhuo* [Harvest] (1982:2): 4–59.

———. "Love Must Not Be Forgotten." Translated by Gladys Yang. In *Love Must Not Be Forgotten*, 1–13. San Francisco and Beijing: China Books and Panda Books, 1986.

———. *Shishang zui teng wo de nage ren qu le* [Gone is the one who held me dearest in the world]. Shenyang: Chunfeng wenyi chubanshe, 1994.

———. *Wuzi* [Wordless]. Vols. 1–3. Beijing: Shiyue wenyi chubanshe, 2002.

Zhang, Jingyuan. "Breaking Open: Chinese Women's Writing in the Late 1980s and 1990s." In *Chinese Literature in the Second Half of a Modern Century: A Critical Survey*, edited by Pang-yuan Chi and David Der-wei Wang, 161-79. Bloomington and Indianapolis: Indiana University Press, 2000.

Zhang, Li. *In Search of Paradise: Middle-Class Living in a Chinese Metropolis*. Ithaca, NY, and London: Cornell University Press, 2010.

Zhang, Li, and Aihwa Ong, eds. *Privatizing China: Socialism from Afar*. Ithaca, NY, and London: Cornell University Press, 2008.

Zhang, Mei. "Rural Privatisation and Women's Labour: Property Rights and Gender Concepts in Inner Mongolia and Xinjiang." In *Women of China: Economic and Social Transformation*, edited by Jackie West, Zhao Minghua, Chang Xiangqun, and Cheng Yuan, 175–92. New York: St. Martin's Press, 1999.

Zhang, Naihua. "In a World Together Yet Apart: Urban and Rural Women Coming of Age in the Seventies." In *Some of Us: Chinese Women Growing Up in the Mao Era*, edited by Xueping Zhong, Wang Zheng, and Bai Di, 1–26. New Brunswick, NJ, and London: Rutgers University Press, 2001.

Zhang, Rui. *The Cinema of Feng Xiaogang: Commercialization and Censorship in Chinese Cinema after 1989*. Hong Kong: Hong Kong University Press, 2008.

Zhang Xipo. *Zhongguo hunyin lifa shi* [A history of China's marriage law]. Beijing: Renmin chubanshe, 2004.

Zhang, Xudong. *Chinese Modernism in the Era of Reforms: Cultural Fever, Avant-Garde Fiction, and the New Chinese Cinema*. Durham, NC: Duke University Press, 1997.

Zhang, Yingjin. "From 'Minority Film' to 'Minority Discourse': Questions of Nationhood and Ethnicity in Chinese Cinema." In *Transnational Chinese Cinemas: Identity, Nationhood, Gender*, edited by Sheldon H. Lu, 81–104. Honolulu: University of Hawai'i Press, 1997.

Zhang, Zhen. "Bearing Witness: Chinese Urban Cinema in the Era of 'Transformation'." In *The Urban Generation: Chinese Cinema and Society at the Turn of the Twenty-first Century*, edited by Zhen Zhang, 1–45. Durham, NC, and London: Duke University Press, 2007.

———. "Mediating Time: The 'Rice Bowl of Youth' in Fin de Siecle Urban China." *Public Culture* 12.1 (2000): 93–113.

———. "Urban Dreamscape, Phantom Sisters, and the Identity of an Emergent Art Cinema," In *The Urban Generation: Chinese Cinema and Society at the Turn of the Twenty-first Century*, edited by Zhen Zhang, 344–87. Durham, NC, and London: Duke University Press, 2007.

Zhao Guangde. "Ganqing shewang yu daode yueshu" [Luxurious love and moral obligations]. In *Gui cheng* [Ghost city], 47–49. Shanghai: Shidai wenyi chubanshe, 2000. Originally published in *Xinhua ribao* [Xinhua daily], September 3, 1980.

Zhao shuli. *Dengji* [Registration]. Beijing: Gongren chubanshe, 1950.

———. "Xiaoerhei jiehun" [The marriage of Young Blackie]. In *Zhao Shuli Xuanji* [Selected works of Zhao Shuli], edited by Xin Wenxue xuanji bianji weiyuanhui [The editorial committee of New Literature], 56–75. Beijing: Kaiming shudian, 1951.

Zheng Yi. "Lao jing" [Old well]. *Dangdai* [Contemporary] (1985: 2): 4–73.

Zhong Chengxiang. "Shenghuo, aiqing, daode" [Life, love, and morality]. *Hongyan* [Red crag], February 1981, 160–65.

Zhong, Xueping. "Hou funü jiefang yu ziwo xiangxiang" [Post–women's liberation and self-imagination]. *Dushu* [Reading] (November 2005):13–20.

———. *Mainstream Culture Refocused: Television Drama, Society, and the Production of Meaning in Reform-Era China*. Honolulu: University of Hawai'i Press, 2010.

———. *Masculinity Besieged: Issues of Modernity and Male Subjectivity in*

Chinese Literature of the Late Twentieth Century. Durham, NC: Duke University Press, 2000.

———. "Mr. Zhao On and Off the Screen: Male Desire and Its Discontent." In *The Urban Generation: Chinese Cinema and Society at the Turn of the Twenty-first Century,* edited by Zhen Zhang, 295–315. Durham, NC, and London: Duke University Press, 2007.

———. "Sisterhood?: Representations of Women's Relationships in Two Contemporary Chinese Texts." In *Gender and Sexuality in Twentieth-Century Chinese Literature and Society,* edited by Tonglin Lu, 157–73. Albany: State University of New York Press, 1993.

Zhongguo Dangdai Wenxue Yanjiusuo qing'ai lunli zuopin zhengming shuxi bianji weiyuanhui [The editorial committee of a series of literary works on love and ethics in contemporary China of the Institute of Contemporary Chinese Literature], ed. *Zhongguo dangdai qing'ai lunli zhengming zuopin shuxi* [A series of literary works on love and ethics in contemporary China]. Vols 1–10. Beijing: Jinri Zhongguo chubanshe, 1995.

Zhongguo daxuesheng jiuye [The job market of Chinese college students]. "2004 Zhongguo zhiye bailing shenghuo zhiliang diaocha" [A 2004 survey of the life quality of Chinese white-collar workers]. *Zhongguo daxuesheng jiuye* [The job market of Chinese college students] (July 2005): 41–42.

Zhongguo funü [Women of China]. "Yu Dan fangtan: Nüren de neixin yao congrong" [An interview with Yu Dan: A woman's inner world should be at ease]. *Zhongguo funü* [Women of China] (2008:1): 6.

Zhou Airong. "Jiexi Chi Li xiaoshuo 'Xiaojie nizao' de dianshiju gaibian" [An analysis of the televisual adaptation of Chi Li's novella *Good Morning, Miss*]. *Zuojia zazhi* [Writer's journal] (2012:12): 210–12.

Zhou Keqin. "Shanyue buzhi xinli shi" [The mountain moon doesn't know my thoughts]. *Sichuan wenxue* [Sichuan literature] (1981: 8): 2–10.

———. *Xu Mao he ta de nüer men* [Xu Mao and his daughters]. Tianjin: Baihua wenyi chubanshe, 1980.

Zhou Xiaohong. *Zhongguo zhongchan jieceng diaocha* [A survey of the Chinese middle class]. Beijing: Social Sciences Academic Press, 2005.

Zhu Lin. *Shenghuo de lu* [The path of life]. Beijing: Renmin wenxue chubanshe, 1979.

Zhu Yaoqun. *Zhongchan jieceng yu hexie shehui* [Middle class and harmonious society]. Beijing: Zhongguo renmin gong'an daxue chubanshe, 2005.

Zurndorfer, Harriet T. "Gender, Higher Education, and the 'New Woman': The Experiences of Female Graduates in Republican China." In *Women in China: The Republican Period in Historical Perspective,* edited by Mechthild Leutner and Nicola Spakowski, 450–81. Münster, Germany: LIT, 2005.

INDEX

Page numbers in *italics* indicate photographs.